SOLDIER
SNAPSHOTS

SOLDIER SNAPSHOTS

Masculinity, Play, and Friendship in the Everyday Photographs of Men in the American Military

JAY MECHLING

University Press of Kansas

Photos courtesy of author's collection.

Published by the University Press of Kansas (Lawrence, Kansas 66045), which was organized by the Kansas Board of Regents and is operated and funded by Emporia State University, Fort Hays State University, Kansas State University, Pittsburg State University, the University of Kansas, and Wichita State University.

Library of Congress Cataloging-in-Publication Data
Names: Mechling, Jay, 1945– .
Title: Soldier snapshots: masculinity, play, and friendship in the everyday
   photographs of men in the American military / Jay Mechling.
Description: Lawrence : University Press of Kansas, 2021. | Includes
   bibliographical references and index.
Identifiers: LCCN 2020048514
   ISBN 9780700632435 (cloth)
   ISBN 9780700632923 (paper)
   ISBN 9780700632442 (epub)
Subjects: LCSH: Vernacular photography—United States. | Male
   friendship—United States—Pictorial works. |
   Soldiers—Recreation—United States—Pictorial works. | Photographic
   criticism.
Classification: LCC TR23 .S66 2021 | DDC 770—dc23
LC record available at https://lccn.loc.gov/2020048514.

British Library Cataloguing-in-Publication Data is available.

Printed in the United States of America

10 9 8 7 6 5 4 3 2 1

The paper used in this publication is acid free and meets the minimum requirements of the American National Standard for Permanence of Paper for Printed Library Materials Z39.48–1992.

For
Simon J. Bronner
and
John Paul Wallis,
two men from different generations,
both coauthors with me and each my friend

Contents

Part IV—Coda

Acknowledgments

I have dedicated this book to Simon J. Bronner and John Paul (JP) Wallis. Simon and I have been friends and coauthors for about four decades, and I owe him an intellectual and friendship debt too long to describe here. I met JP just as I retired from teaching American studies at the University of California, Davis, in 2009 after thirty-eight years. He is a Marine veteran of two tours in Iraq, and our collaboration began with my helping him with his senior honors thesis in American studies, and that led to our writing two articles and a book together. I have learned a great deal from both men.

This project began with a book chapter I wrote for a volume of military folklore edited by Tad Tuleja and Eric Eliason, and I am grateful that they invited me into the project. Later, Tad was our editor for a book chapter I wrote with JP for a volume on resistance in the military.

Over the years Jon Wagner has been a good friend and intellectual playmate. I always learn from him.

This book benefited greatly from commentary by John Ibson and Richard Burns, for which I am grateful.

I deeply appreciate the confidence in the project and the encouragement from Joyce Harrison, editor in chief at the University Press of Kansas.

Finally, I am nothing without the love and support and advice from my spouse and longtime coauthor, Elizabeth Walker Mechling. Always.

Introduction

The snapshot opening this Introduction sets the tone for what is to follow. As is typical of the snapshots in this book, I do not know the names of the two men in the snapshot. I do not even know their branch of service, so I will just call them "soldiers." The bed and metal lockers behind them suggest they are in a more formal and comfortable barracks than a tent in a field. They are looking at an array of snapshots spread out on the bed, and from what we can tell the snapshots are of women, probably girlfriends or family members or both. The snapshot of the two soldiers, though, conveys more. These two soldiers are "buddies," and they are experiencing a moment of strong bonding looking at these snapshots together, doing something "side by side." The snapshots on the bed probably belong to just one of the soldiers (my guess is the one on our right, given his primary body position over the snapshots and the buddy's body position from the side). They are smiling, and if we see the snapshot as a moment in an ongoing story of their relationship, we might guess that the owner of the array of snapshots (possibly recently sent from home) has been telling his buddy stories about the people in the snapshots. Moreover, the men are not afraid to be touching shoulders. Their friendship permits casual touching. We know nothing about these two men, yet this snapshot of them tells us a great deal. That is the point of this book.

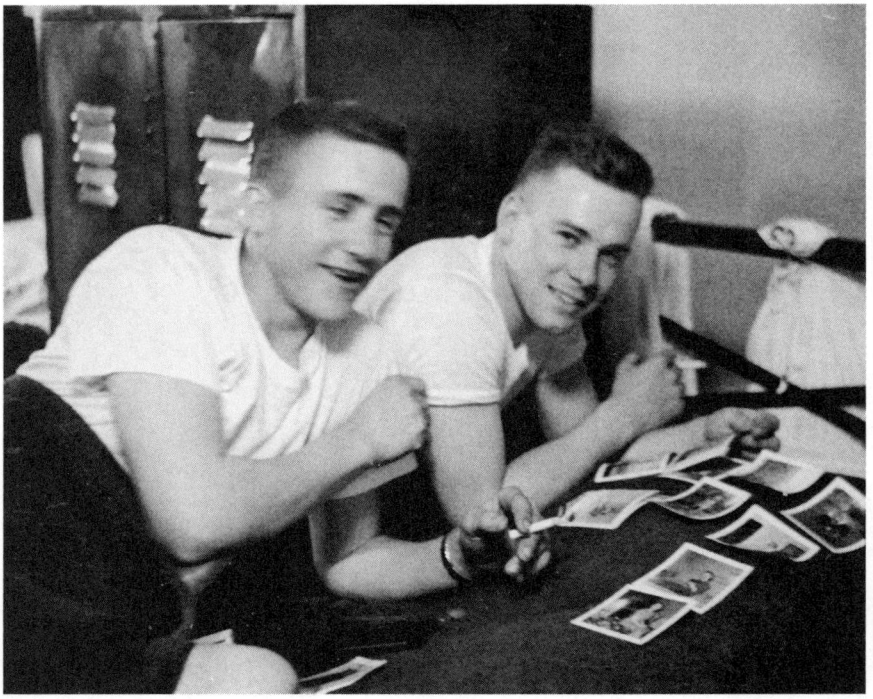

Snapshot I.1

This snapshot also points to two fundamental themes explored in this book. The first theme is how American men socially construct their performance of masculinity in everyday life in all-male friendship groups. The construction of masculinity is not an easy "project" for the individual, as we shall see. The male friendship group creates paradoxes for that project. The second theme, therefore, is how men use their folk practices in the male group to manage the paradoxes of their friendship and comradeship (not the same thing) under sometimes stressful conditions. Most of the folk practices, the folklore, the "vernacular," everyday culture, have elements of play. They use play to manage their friendships and to manage their feelings. The title of this book conveniently includes these keywords: masculinity, play, and friendship.

This is an interdisciplinary American studies book. As in all of my scholarship, the "subject" of the book or essay is American culture. I seek an understanding of American culture by subjecting particular bits of evidence to scrutiny to see how the part can reveal the whole. The book in your hands is about vernacular photography, "snapshots," by American soldiers, sailors, Marines, and aviators; the snapshots are the evidence, the parts I suspect will reveal something about the whole. And since almost all of the snapshots I have available in my pool of evidence are photographs taken of men most likely by other men, this is also a book about the social construction, performance, and repair (if necessary) of American masculinity. From snapshots to ideas about the everyday lives of male soldiers to ideas about the lives of men in groups to ideas about American culture. Parts and wholes.

In this Introduction I explore some key issues always involved with the study of cultures. I have never put together in one place my thoughts about how one undertakes the interdisciplinary study of American culture, and this Introduction is as good a place as any to do that. This Introduction also introduces you to the voice I use in writing—it is a very personal voice and I know that I break many norms of scholarly writing. Those norms sometimes need to be broken.

I also try to explain some complex ideas in everyday language easy for all readers to understand. I joked in one article I wrote, laying out ten axioms for doing American studies, that the writer should "eschew obfuscation" (Mechling 1997). Accordingly, I avoid the specialized jargon found in the disciplines I must often tap, and when I must use a word or phrase for which there is no easy substitute, I explain the meaning of that word or phrase. My intellectual hero is William James, one of the "fathers" of American psychology and the philosopher who founded the American school of philosophy still alive today—Pragmatism. James gave public lectures in which he introduced his complex ideas in language the lay audience, often schoolteachers, could understand. James was announcing a radical idea that truth is "something that happens to an idea," that there are no absolute truths except as people construct them and agree to the construction. Those truths are always tentative. Imagine a late-nineteenth-century or early-twentieth-century audience hearing that radical idea. James's *Pragmatism* (1907/1975) was the first book I read in college, and years later I read Peter Berger and Thomas Luckmann's *The Social Construction of Reality: A Treatise on the Sociology of Knowledge* (1967), a book very much in the tradition of American Pragmatism (Mechling 1985; Mechling 1986; Mechling and Mechling 1999). The present book's focus on the actual everyday practices of Americans, in this case "soldiers" (which I use often as shorthand for soldiers, Marines, sailors, and aviators), works from that Pragmatic tradition.

When I wrote my book on the Boy Scouts, *On My Honor* (2001), after nearly two decades of writing scholarly articles based on that fieldwork and historical research, I aimed to write a book that would be readable by both the scholarly audience and the general audience, especially by men for whom the scouting experience was as important in their lives as it was in mine. When John Paul Wallis and I (2019) came to write a book about post-traumatic stress disorder (PTSD) and the folklore of the male friendship group in the military, we also had in mind two audiences—folklorists and other scholars were one audience, and veterans themselves (of which Wallis is one) were the other. My aim in the present book is the same. I have tried to write about soldier snapshots for both a scholarly audience and for veterans of the military experience captured by the snapshots.

In his 1983 essay "Common Sense as a Cultural System," the anthropologist Clifford Geertz notes that one of the characteristics of common sense, of taken-for-granted, everyday reality, is its "earthiness," which is one way of saying that common sense, expressed through folklore, is often obscene and profane. Because I am looking at the everyday folk practices of the men in these snapshots, I will often use folk terms like "piss" and "shit" and "butt" and "fuck." This is the language used by the men themselves in their everyday lives in the military, so it seems appropriate to me, when analyzing the military folklore of men, to use the "earthy" folk terms.

Beginning with Raymond Williams's 1976 book, *Keywords: A Vocabulary of Culture and Society,* scholars have picked up his idea to create books on keywords in a discipline or field, including Burt Feintuch's (2003) on folklore, "expressive culture." My title already announces three keywords—masculinity, play, and friendship—that readers will encounter throughout the book. The remainder of this Introduction offers a concise discussion of four keywords addressing the theory and methods undergirding my study, perhaps naming issues, really, guiding my work. Those are interpretation, generalization, interdisciplinary, and unconscious.

THE ACT OF INTERPRETATION

I am engaged here in acts of interpretation. That is what scholars do: they try to make sense of something that intrigues them. That has always been my modus operandi, my MO as a detective might call it, through most of my scholarly life. I see a puzzle and often cannot rest until I solve it.

In many cases I am attracted to puzzles of everyday life, to things that might seem trivial, everyday, ordinary. Some American studies scholars focus on the products of high culture, texts like novels and paintings and unique buildings, significant works of art. We study those products because we believe we can see through the eyes and ears of a perceptive individual some "truths" about the meanings of life in the colonial and postcolonial United States (America, for convenience). Some American studies scholars choose to study, to describe and interpret, the products of popular culture, sometimes called mass-mediated culture, sometimes called commercial culture. We study these texts, texts usually produced by anonymous makers and consumed by anonymous audiences, because we assume that if the audience is willing to pay to consume the products (popular fiction, popular music, comic books, television, films, video games, and more) then the audience must be getting pleasure out of that consumption, and sorting out the pleasure of consumption tells us about the meanings of the lives of the consumers. Some American studies scholars study vernacular culture, the everyday, the ordinary. Folklorists carve out this territory as a matter of course, but other American studies scholars not grounded in folklore studies still find themselves drawn to the everyday cultures of Americans. In some ways the scholar working on folk cultures aims "to make the familiar strange and the strange familiar," a catchphrase common in anthropology but also appearing in many other disciplines that study taken-for-granted, everyday life.

We distinguish these three realms of American culture—high culture, popular culture, and folk culture—not as the end of our classification and analysis but merely as a convenient place to start, because, in truth, "texts move" between these realms. Authors of high culture novels sometimes appropriate materials from popular culture and folk culture as literary devices in their unique creations. Sometimes popular culture appropriates materials from both high culture and folk culture to create commodities to sell. And sometimes folk cultures appropriate materials from high culture and popular culture.

Understanding, even in as cursory a way as I present it here, the notion that texts exist in a world of other texts, moving between levels of culture and poaching from other texts, helps us see that a snapshot is suspended in a "web of significance," a phrase used by Max Weber and adopted by Geertz (1973b, 5) to describe culture. Those webs are contexts for understanding the meaning of texts, and scholars commonly look at historical, social, and cultural contexts for a text. Other texts can also provide context for a text's meanings, and scholars often talk about "intertextuality," references in one text to those in another. This notion of intertextuality is relevant to the study of snapshots, as most amateur photographers come to take a picture with a history of exposure to both professional and vernacular images.

So what does it mean to "interpret" a snapshot, a vernacular photograph taken in most cases by an unknown photographer? It means making guesses, but that does not mean that all guesses are equal. I have always liked the claim the cultural anthropologist Clifford Geertz makes that "interpretive anthropology" is "scientific," but not in the mode of deductive sciences, like physics. Interpretive anthropology, says Geertz (1973b, 26–27) is an inductive science on the model of "clinical inference" in medicine.

When I was teaching and tried to explain clinical inference to students as a scientific method, my job became much easier with the rising popularity of the television series, *House* (2004–2012), which most of my students had seen. A patient presents to a physician a number of "symptoms" (I put that word in quotation marks for a reason I shall explain shortly). The physician collects information (data, facts), which usually starts the moment the physician lays eyes on the patient because many ailments present themselves with distinctive visible and olfactory (smell) symptoms. The patient tells the doctor a story, providing more information. The physician examines the patient, taking vital signs. The physician may order lab tests, yet more information. At some point the physician believes that she or he has enough information to formulate a diagnosis, a hypothesis that makes "best sense" of the symptoms, realizing that not every bit of information is actually relevant. The physician then applies a treatment based on that hypothesis (diagnosis) and waits to see what happens. If there is no improvement, the physician might repeat the examination and testing, gathering new information as the basis for a new diagnosis that makes best sense of the new data. And so on.

Geertz's useful insight is to see that the interpretive anthropologist's method resembles the method of clinical inference. The scholar is presented with a puzzle, gathers information, and then formulates a hypothesis about what "story" makes best sense of the data. When Sigmund Freud used folklore (myths, jokes, slips of the tongue, and so on) as psychological "symptoms" in some of his most famous writing, he provided folklorists and other interpreters of culture a lovely example of how we might see the practices of everyday life as "symptoms" of underlying meanings and causes. Think of snapshots as symptoms, as data points to be interpreted.

Of course physicians in many cases get to see the results of a test of their diagnosis: the patient gets better or doesn't. There is no parallel in interpreting culture. The hypothesis—that sounds so much more scientific than my preferred words "guess" and "hunch"—that makes best sense of a cultural practice in most cases cannot be tested, as can clinical diagnoses. It should be clear, though, that interpretation must be evidence-based; not every interpretation makes best sense of the meanings of the practices.

Above I used the word "story" a few times in describing clinical inference. The patient tells a story about the symptoms that bring her to the physician, and the physician formulates a story that makes "best sense" of the evidence and proceeds to prescribe a treatment based on that diagnosis. It may seem strange to call both the patient's narrative and the physician's diagnosis stories, but that is what they are. Which reminds me of a story.

The great anthropologist Gregory Bateson (whose ideas about play we shall encounter often in the coming chapters) recounts this story (dated as some of the technical references are):

> A man wanted to know about mind, not in nature, but in his private large computer. He asked it (no doubt in his best Fortran), "Do you compute that you will ever think like a human being?" The machine then set to work to analyze its own computational habits. Finally, the machine printed its answer on a piece of paper, as such machines do. The man ran to get the answer and found, neatly typed, the words: THAT REMINDS ME OF A STORY. (Bateson 1979, 13)

Humans think in terms of stories. Bateson firmly believed that cultures are systems of parts all connected into a whole. Parts and wholes. In that respect, Bateson was as comfortable talking about redwood forests' "thinking in terms of stories" as he was talking about the human mind. A story connects the bits and pieces into a pattern through time, its context (Bateson 1979, 14).

Following Bateson, and bypassing the long history of attempts to define the "culture" concept, I understand culture as the stories people hear and tell each other to make sense of their experiences, to bring order to the "blooming buzzing confusion" of everyday lives (William James again). Some of the stories are grand, worthy of being called mythologies. Some are simply everyday conversations. Adopting this view of culture requires us to expand what counts as a story beyond what we normally think of as a story. For my purposes here, I need to see a snapshot as a moment in a story, even though I do not have the direct evidence of the story captured by the snapshot, of what happens to the people in the photo before and after the snapshot is taken. I do not know the names of the people in the snapshot. But I am familiar with patterns in American culture, "patterns which connect," as Bateson puts it (1979, 8). For me, then, the act of interpreting these snapshots consists of figuring out the story, the pattern, of which the snapshot is a part.

Scholars choose to study some texts over others. If Bateson is correct about cultures as whole, connected systems, then in theory one could choose any text at random and, with sufficient time and effort, formulate a hypothesis about how that part is connected to the whole. In actual practice, though, a scholar chooses some texts to study. I shall bypass the very interesting question of how the scholar's life experiences may steer her toward one text or another. I do know that curiosity plays a large part in the choices.

I said earlier that I know I tend to choose genuine puzzles to study, and everyday life is full of puzzles. When Wallis and I decided to write about playfighting in the combat zone (Wallis and Mechling 2015; Wallis and Mechling 2019, 67–87), what piqued our curiosity was a color photograph (by Tim Hetherington, 2010) on the back of the dust cover to the hardbound edition of Sebastian Junger's *War* (2010). Wallis had served two tours as a Marine in Iraq, and his own experiences confirmed how common it was for warriors to have rough-and-tumble playfights in the combat zone, a truly puzzling phenomenon (see Chapter 10 here on playfighting in the snapshots). I mention this example of the Hetherington photograph because that was the "text" that launched our inquiry. Wallis has engaged in such playfighting as a Marine; it was part of his everyday, taken-for-granted reality. Now he wanted to join me in stepping back from the text to employ our intellectual equipment (ideas and approaches) to make best sense of that puzzle.

Since I have been mentioning key intellectuals (James, Berger and Luckmann, Bateson, Geertz) who have influenced my thinking about my craft of cultural interpretation, I should add another example—Stephen Jay Gould (1941–2002), the Harvard paleontologist and evolutionary biologist who also wrote articles for the general reader. For many years he wrote a monthly column for the magazine, *Natural History*, and occasionally he would gather some of those magazine articles into books. The articles he wrote for *Natural History* are such fine examples of essay writing that some of them are used in university composition courses as models to emulate.

What I love so much about Gould's essays is that many of them begin with a true puzzle, asking a childlike question so simple and yet so revealing in the discovery of a solution. For example, is a zebra a white animal with black stripes or a black animal with white stripes? Gould (1983) then proceeds to answer the question. Sometimes he follows a hypothesis (a guess or hunch) for a while but finds it a dead end. He returns to the question and follows another line of reasoning and evidence until he arrives at a "best answer," even though it might carry some troubling ambiguity.

My use of the phrase "best answer" requires a brief explanation, as it names an idea from the sciences (including the clinical induction discussed by Geertz) I adopt in my acts of interpretation. In his well-known discussion of the process of change in scientific ideas, Thomas Kuhn (1970) argues that when scientists discard one scientific paradigm for another, their embrace of the new paradigm is never based solely on evidence but involves a great deal of faith. He likens the change in scientific ideas to a religious conversion. At the same time, evidence matters. Among the ways evidence matters are these: the new paradigm must explain the "anomalies," evidence that does not fit the old paradigm; the new paradigm must predict things not predicted under the old paradigm; and the new paradigm must be aesthetically pleasing, which includes simplicity (Occam's razor) and ineffable beauty. This is why mathematicians can consider a proof "elegant" and why scientists can speak of the "beauty" of an explanation.

To return to my interpretive task, then, I seek an interpretation of a photographic image that makes "best sense" of the motive for taking the snapshot and for the behavior captured by the snapshot. Another scholar or even lay observer might have a different interpretation of a snapshot I analyze here, but if so I would say something like, "Well, then, you tell me why the men in this snapshot are dressing like women." Niobe Way (2011, 25) distinguishes between "thin culture interpretations" and "thick cultural interpretations" (drawing on Geertz, as I do), and my goal in this book is to move beyond the thin interpretation of each snapshot to a thick interpretation of all the layers of meaning captured in that artifact.

Another thing I like about Gould's essays is that they violate one common rule composition teachers give their students: put a clear thesis in the first paragraph. Gould saves the thesis for the end, beginning with a puzzle and giving us a tour through the ideas, some dead ends and some productive leads, until he arrives at what easily could have been stated in the first paragraph. But why ruin the fun?

GENERALIZATION

The second keyword I want to explore briefly in this Introduction is "generalization," the challenge of generalizing. And that reminds me of a story.

Several years ago the chair of women and gender studies at my university and I team-taught a graduate seminar on "Masculinities." At the time she was studying men's social movements (Newton 2004), and I had been writing about and teaching about masculinities for decades. Judy and I sat at opposite ends of the long seminar table, with about twelve students seated on the sides. There were four graduate students from English, three from history, and a scattering of students from other departments and programs. One night a strange discussion emerged across the table between the English graduate students and the history crowd. For a while I was puzzled about the argument, and then it dawned on me. Somewhere or from someone the graduate students in English had learned that generalizing was "essentializing," and that is bad, especially if one is essentializing gender and sexual identity as grounded in biology. The history graduate students were having none of that. As historians they knew that generalizing was their scholarly responsibility, and perhaps sometimes their burden. Historians have to generalize; that is the nature of the discipline. Literary critics tend to look at single texts or authors, but social and cultural historians look across many texts, seeking patterns, patterns that connect and lead to generalization. The discussion moved on to other topics, as that one would never be resolved in the conversation between those two disciplines.

Back the early 1960s the Social Science Research Council assembled a panel of historians to discuss the problems of generalization in the writing of history. That project resulted in a book edited by Louis Gottschalk (1963). As an undergraduate American studies major taking a course in 1965–1966 on "American National Character," I skimmed that book but read carefully the article by Walter Metzger (1963) on generalization in writing about national character. The study of national character had arisen out of the need in World War II to understand German and Japanese cultures, but also the cultures of Pacific Islands occupied by the

Japanese and then liberated by the Allies. At the same time, the school of culture-and-personality studies arose in anthropology, a reflection of the hope for an interdisciplinary study of culture, one that included psychology and sociology.

Social movements and their counterparts in the academy eventually ended interest in national character studies, as the study of women's lives (and the women's rights movement), ethnic studies (the civil rights movement), folklore studies, popular culture studies, and eventually gay studies challenged the generalizations about national character based on the lives of white men. Of course, making generalizations about "group character" did not go away; the size and nature of the group changed, but not the understood mission to generalize about the group. Historians and social scientists kept up their worries and conversations about the act of generalizing. I recall reading Metzger's essay in the 1963 book and have never forgotten this point of his. From one point of view, all human beings are the same. From another point of view, every human is different, even identical twins. The challenge is to find generalizations between these two truths, generalization large enough to be useful but not so large they wash out important variation in people.

What this means in practice for this study of soldier snapshots and what they reveal about the everyday lives of men in the military is that I will make generalizations along the way, knowing full well that what I say about the men taking these snapshots and appearing in the snapshots may not be true of everyone. Although American culture musters lots of forces in support of normative male heterosexuality, we know enough about human sexuality that both gender identity and sexual identity are diverse and, for some people, fluid. I would find it awkward for the flow of my narrative to say every time I make a generalization that I know it might not be true for every man, so I am making that declaration here.

INTERDISCIPLINARY THINKING

The word "interdisciplinary" gets used a lot in research and teaching, but in many of those cases the user really is meaning cross-disciplinary or multidisciplinary. I have strong feelings about the meanings and practice of interdisciplinary scholarship, and this Introduction is an excellent place to have my say.

All of my degrees are in American studies. If American studies defined itself by its subject matter—all of American history, literature, art, architecture, music, social thought, and so on—that would set up an impossible task. But if we define American studies as a cognitive style, as a way of thinking about culture, then the task becomes manageable, especially if (following Bateson, again) we conceive of the task as one of connecting things. The patterns that connect. This still does not define "interdisciplinary."

American studies began in the 1930s when teachers of American history and literature began creating team-taught courses connecting the history and the literature. Sometimes they brought in American art history, so some of the early programs were called American HAL programs, for history-art-literature. These were cross-disciplinary in my usage, where a scholar trained in one discipline crosses over into another to make connections with the "home discipline." Many scholars I have chatted with think that learning a discipline is hard enough that (at best) someone can learn one other discipline to add to his or her repertoire of ideas and approaches.

I shall not write a history of American studies here, as there are some fine histories. My aim here is to describe my own interdisciplinary practices, practices on view in this book.

I have no "home" discipline. Instead of defining my way of thinking as interdisciplinary or cross-disciplinary, I would say my method is convergent-disciplinary. Since my goal is to take a puzzle, a "text," a "part," and find its connections within the pattern of the "whole," I put the text at the center and then look around the circle of disciplines (I have a visual image of this in my mind) to see what disciplines might have something to add to thinking about the text. For this book, the task is to entertain (to "play" with) what ideas and approaches from different disciplines might help make best sense of a snapshot. I draw from history, folklore, anthropology, sociology, rhetoric, and psychology. Then there are the interdisciplinary fields—gender and sexuality studies, ethnic studies, popular culture studies, and visual studies.

A truly interdisciplinary field founded in the humanities and social sciences should also include the natural sciences. In my work on the social construction, maintenance, and repair of masculinity, I have found it useful to consult the work of ethologists (those who study animal behavior), primatologists, evolutionary biologists, and the brain scientists (Mechling 2000; Mechling 2019). The book Wallis and I (2019) wrote on PTSD and folk therapy, for example, relied heavily on the neuroscientific work on PTSD, including neurobiology, endocrinology, and brain science.

Whenever I make the case for a broad sweep of humanities, social science, and natural science disciplines in doing American studies, I usually bump into the view that learning one, maybe two disciplines in a lifetime is hard enough. People ask, How can one possibly become competent in the many disciplines you list?

The key is knowing what you need to know for a particular task of interpretation and knowing how you can go about learning as much as you need to know without absorbing the entire discipline. One of my favorite examples of this is recounted by John Watson in his book, *The Double Helix* (1968), describing for the general audience the search (with Francis Crick) for the structure of DNA. Watson and Crick knew that whoever unlocked the secret of the structure of DNA would win a Nobel Prize, but they also knew that the famous chemist, Linus Pauling, was on the hunt as well. There were big gaps in Watson and Crick's training in chemistry, so what did they do? They read Pauling's book, *The Nature of the Chemical Bond* (1939)! They knew what they needed to know, and they knew how to find that specific information.

I like anthropologist's Anthony F. C. Wallace's (1970) notion that we carry around in our heads "cognitive maps" of the interconnected system we call culture, so one way to describe what Watson and Crick did is to say that they had a cognitive map of all of the information and disciplines they needed to solve their puzzle. For the interdisciplinary American studies scholar, a combination of cognitive maps of the disciplines and a cognitive style comfortable with navigating those maps makes possible the convergent-disciplinary approach I employ. It helps that there are specialists who write books for general audiences. I have found the books by primatologist and neurobiologist Robert Sapolsky (1997, 2004, 2017) to be valuable for writing about masculinity, for example.

UNCONSCIOUS MOTIVES

One body of theory and practices I draw upon here is folklore studies, an interdisciplinary field that takes as its object of study the vernacular, everyday culture of people as they strive to make their lives more meaningful. That describes precisely my goal here, looking at the vernacular photography by soldiers, sailors, Marines, and aviators. Taking snapshots is a folk custom, with its own traditions.

As in only a few other scholarly fields, folklorists seem to agonize end-
lessly over how to define their discipline, in part because many people use
the dismissive phrase "that's just folklore" to tag some belief as untrue. On
the contrary, folklore describes the most basic genres of communication
between people in their everyday lives and reflects the most basic patterns
of beliefs and values of people. It describes their common sense, "common" both because it is everyday, ordinary, and because it is widely shared
in a group (see Geertz 1983).

In my own work I prefer Elliott Oring's approach, setting aside the pursuit of a neat definition of folklore and opting, instead, to see folklore as
an "orientation":

> folklorists seem to pursue reflections of the *communal* (the group or collective),
> the *common* (the everyday rather than extraordinary), the *informal* (in relation
> to formal and institutional), the *marginal* (in relation to the centers of power and
> privilege), the *personal* (communication face-to-face), the *traditional* (stable
> over time), the *aesthetic* (artistic expressions) and the *ideological* (expressions
> of belief and systems of expressions. (Oring 1986, 17–18, emphasis in original)

Not every folklorist at every time incorporates every one of these orien-
tations, but you will find in this book attention to most of these as I write
about the soldier snapshots.

My own approach to studying folklore also aligns with Simon J. Bronner's (2017) understanding of folklore as everyday *practice,* praxis, an
approach with its roots in the American philosophical school, Pragmatism,
founded by William James (1842–1910). One can trace the pragmatic tradition in folklore studies (Mechling 1985) up through Roger Abrahams
(2005) and Bronner's scholarship. Kenneth Burke (1897–1993), also
working in the Pragmatic tradition, proposed a list of five rhetorical elements in his "Pentad"—act, scene, agent, agency, and purpose (Burke
1945/1969)—that I have adopted in my work to describe the complex
questions a folklorist should ask when encountering any performance of a
folk tradition: Who performed what tradition, when, how, for what audience, and for what purpose? What was the outcome?

Notice that nearly all of these elements can be directly observed in fieldwork, and even in the case of material culture (which is what a snapshot is)
we can make pretty good guesses about the actor who took the photograph,
when and where he did it, how he composed the image through the lens

(including how his previous experience with the "tradition" of snapshot photography is revealed in the image), and who was the intended audience for the snapshot. The question in the folklorist's version of Burke's Pentad regarding motive, or purpose, is the one requiring the most speculation. Motive is not directly observable, and asking a person why he or she performed a traditional practice usually yields a useless answer. The strong interpretation of motive requires a theory of the unconscious.

At times in this book I shall draw upon psychoanalytic theory to help make best sense of a snapshot and of some cultural practice the snapshot captures. I know full well that many people have an aversion to psychoanalytic theory, or what they take to be psychoanalytic theory, and in my book on the Boy Scouts I put the psychoanalytic interpretations of some of the folklore at camp in a separate chapter, with the advice to readers that they could skip that chapter if their aversion to psychoanalytic theory was strong. You can skip the chapter and still get a good understanding of the central points of the book, I told readers, but you will be missing an interesting key to understanding the unconscious meanings of some of the boys' practices.

The key word in that last sentence is "unconscious." Explicitly or not, the critic interpreting specific cultural practices (in this case, both the practice of taking a snapshot and the practices captured in the snapshot) postulates a motive or set of motives for the practices. Some motives are conscious, and the person performing the practice can usually articulate the motive. But many motives are unconscious. In fact, there are good reasons to believe that if an unconscious motive is brought to the conscious level, the psychological and social value of the practice might lose its usefulness. If, for example, I could convince the boys who played the game of poison pit at the Boy Scout camp I studied (2001) that they are enacting in the game their adolescent anxiety about female bodies, knowing that would probably ruin the game for them. Discovering unconscious motives requires some sort of depth psychology, of which psychoanalytic theory is the best-known.

Note that I wrote "psychoanalytic theory" and not "Freudian theory." Freud is the father (or one of the fathers) of psychoanalysis, certainly, but the rise of a feminist psychoanalytic theory modified Freudian thought for a more nuanced understanding of masculinity. Melanie Klein (1882–1960) and Karen Horney (1885–1952) led the way, but the crucial turn came in the 1970s when feminist theorists like Nancy Chodorow (1978) turned their analytical gaze away from women and onto men. The ideas of those feminists who reinterpreted Freud very much inform my understandings of the dynamics involved in the creation, maintenance, and repair of masculinity.

Not that Freud is absent from these pages. Working on my interpretations of the cultures at the Boy Scout encampment I was studying in the 1980s and 1990s, some of my "aha" moments came when I realized that psychoanalytic approaches to folklore unpacked for me some puzzling customs, like the food = feces folk speech of the boys and the meaning of the game of poison pit they played in a day of scout contexts and games (Mechling 2001, 83–85). When I turn in this book to psychoanalytic theory about social masochism, in Chapter 11 on "Hazing," Freud makes his appearance again, though modified by his student, Theodor Reik (1888–1969). While some scholars might believe you can interpret a photograph without any recourse to speculation about unconscious motives, I think an interpretation without some consideration of unconscious meanings is incomplete, not the interpretation making best sense of the text.

A MAP OF THIS BOOK

Part I introduces a brief history of war photography and establishes the nature of vernacular photography, the snapshot. The chapters in Part II establish many of the ideas about masculinity and the vernacular practices of men in groups, exploring male friendship, the role of the play frame in men's relationships, and (perhaps surprisingly) the ways "animal buddies" adopted by male friendship groups actually tell us even more about male friendship and issues of trust.

The chapters in Part III establish a main point about the snapshots—namely, that the male body is the complex symbolic site. The male soldier forms strong bonds with his "buddies" in his friendship group, and the chapters in Part III explore how the men employ different folk practices—including rough-and-tumble playfighting, building human pyramids, bathing naked in public, cross-dressing, hazing, and the darker sides of deep play—in order to manage their relationships. Regardless of the man's sexual orientation and sexual identity, the very strong heterosexual norm in the military means that the men must find ways to understand and even enact or perform their feelings of bonding while still defining those feelings and acts as heterosexual.

I shall warn you now that the Coda at the end of the book is not your usual academic Conclusion to a book. I decided to write a very personal Coda.

Some chapters conclude with an "excursus," an aside, really, a commentary on a single snapshot that both fits and does not fit with the others in the chapter. The excursus is a narrative device I borrowed from Peter Berger (Berger, Berger, and Kellner 1974) in writing *On My Honor* (2001). The excursus sometimes is a mini-essay that takes the place of a long footnote (you will find no footnotes here). I had not intended to use that device in this book, but I have in my collection snapshots that don't seem to fit the chapter categories and yet are very revealing about masculinity.

PART I
The Military Snapshot

1

The Military Snapshot

Time and again historians of war point to publication of a photograph or a thematic series of photographs (a "photo essay" in a newspaper or magazine, perhaps) as the turning point in public perception of the war. Those iconic photographs, which appear in newspapers, magazines, and on television, may shock or inspire the public, ramping up patriotic support for the war or turning public opinion against the war (e.g., Zelt 2012). Images of the dead bodies of both civilians and fighters, images often censored by the authorities, can have enormous impact on the public, but images of the awful destruction of whole cities, seemingly of civilization itself, also elicit an emotional response by the public. The pen might be mightier than the sword, but so is the camera.

Most of the scholarship on war photography, sometimes called "combat photography," reprints and offers some sort of analysis of the photographs taken by official military photographers and by "commercial" photographers—the photojournalists working for publications, or for collectives or agencies of professional photographers such as Magnum. The professional photographers who work for the military or for commercial organizations document a war in the role of participant-observers. They carry a camera rather than a lethal weapon, and they carry their cameras into combat situations at great risk to themselves (Coons 2011). The powerful, award-winning documentary film *War Photographer* (2001), directed by Christian Frei, uses the life and work of famed war photographer James Nachtwey to convey the sense of mission that drives combat photographers, leading them into danger that often takes their lives. Such war photographers, involved as they are, are still observers, making choices of what to photograph and what not to photograph, what to send to their superiors and what to hold secret. They are not warriors themselves, but they experience much of what warriors experience without the extra, nontrivial act of taking human life. Good war photographers spend a lot of time with their "subjects," often building friendships with men and women whom they then see wounded or die. Some of the best war photography captures the range of emotions felt by soldiers, from laughter to tears, from fear to grief, from anger to the stunned blank expression that warriors call "the thousand-yard stare."

This book looks not at the professional war photography, of which there are plenty of fine illustrated histories (e.g., Moeller 1989; Fox 1996; Howe 2002; Knightley and Keegan 2003), but at the amateur photography by the soldiers, sailors, Marines, and aviators who also carried cameras and documented their military experiences from deep inside the experience. Members of the military, just like the professional photographers beside them, are participant-observers of the mundane, everyday lives of warriors. One difference is that the professional war photographer keeps "shooting" photographs when the actual shooting of weapons begins, whereas the warrior is too busy doing the shooting or trying not to get killed. Another difference is that the professional photographer takes the photograph for public consumption, whereas the amateur photographer might be taking the photographs for personal viewing or viewing by a small circle of fellow soldiers, or sometimes by family and friends back home.

Even though my topic here is not professional war photography, it may be worthwhile recounting briefly the history of photography that led to a soldier having in his or her hands a small, lightweight camera for taking "snapshots," a word borrowed from hunting to describe a photograph taken hurriedly and on the spur of the moment (Kouwenhoven 1982, 161–162). The hunting term seemed so appropriate that by the 1940s both professional and amateur photographers talked about "shooting" photographs (Greenough et al. 2007, 2).

Photography was invented in 1839, and by the Crimean War (1853–1856) and the American Civil War (1861–1865), professional photographers were hauling their heavy, bulky photographic equipment—large cameras, heavy wet plates, chemicals for developing photographs—into the field, not during the combat but in its aftermath. Not until R. L. Maddox (1816–1902) invented the gelatin-coated dry plate in 1871 and then George Eastman (1854–1932) patented a coating machine in 1878, freeing photographers from carrying so much equipment, was the snapshot possible. Eastman's Kodak No. 1 camera, introduced in 1889, was the first truly portable camera, small enough to be handheld and containing a 100-exposure roll of film using paper negatives. When all 100 exposures were taken, the amateur photographer sent the entire camera to the Eastman labs in Rochester, New York, to be developed. The resulting 2.5-inch, round snapshots were then sent back to the customer with the camera reloaded with another roll of film. In 1889 Eastman also introduced the Kodak No. 2 camera, which made larger round prints (3.5 inches in diameter) from roll film on a transparent (celluloid) base (King 1984, 6). With the introduction of the Brownie camera in 1900, a camera easy enough for children to use, Eastman put into the hands of ordinary people small, lightweight, easy-to-use cameras for taking snapshots amassing a visual history of their everyday lives.

Both European soldiers fighting in World War I (1914–1918) and, with the entry of the United States into the war in 1917, American soldiers added their own snapshots to the body of vernacular photography documenting that war. The Houghton Company in London made the Ensignette No. 1, patented in 1907 and released in 1909, a folding brass camera compact enough to be carried in a soldier's pocket. The popularity of that camera with troops was eclipsed by the introduction in 1912 of the Kodak Vest Pocket camera, also a folding camera, in this case constructed of aluminum and marketed as "the soldier's camera" (much like the camera in Snapshot 1.1). Kodak earlier (1907) had marketed the Kodak No. 2A Model B box camera, which was not as compact as the Vest Pocket camera but was still small and light enough to be carried to the front. That camera used 116-size film and produced postcard-size negatives that could be contact-printed; for this reason some snapshots we have from World War I appear to be postcards, though they were not produced by commercial postcard companies. By World War II soldiers carried equally small and lightweight 35 mm cameras (Snapshot 1.2). In short, the twentieth-century wars fought by Americans and Europeans generated a large number of snapshots.

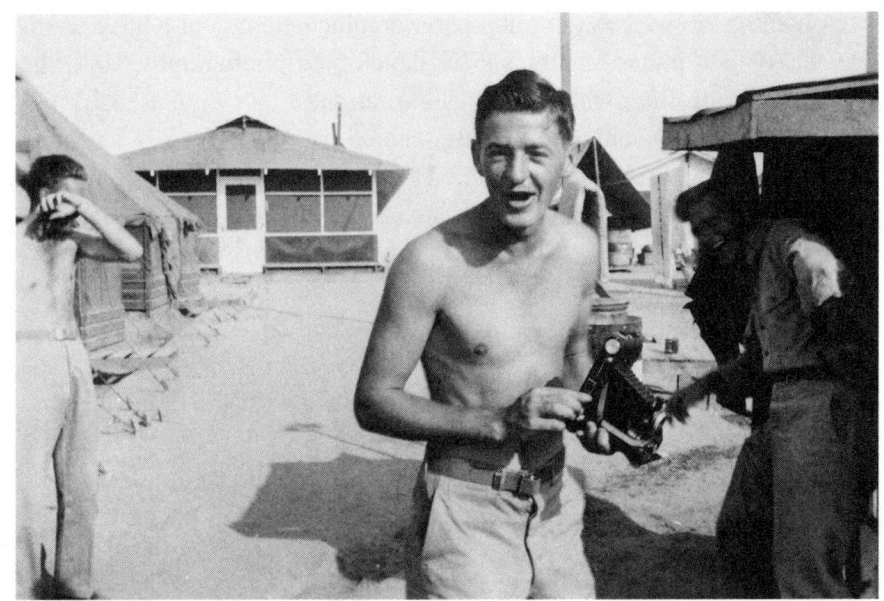

Snapshot 1.1

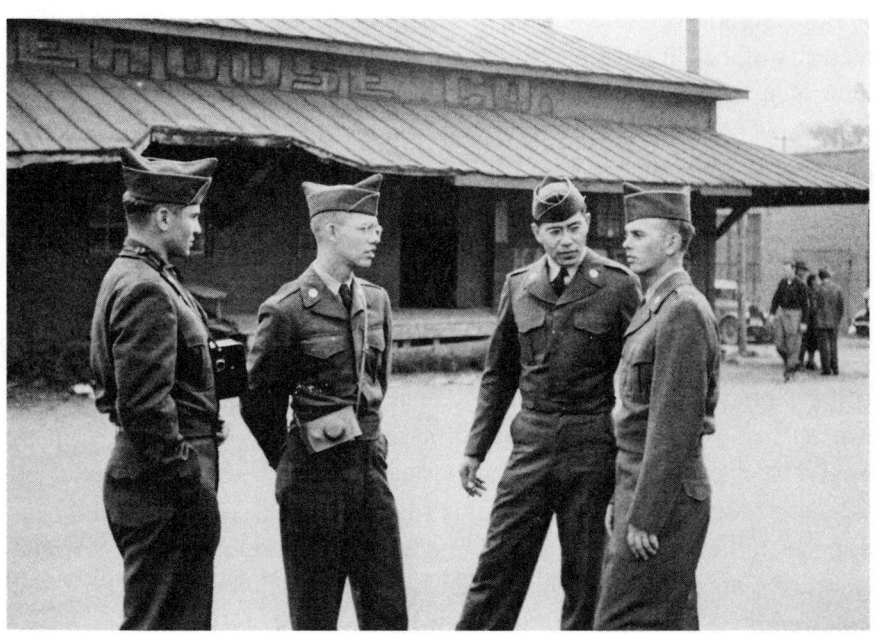

Snapshot 1.2

THE SNAPSHOT

In her introduction to *The Art of the American Snapshot, 1888–1978* (2007), a collection of essays and images accompanying an exhibition mounted by the National Gallery of Art in Washington, DC, Sarah Greenough uses Charles M. Taylor's little-known 1902 book, *Why My Photographs Are Bad,* to describe the elements of the photograph that mark it as a snapshot, as a photograph taken by an amateur rather than a professional. We recognize these elements—blurred images, tilted images, double exposures, off-center positioning of a subject, and the accidental inclusion of the shadow of the photographer—as markers of bad photography, but Greenough invokes Taylor's distinctions between "good" and "bad" photographs to make the point that Taylor's "'good' photographs are, not surprisingly, stiff, bland, and boring. Not only do they possess none of the humor of the 'bad' photographs, but they have none of their immediacy or authenticity" (Greenough 2007, 2). This is the great paradox of snapshots as documents of our lives, that we view the snapshot as "true," as "authentic" (King 1984, 49–57, 179).

These qualities of the amateur snapshot attracted the attention of the professional art photographers embracing the Modernist aesthetic and philosophy after World War I, and several of those photographers appropriated these elements of bad amateur snapshots to add elements of truth and authenticity to their art photographs. This led to museum curators' recognition that the lowly snapshot deserved serious attention from historians of art and photography. The Museum of Modern Art in New York City mounted an exhibition, *The American Snapshot,* in 1944, and there were subsequent major exhibitions of snapshots at the San Francisco Museum of Modern Art in 1998 and at the Metropolitan Museum of Art in 2000 (Greenough 2007, 3).

My interest here, of course, is not in the snapshot as a work of art but as a piece of evidence for writing the history of the everyday lives of Americans. When historians turned from writing about human players on the large stages of politics and war to attempting to reconstruct the everyday lives of ordinary people, the nature of the evidence changed. Ordinary people usually do not leave boxes of papers and correspondence for historians to peruse in libraries and museums. They do leave snapshots. Soldiers, sailors, Marines, and aviators leave snapshots for us to gaze upon, snapshots possibly bearing information about their everyday lives as ordinary people in a large war machine.

Many historians of everyday life in the United States have been drawn to vernacular photography as a rich sort of evidence for their work. John Ibson, whose book *Picturing Men: A Century of Male Relationships in Everyday American Photography* (2002) is an outstanding example of this genre of social history, provides the reader an epilogue—"Out of the Attic—Vernacular Photography and Cultural Studies"—that briefly surveys the American studies and American history scholarship relying on vernacular photography to write social history, and he explains to the reader his own approach to interpreting the photographs in his vast collection (some more formal studio photographs and posed photographs, some more informal snapshots). I shall not duplicate Ibson's survey of previous work, but I do owe the reader of this book some insight into my own approach to understanding the military snapshots I present here as cultural "texts" worth our thoughtful attention.

Ibson and I are both interested in what vernacular photographs of boys and men tell us about the friendships and emotional lives of American men. Ibson pays special attention to the body language and spatial arrangement in the snapshots, so I have not added much in that regard as I consider the snapshots I present here for analysis. What I do add to the conversation are ideas from the social scientific corners of folklore studies (especially frame theory) and from depth psychology. While Ibson "reads" the performance of male emotions and friendship in the snapshots as revealed in patterns of touching and distance, I tend to read the snapshots for the folk practices documented by the photographs. Our analysis is complementary, reflecting our slightly different training and interests.

Like Ibson and other scholars who work with snapshots, I have been collecting these vernacular photographs for several years, buying some in online auctions, some in antique stores, some at shows for collectors of photography. At the time he published *Picturing Men* (2002), Ibson was working from a personal collection of about five thousand snapshots. The eighty-one snapshots I analyze here come from my personal collection of about seven hundred soldier snapshots, but (like Ibson) I have also seen hundreds of other vernacular photographs on my topic, enough to make me confident that my collection pretty well covers the genres of practices captured by the photographs. These are, in most cases, "orphan" photographs, by which the collector means that we have little or no contextual information about the photograph, its subjects, and the photographer. If we bought an album assembled by a family or by an individual military service member, we might have some contextual information, and in some cases an individual snapshot might have some writing on the front or back. Many of the military snapshots I present and analyze here, for example, have written on the back of the photo a list of names of the men pictured in the snapshot. A few snapshots have more elaborate messages written on the back, likely because the soldier sent the photo back home to family or a friend and wanted to use the back to write some context and a message. One of the snapshots I analyze in the chapter on cross-dressing has a long note on the back, and these brief snippets of writing help flesh out the world captured by the snapshot and the thoughts and feelings of the photographer as he offers the snapshot to friends and family.

The snapshot captures a split second, literally, in the everyday life of the person taking the snapshot. Some snapshots are posed, and there are several examples of posed snapshots here. Some are "candid" snapshots, photographs taken more hurriedly than the posed scene and, therefore, often evaluated by the viewer as more "authentic" than the posed snapshot. At times the hurried aspect of the candid snapshot results in qualities that help certify the snapshot as capturing a "true," unpolished, and unrehearsed moment in the lives of the people in the snapshot. As I have noted, those qualities include blur, off-center composition, double exposures, and the shadow of the photographer in the image.

Evaluating the evidentiary value of the snapshots, we also must keep in mind that any snapshot has gone through several stages of editing. First, the photographer edits the snapshot through the lens. The photographer chooses a subject, chooses to photograph the subject, and chooses how to frame the scene through the viewfinder and lens. The photographer then decides whether to develop the snapshot, and if so, there is another point at which the snapshot might be censored by the developer. Once printed, a snapshot still has to find its way to a collector. Individual snapshots and whole collections can be discarded at some point in their history. Even if a dealer buys a collection of snapshots at a yard sale or estate sale, that dealer will go through the collection and discard any snapshot deemed not interesting enough for other collectors to buy. This brief history of a snapshot explains why any collection of snapshots a scholar uses to write the history of everyday lives is nothing like a random sample. It is a sample, though, and historians and others who study visual materials work with what they have.

Let me pause here a moment to mention what evidence we don't have.

I, personally, don't have in my collection snapshots I did not buy, either because they were too expensive at a show or I was outbid in an online auction. Sometimes I might refer here to unpublished snapshots I have seen but do not own; at times I refer to snapshots published elsewhere.

Beyond the vagaries of my own collection, there are moments that tend not to show up in the snapshots. Amateur photographers tend to capture moments when the people (the friendship group) are happy, often smiling. The warriors who took the snapshots almost never photographed extreme pain or grief. I have never seen, for example, a snapshot version of the famous image of one soldier embracing and comforting another taken in 1950 taken by Al Chang, a war photographer covering the Korean War (Bernstein 2007; Hanson 2014, 17). Judging from the military snapshots I have seen over the years, the amateurs seemed to respect (or at least could be forced to respect) the official policies about showing dead bodies, though this policy changed (Roeder 1993). Similarly, as we shall see in more than one chapter that follows, most of the soldiers taking snapshots of their buddies partially or fully naked follow the custom of showing only buttocks (butts), though in a few cases the snapshots show male genitals, which we would not see in professional photographs published in newspapers, magazines, and even advertisements (e.g., the wartime Cannon towel series of advertisements). Military snapshots also rarely show activities that are illegal or at least against military regulations, though we really don't know what kind of cigarette a soldier is smoking with his buddies in Vietnam.

Digital photography changes everything, of course. The digital camera or the smartphone that takes digital snapshots increases exponentially the number of military photographs and their subject matter. In the wars in Afghanistan (2001–present) and Iraq (2003–present), almost every American participating in the wars carried smartphones if not digital cameras. The editing process of the photographer who uses film is very similar to that of the amateur photographer taking digital snapshots—the photographer chooses the subject, edits the image through the lens, immediately can see the snapshot taken, and decides to save or discard (erase) the digital image. The digital storage chips in both cameras and phones can hold hundreds, or in some cases thousands, of images, some of which might be printed later.

I include no digital snapshots in this book, but I raise the topic here because digital photography makes possible the creation and saving of snapshots of forbidden events. A case in point is photography of wartime atrocities. Professional war photographers have photographed the aftermath of atrocities, such as the exhumation of mass graves or the liberation of Nazi concentration camps. What we do not see are professional photographs of wartime atrocities as they are happening. We know from the testimony of participants and witnesses that American soldiers have murdered unarmed prisoners of war when it was deemed too risky to convey the prisoners to a safe place, as required. Such atrocities happened at least as long ago as World War I (see the 1933 novel *Company K* by William March, based on his experiences in that war), though I know of no photographic record of executing unarmed prisoners of war. Similarly, the infamous My Lai massacre on March 16, 1968, was not photographed as it was happening.

In our book *PTSD and Folk Therapy*, John Paul Wallis and I (2019) distinguish "hot atrocities," taking place when the combatants are in what psychiatrists call "the berserk state" (Shay 1994), and "cool atrocities," committed in cold blood, after the hot-blooded experience of combat. Two dramatic examples of digital snapshots and digital video capturing cool atrocities make the point that digital photography changes everything. In 2004 digital photographs showing horrendous abuse of Iraqi prisoners by American soldiers and CIA operatives at the notorious Abu Ghraib prison near Baghdad became public, setting off a firestorm of criticism (Hersh 2004; Morris 2011; Sontag 2004). Eight years later, in January 2012, a thirty-nine-second video of four Marines in Helmand Province, Afghanistan, urinating on the bodies of three dead Taliban fighters became public (Bowley and Rosenberg 2012). A shocked public demanded action from the military establishment. In both cases digital media taken by American warriors themselves revealed criminal behavior, perhaps behavior that was uncommon but certainly counts as how the soldiers actually experience working, living, and fighting in the combat zone.

In the news as I write these words is the story of the outrage over Navy SEAL special operations chief Edward Gallagher, who (in May 2017) texted to a friend a digital photo showing Gallagher holding the head of a limp, dead, teenage ISIS fighter, along with Gallagher's boast that "I got him with my hunting knife" (Szoldra 2018). Gallagher's subsequent court-martial exonerated him of a crime, but the photo is a violation of regulations so Gallagher was demoted (Chappell 2019). President Donald Trump took the controversial step of pardoning Gallagher. Again, it was a digital snapshot taken in the combat zone that revealed the dark side of American "cool atrocities" in war.

As I said, I have no snapshots on film revealing forbidden behavior, though some of the shots discussed in Chapter 12 come close. We do have a unique published volume of snapshots taken by American military personnel during the first few years of the war in Iraq. *GQ* magazine accepted journalist Devin Friedmen's proposal that they publish a volume of such photographs, initially publishing a photo essay in the magazine in 2005 and then a book, *This Is Our War* (2006), selecting 256 images from over ten thousand submitted by military personnel. As Friedman puts it in his introduction to the volume, "These pictures reveal not only what the servicemen and women saw but the way they saw things. What they were curious about. What they felt proud of. What felt remarkable to them, what felt funny. . . . They showed us their war" (Friedman et al. 2006, 19).

It should surprise no one that the snapshots in *This Is Our War* (along with direct quotations from the warriors providing the snapshots) draw upon the same repertoire of subjects and genres I find in my collection of analog snapshots: pictures of buddies embracing, warriors holding pet animals, soldiers showing off their weaponry, destruction, wounded bodies, dead bodies, funerals, exhausted fighters catching a little sleep, soldiers sunbathing, soldiers playing cards and other games, a barracks wall covered with pinups of half-naked women, Iraqi prisoners on the battlefield, heroic rescues, emergency medical care, Marines burning half barrels of feces from the latrines, and even a single snapshot of a prisoner being beaten at Abu Ghraib prison. A major difference between my snapshots and those published in *This Is Our War* is the presence of women warriors in the Iraq War photos. Otherwise the snapshots taken by American soldiers at work and play are pretty much the same over the past one hundred years.

INTERPRETING SOLDIER SNAPSHOTS

Collecting and categorizing these military snapshots are necessary steps, but the goal here is to use the snapshots as historical evidence. Some historians and cultural critics are explicit in their methods and concepts for interpreting snapshots; other scholars are less explicit. I want to explain here in detail how I approach the snapshots. It is one thing to use photographs as illustrations for a written analysis; it is another to use a photograph as an actual "text" to be "read" in the same way a historian reads documents. I expand here on some of my discussion of interpretation in the Introduction.

About halfway through the book *War/Photography: Images of Armed Conflict and Its Aftermath* (Tucker et al. 2012), based on the exhibition mounted by the Museum of Fine Arts in Houston, is the transcript of an interview conducted by the prime curator, Anne Tucker (AT), with two important contributors to the project—Hilary Roberts, head curator of the Imperial War Museum Photograph Archive in London, and Jeffrey W. M. Hunt, director of the Texas Military Forces Museum in Austin. At one point deep in the discussion Roberts (HR) and Hunt (JH) have an exchange about the nature and value of the sort of vernacular photography examined in this book, and it is worthwhile to reproduce some of their discussion. Here they have just acknowledged one of the most disturbing sorts of events behind the line of combat: the killing of unarmed prisoners of war by a few soldiers who do not want to be separated from their unit while delivering the prisoners to the far rear.

> AT: You brought up an important point—that they did not want to be detached from their unit. I think the hard thing for a photograph to convey is how important the "band of brothers" is.
>
> JH: The camaraderie. Your unit is your family.
>
> HR: This is where the personal photography, the soldier's snapshots, the servicemen's snapshots, play a key role in bringing this across.
>
> JH: And why they so often look like family vacation pictures. Most of these snapshots are of their friends and their day-to-day living conditions.
>
> HR: They show aspects of life, food, sanitation, moments of pleasure, children, animals—the highlights of a serviceperson's daily life. And they show individuals, some of whom are here today and gone tomorrow. These photographs are intended to preserve memories. In some cases they can appear quite monotonous and the quality might vary. But every so often there will be an absolute treasure, something that no other camera has recorded. (Tucker et al. 2012, 283)

In truth, we can do a pretty good job of writing the social history of everyday lives in the United States without the snapshots. The wished-for goal, however, is to find and analyze snapshots that show us things not obvious in the written or even material culture evidence.

Sometimes snapshots reveal customs not found in other evidence, such as snapshot 1.3 of three soldiers showing off a chain of dollar bills. The online seller of this snapshot thoughtfully clipped the portion of the black paper album page with "Short Snorters" written in white ink as the caption (as people often did). Without that caption I would not have known what it was they were holding. It turns out the snapshot records a common military folk custom, one probably well-known in the military but unknown to me, wherein people who share a transoceanic flight autograph dollar bills and link them together in a chain as a souvenir of the flight (Marotta 2002). This folk custom marking a shared experience resembles the "Crossing the Line" festival discussed in Chapter 11.

Most often, though, a snapshot conveys additional information nonverbally. The snapshots I present and analyze here use the language of touching to communicate the expression of feelings or emotions.

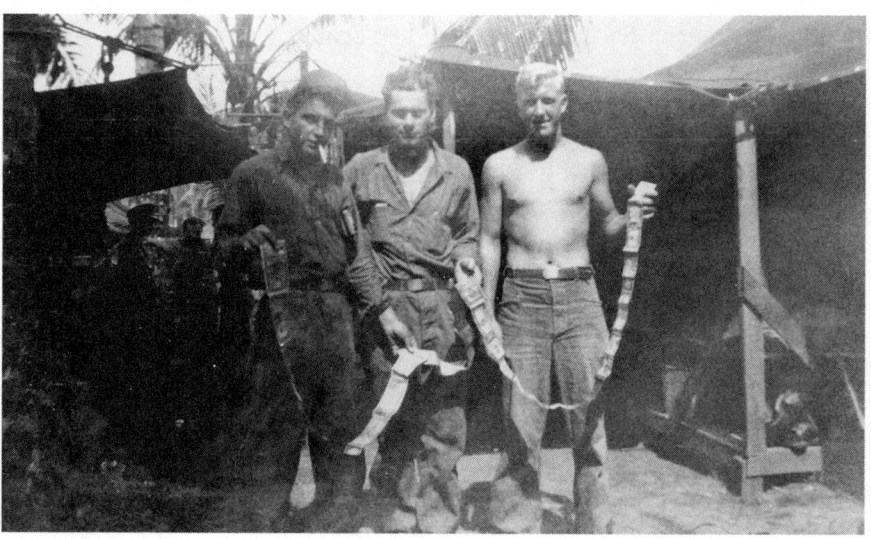

Snapshot 1.3

THE LANGUAGE OF TOUCHING IN
THE SNAPSHOTS

The verbal documents created by Americans in military service take us partway toward an understanding of how those people experience the military institution as they work, play, and fight, often in the combat zone. War memoirs, collections of letters, the occasional war diary, and oral histories all provide glimpses into the actual experiences of the average service member, from the mundane to the terrifying. Words, though, are not always the most reliable evidence of the emotions being felt by the service member. John Crawford titled his memoir of his experiences in the Iraq War *The Last True Story I'll Ever Tell* (2005), letting us in on the knowledge that the stories veterans tell might not always be "true."

In our everyday experiences we know that the body language and facial expressions of someone telling us a story might be sending us confusing signals, signals that seem to contradict the words. In Chapter 3 I introduce Bateson's notion of the play frame (1955/1972), and we shall see in that discussion how humans use not just verbal language but also nonverbal "body language" to construct a shared social reality. If "culture is communication," then we must attend as much to nonverbal communication as to verbal communication. Snapshots uniquely capture the nonverbal ways male soldiers use their bodies to communicate meaning, and my analysis of several snapshots in this volume draws our attention to the body language of the soldiers.

Anthropologists, sociologists, and psychologists began clueing us in to the importance of nonverbal language by the early 1970s. E. T. Hall's *The Silent Language* (1959/1973) was a popular best seller, but in visual studies Erving Goffman's *Gender Advertisements* (1976) provides the best introduction to the ways we can read photographs for information about the relationships between the humans depicted. In that book Goffman is interested in analyzing "gender displays" in the photographs in advertisements, an interest stemming from his sociological approach to all social interaction as a kind of stage drama, with actors, scenes, scripts, props, onstage zones, and backstage zones. Looking at advertisements, Goffman is interested in what the gender displays tell us about gender and power.

In some ways the most interesting commentary in *Gender Advertisements* is not the theoretical setup over a few dozen pages but the shorter texts accompanying clusters of images from advertisements. Thus, Goffman is interested in how power relations might be communicated by image size and by body rituals of subordination. Most of what Goffman has to say unpacks for us how the body language in the advertisements puts on display normative gender relationships in 1970s America (women's bent legs, patterns of touching, patterns of eye contact, etc.). Since the soldier snapshots I analyze here feature men with men, I shall mention here some of Goffman's points that help us read the snapshots I present.

Goffman argues that some of the gestures in the advertisements—the man's extended arm, the "arm lock," the "shoulder hold," and "hand-holding"—signal the male's "ownership" of the female in the photograph, and the typical difference in the gaze (the women looking down, the men looking away) or in the positioning of the figures (one behind the other) reinforce the power relationship in the gender displays. None of the individual gestures Goffman analyzes (save possibly his comments on "snuggling" and "nuzzling") easily translate into what we see in the soldier snapshots, but Goffman's analysis does give us a model for what to pay attention to in snapshots featuring two or more men, men who are as much engaged in gender display as the male-female couples in the advertisements.

We can appreciate Goffman's drawing our attention to the unconscious meanings of the gestures and body language in photographs, though his primary interest in gender relations has its limitations when looking at men touching men in the snapshots I present here.

SOLDIER SNAPSHOTS AND EMOTIONS

The more I have worked with the military snapshots in my collection, the more I realize that the most important information communicated by images is about the emotions, the feelings, being experienced by the men in the snapshots, and the more I realize that what the snapshot is preserving for the photographer who carries the snapshot back home as a "souvenir" is the remembrance of those feelings.

Brian Sutton-Smith, a developmental psychologist who was the founder of the modern study of play, especially children's play, and who wrote extensively about play and folklore, returned to his developmental psychology roots in his final book, *Play for Life: Play Theory and Play as Emotional Survival* (2017), published posthumously. Sutton-Smith was a very important scholar in my thinking about play, and when I was invited to write an essay for a festschrift for another famous folklore scholar, I realized that Sutton-Smith's main argument about play as the folk practice we use both to display and to manage emotions could be extended to all folklore. I titled the essay I wrote for that festschrift "Folklore and the Emotional Brain" (Mechling 2019). For scientists, emotions are an unconscious physiological thing that happens in the body, whereas the word "feelings" names the conscious experience of those emotions. In that essay

I rather boldly claimed that the significance of folklore is that it is the means by which we display and communicate to others our feelings.

Reading Sutton-Smith's last book and writing that essay on folklore and the emotional brain suddenly made me realize that the military snapshots convey in a much better way than even the words in war memoirs and letters the range of emotions being felt and managed by the men in the snapshots. I return to this point in Chapter 4.

THE SOLDIER SNAPSHOT AND THE SCHOLAR'S GAZE

Holding in my hand one of the snapshots in this book or any snapshot in my collection, I cannot ignore the variety of emotions the images evoke. Like other collectors, I buy a particular snapshot because it interests me in some way; perhaps a snapshot fits one of the categories that emerged as I worked on this project. Or perhaps a snapshot attracted my attention for reasons I cannot fully explain.

I am sure that other scholars who work with vintage snapshots as their texts have the same experience as I. We are looking at a snapshot that once meant a great deal to the person who chose to save it. That person likely is gone now, and the snapshot became an orphan as it moved into the impersonal world of commerce, sometimes in a yard sale, sometimes in an estate sale, and then into a dealer's hands. We are voyeurs into the everyday lives of the people in the snapshots, and in most cases we see their moments of joy and good humor. As my wife says, reflecting on her pleasure scrapbooking our family's story, people almost never take snapshots of the terrible moments in their lives, moments they would rather forget. People take snapshots of moments they want to remember. Snapshots are souvenirs, literally aids-to-memory, aids to "looking again" at moments of pleasure (Stewart 1984).

Military photographs carry their own baggage of meanings and emotions. When I look at one of these soldier snapshots, I carry all of my reading of war memoirs and novels and reportage I have done for my teaching and writing. I do not know firsthand the military experience, but I know from my reading the sometimes awful, everyday world of the soldier and sailor and Marine. I know the terrible things they have seen and sometimes done.

As I look at the smiling faces in these snapshots, I wonder about the fate of these young men. Did they die after the snapshot was taken? Did they survive to return to civilian life physically or mentally wounded? I know what they don't know. I know how the wars turned out. And many of them know something I don't know. They have experienced combat.

They are smiling in the snapshots, while I am often sad looking at them.

PART II
Men in Military
Groups

2

Manhood as a Project

The "topic" of this book is American masculinity as revealed in vernacular photography by American soldiers, Marines, sailors, and aviators in the armed services. So, of course, I turn to the subject of manhood in this early chapter before moving on to the snapshots themselves and my reading of their contexts and meanings.

Writing this chapter in 2020, though, is not as straightforward as it might have been twenty years ago, when I was revising my Boy Scout book, *On My Honor* (2001). Immersed in the surge of masculinity studies from the 1980s and 1990s, I was fairly certain then about the theoretical foundation of masculinity studies in feminist theory, mainly in the line of feminist psychoanalytic thought. The first generation of feminist psychoanalysts, including Melanie Klein (1882–1960) and Karen Horney (1885–1952), were dissatisfied with Freud's account of gender and sexuality, so they formulated alternative ideas. Object relations theory, which Nancy Chodorow (1978) uses for her formulation of a theoretical foundation for understanding the creation of gender, arose in that first wave of feminist psychoanalysis. Chodorow's work became a starting point for masculinity studies based on the feminist revision of psychoanalytic thinking.

The theory has not changed much in forty years, but the boys and young men reared in the United States have been affected by history and new developments in society and culture. Historians' shorthand for these changes is to write about generations. The boys have changed, but so have the girls, so while this book is about American masculinity revealed in the soldier snapshots, I will comment as well on how differences in expectations for girls and women create new forces for change in previously all-male institutions like the military.

My reliance on Chodorow's ideas helps us be sensitive to historical change. Chodorow's approach, as we shall see, assumes that the particular shape of masculine development in American boys in large part results from the fact that in American culture "women mother," thus recognizing that boys' gender and sexual identity often originates in the need of the boy to separate his identity from that of the major caretaker. Chodorow and others writing about the particular pattern of American boys' development recognize that this could change if men took a role in the early care of infants and boys. The personality patterns resulting from particular child-rearing practices are malleable as the practices change and as other forces affect the male child's understanding of what it means to be a man. Writing about masculinity in 1980, for example, did not entertain the notion of the "fluidity of male sexual identity and practices," but in 2020 it is impossible to write about masculinity without acknowledging that fluidity (Savin-Williams 2017).

I have tried to capture the complexity of the story of "manhood as a project" in this chapter, trying not to get lost in the hurricane of changing variables involved with the social construction, maintenance, and repair of masculinity. While writing this chapter I have been ever-mindful of the discussion about generalization in the Introduction. Here I attempt to make generalizations about the project of manhood, trying to couch them in ways that do not do too much damage to individual differences in boys and men. The reader will have to judge if I have succeeded.

THE BIOLOGY

Robert Sapolsky is a primatologist, neurologist, and evolutionary psychologist who offers a very helpful scientific basis for our thinking about the forces that create masculinity. A biologist, he rejects biological essentialism, a view taken by some who write about gender, to show how the behavior of human males, including the behavior of the primates closest to us (notably bonobos and chimpanzees), must be seen as the product of a complex interaction between nature and culture. In understanding male behavior, says Sapolsky (1997, 156), "No biology. No environment. Just the interaction between the two."

When people generalize about male behavior, they often focus on aggression and violence. There is no doubt that across time and space, males have been more aggressive and violent than have females, but Sapolsky is quick to point out that although some hormones, mainly androgens and anabolic steroids (which, for simplicity, he lumps together under "testosterone"), are heavily implicated in male behavior, especially aggression and violence, the testosterone does not cause the aggression; "it's *exaggerating* the aggression that's already there" (1997, 155, emphasis in original). Put differently, any tendency toward aggression and physical violence we observe in males is as much a product of the socialization of boys as their biology. Even a cursory look at American culture, especially the popular culture narratives consumed by boys and male adolescents, reveals the omnipresence of aggression and violence in those narratives. The popular culture does not cause male aggression; we must not make that error. But if the adolescent male statistical tendency toward aggression and violence comes from the interaction of the boy's biology and the forces of socialization, we must look at both forces (Wallis and Mechling 2019, 13–38).

The study of masculinity, however, is full of paradoxes. The very same hormones that might push a boy toward being aggressive, even violent, can also play a role in emotions other than anger. The first scientist to write about male adolescence, G. Stanley Hall (1904), was impressed by the tendency toward romance and service to others that adolescent male hormones created, a point noted by the founders of the Boy Scouts of America in 1910 and by other adults who worked to direct the energies and "nature" of boys into socially positive activities (Mechling 2001; Mechling 2016a). Subsequent research has confirmed that testosterone can as often lead to altruistic behavior in the group as to aggression (Sapolsky 1997; Reimers and Diekhof 2015; Sapolsky 2017).

Let us fast-forward from male childhood and adolescence to explore this interaction of socialization and biology in the eighteen-year-old male recruit in the military. His biology, from his hormones to the structures of his still-maturing brain, present the institution (in the person of the basic training drill instructor) with raw material (but not a blank slate) for creating a young man who will bond with the group, follow orders, and be willing to kill other humans. It is not so easy to train a person to kill (Grossman 2009).

The point I want to make here, without plunging deeper into the biology of the male soldier in his late teens and twenties, is that male biology is as important a foundation for male bonding as it is for male killing. Traditional war photography shows plenty of killing; the soldiers' snapshots show plenty of bonding and very little killing.

It turns out, then, that understanding the biology of masculinity does not lead us very far in understanding the snapshots, so let me turn to developmental psychology.

DEVELOPMENTAL PSYCHOLOGY

Feminist psychoanalytic thought provides a lot of the ideas I tap for understanding the social construction of masculinity in the United States, as revealed in the soldier snapshots reproduced here. Freud's initial formulation of the Oedipus complex—with its ideas about the young boy's attachment to his mother, his jealousy of his father's access to the mother, his fear of castration by the father, and his subsequent identification with the father and distancing from the mother—mistakenly treats this as a universal phenomenon rather than as a product of the family arrangements found in middle-class European and American patriarchal society.

Chodorow sees in the gender arrangement in most American families, where the mother or another female takes primary responsibility for the care of the child, the roots of the "othering" of the feminine (Chodorow 1978, 1994; see also Connell 1995). The sexual potential in infants and young children can be shaped by socialization, as can their gender identity. In patriarchal cultures, women tend to be the primary caretakers of infants and young children. In this pre-Oedipal stage, the primacy and intensity of the attachment of the male child to the mother creates ambivalence (Mitchell 1974, 57). This is where the object relations theory developed by Klein, Winnicott, Chodorow, and others (see Greenberg and Mitchell 1983) enters the psychoanalytic picture. The power of the attachment of the male child to the mother, the source of his primary socialization, creates a "problem" from the point of view of patriarchal society. The "proper" gender identification of the male child is with the father, so the male child embarks on a course in which he distances himself from the feminine in order to identify himself as masculine. This means, as Stephen Frosh puts it, that "masculinity is defined negatively, as that which is not feminine" (1994, 79).

Despite the common appearance of masculinity as a strong, confident identity, the masculinity created by the patriarchal family is really very fragile. That fragility is the great "secret" held by boys and men, a fragility that causes them anxiety and leads them to pursue practices that mask the vulnerability. Defined as a "lack," as the negative state "not feminine," masculinity constantly needs reinforcement and repair when damaged. Things for the boy are even more complicated by the fact that he retains elements of the attachment to the mother and, accordingly, attachment to the feminine elements of his own self. Thus, while the boy learns to repress the feminine side of his second nature through expression of misogyny and homophobia, there are also psychic costs to that repression. Horney (1932) argues that boys "dread" women's omnipotence and intimacy in early child-rearing, but the boy also finds his mother's care and love "seductive and attractive" (Chodorow 1978, 183). He lives with powerfully ambivalent feelings about the feminine and, accordingly, about his own masculinity.

The male friendship group polices this situation, defending the border between the masculine and the feminine, even at great psychic cost to the boy. So I turn now to the socialization of the boy in the male friendship group.

SOCIALIZATION: THE BOY CODE AND THE GUY CODE

Boys learn to be men in the male friendship group and in the everyday interactions with other boys (Bronner 2005). Working with American boys in his therapeutic practice, William Pollack (1998) sees at work in the boys the effects of the "boy code" (Brannon and David 1976), which contains the following admonitions:

- The "sturdy oak." Men should be stoic, stable, and independent. A man never shows weakness. . . .
- "Give 'em hell." This is . . . a stance based on a false self, of extreme daring, bravado, and attraction to violence. . . .

- The "big wheel." This is the imperative men and boys feel to achieve status, dominance, and power. . . . Boys and men are taught to avoid shame at all costs, to wear the mask of coolness, to act as though everything is under control, even if it isn't. . . .
- "No sissy stuff." Perhaps the most traumatizing and dangerous injunction thrust on boys and men is the literal gender straightjacket that prohibits boys from expressing feelings or urges seen (mistakenly) as "feminine"—dependence, warmth, empathy. (Pollack 1998, 23–24)

In his book *Guyland* (2008), the sociologist Michael Kimmel, a prominent figure in masculinity studies, devotes a chapter to "'Bros before Hos': The Guy Code" (2008, 44–69). Building on the boy code, Kimmel notes that longitudinal studies of young men in high school and college continually affirm that the boy code is still in place and enforced by the male friendship group (Kimmel 2008, 46). Key to the enforcement is the fact that a young man must "prove" his masculinity. As Timothy Beneke (1997) puts it, the young man experiences a "compulsion" to prove his masculinity, to prove that he measures up to the norm of the heterosexual male. The young man proves his masculinity by passing tests, mainly provided by his peers. Thus, a young man can never be comfortable with his masculinity because he moves from test to test, with the possibility of failure at every test. Normative, "compulsive masculinity" (Beneke 1997, 36) is never achieved finally; it is always fragile and always a work in progress.

The generalizations from this body of theory are extremely useful in understanding many commonly observed practices of men, many of those displayed in the snapshots I analyze in the following chapters. The theory makes sense of many otherwise puzzling folk customs in the male friendship group, as we shall see.

Another factor to consider about social and historical contexts for the pattern of "mother-raised boys" is the media environment. The boy's male friendship group is a primary source of the enforcement of the learned boy code, but popular culture (mass-mediated culture) reinforces the code's messages. The patterns of male heroes in American popular literature (from the dime novels of the late nineteenth century to the manga and graphic novels of the twenty-first century), film, television, and video games are well-enough known that I do not need to elaborate this point.

Between the boy's male friendship group and the narratives boys consume in their everyday mass media environment, it would seem that the boy code, and by extension the guy code, amounts to a juggernaut of messages to be strong, stoic, independent, daring, brave, aggressive, and wary of values and behavior the culture customarily attributes to the feminine—namely, dependence, warmth, and empathy.

Some cultural critics, though, alert us to patterns of male resistance to this hegemonic boy code and its continuation in the guy code.

SOCIALIZATION: THE RESISTANCE

In his 1973 book, *Home from the War,* psychohistorian Robert Jay Lifton uses his "rap sessions" with Vietnam veterans, many of them active in the Vietnam Veterans against the War movement, to understand what other Americans might learn about human nature and society from the experiences of those veterans. In a chapter devoted to the infamous massacre at the village of My Lai on March 16, 1968, Lifton recounts his conversations with the lone member of that platoon who did not fire his weapon while his comrades murdered hundreds of women, children, and old men in the village (Jones 2017). Lifton was interested in the sources of strength of character a man could bring to resisting peer pressure in his male friendship group. In the case of that lone resister, Lifton found that he had some religious background, but the most important source of strength was the soldier's strong sense of military discipline and honor. He simply thought that participating in the massacre would be dishonorable. Another hero of the day was Hugh Thompson, a helicopter pilot who (with his crew) arrived on the scene and effectively stopped the massacre (Wiener 2018).

Men every day resist the messages forced upon them by their male friendship groups, the institutions they live and work in, and the mass media. Despite strong peer pressure, young men sometimes walk away from fraternity or sports team hazing. In *Burning Sands* (2017), a Netflix movie about an African American fraternity "hell week," one of the five pledges walks away from the hazing. Even military service members, who work and play and fight in a total institution (Goffman 1961), can use their bodies for "microresistance" against the regulations and customs of the institution (Wallis and Mechling 2020).

In Niobe Way's 2011 book on boys' friendships, one of the bodies of research she delves into is on boys' "processes of resistance to cultural conventions, dictates, stereotypes, and expectations" (Way 2011, 67–74). In her own longitudinal research with adolescent boys and her survey of the literature on boys and their friendships, Way discovers in some of her interviews the sorts of resources boys bring to challenging the larger cultural narrative that they are less emotional than girls and that their friendships differ from those of girls. In Chapter 4 I take up what Way discovers about patterns of male friendship, but here it is enough to say that boys often have support at home for resisting gender stereotypes. And these boys in her samples are culturally diverse.

MORE COMPLICATIONS

If the neat picture of psychological development in young men is getting a bit fuzzy the more we take into account changes in the patterns of family and socialization, two other changes over the past forty years further threaten generalizing from the feminist psychoanalytic model. The first is an evolution in female development, and the second is a shift in boys' understanding of agency in defining their sexual and gender identities.

Since boys and young men tend to define themselves as "not women," we should look at how girls and young women have been changing in the late twentieth and early twenty-first centuries. I can sketch these changes briefly, based mainly on ethnographic research by folklorists, sociologists, and anthropologists who actually study young people in their "natural settings"—playgrounds, schools, summer camps, and so on.

For decades those who studied the friendship groups of children thought the stereotypes were true, that girls' play in groups tended to be more passive and cooperative than boys' play, which was seen as active, aggressive, and competitive. Scholars thought girls' friendships tended to be dyads and less resilient than boys' friendships, which often involved larger groups and were more resilient, less easily broken. These generalizations did not quite get things right; only with ethnographic studies of girls' play and friendship groups in the 1970s, for example, did scholars begin to understand that girls were just as aggressive and competitive as boys, but girls learned to mask those "masculine" qualities (e.g., Hughes 1993). Second-wave feminism in the 1970s also enabled girls to have experiences more like boys', including team sports. We cannot overestimate the effect of Title IX of the Educational Amendments of 1972 and the opportunities it gives young women to participate in team sports. The 1970s also saw increased attention to the psychological development of girls (e.g., Pipher 1994). In short, the play experiences and friendship groups of girls and young women were becoming more like those of boys and young men.

The war memoirs by women veterans of the wars in Iraq and Afghanistan speak clearly to the consequences of the changes in the early socialization of girls and young women (Wallis and Mechling 2019). Some of those female veterans cite team sports as the source of their understanding of the male friendship cultures of the military units they were joining. Some were raised with brothers or otherwise thought of themselves as "tomboys" more comfortable playing with boys than with girls. The women who join the modern American military services are not a random sample of women, but they add to the evidence that young women in the first decades of the twenty-first century generally do not fit the stereotypes of "the feminine" used in the boy code and the guy code.

I raise this issue here without being able to pursue it in these pages, tagging it as a cultural change worth analysis. Put simply, if the unconscious dynamics of the construction of normative masculinity as "not female," as feminist theory has it, responds to the facts that women mother and that young women behave in certain stereotypical ways, how does female movement away from the stereotypes change the male developmental dynamic? We cannot overstate the fact that so many young women encountered by young men in their everyday lives do not fit the code stereotypes. For many young men, "not female" loses its meaning if they encounter young women every day who demonstrate none of the dependence, emotional variability, and other factors previously associated with "female" and instead meet young women who are more and more like themselves. The young women who pass the test of basic training, even becoming members of the elite fighting groups, signal the "new woman" many young men are living, studying, working, and fighting alongside (Lacdan 2019). This in no way changes what was true in 1917 or 1942 or even 1968, so I feel comfortable sticking to the feminist psychoanalytic understandings of the men in the snapshots from earlier eras and wars.

It is possible that the changes in young women's behavior will not cause the young men in the military to abandon the guy code, which, if anything, is a code "on steroids" in the military. I can imagine male warriors concluding that "some women" are just like men, that those female warriors adopt some version of the guy code to "fit in" to the very male culture of the military unit. This raises very interesting questions I cannot answer here, especially without sufficient ethnographic evidence exploring the attitudes of women in the military toward the guy code. Tantalizing questions linger.

At present we lack strong evidence about how the increasing presence of women in American military units and their new roles there change the dynamics of the previously very male folk cultures of military groups. When we turn our attention to the changing landscape of male sexual and gender identity in the military, the evidence is more plentiful. Again, I have to be brief here.

Ever since the research on male sexuality by Alfred C. Kinsey and his colleagues (Kinsey, Pomeroy, and Martin 1948), researchers and the public alike have understood that male sexual practices and sexual identity are not binary, not simply heterosexual or homosexual, but far more diverse and fluid. Although the institution of the American military does everything it can to create warriors who fit the cultural norm of strong, heterosexual masculinity, the actual men in the military have lived the Kinsey scale. Allan Bérubé (1990) has compiled the most comprehensive history of gay men in the military, and the books by Steven Zeeland (1993, 1995, 1996, 1999) provide voluminous testimony about the actual sexual practices of military men, with many of the accounts featuring men having sex with other males.

Jane Ward (2015) uses interviews and other evidence to argue that many men who see themselves as heterosexual, or "straight," are capable of having sex with other men under certain circumstances, while still hanging on to their straight identity. Ritch C. Savin-Williams (2017) uses his interviews with young men to attempt to parse out the sexual identity of those men he calls "mostly straight," describing them as having a "fourth sexual identity," not straight, not bisexual, not gay, but "mostly straight." Other scholars writing about millennials and the iGen (Generation Z) come across the same truth—young men in the United States in 2020 view sexual identity and gender identity as fluid, and the same goes for sexual practices. Young men often see this fluidity in themselves, and even if they don't see it as defining them, they are tolerant of it in others.

The relevance of this trend lies in the increasing presence in the US military of men openly declaring their nonnormative sexual identity, and even gender identity. The end of "Don't Ask, Don't Tell" permitted many men to be open about their sexual orientation. And the policy permitting trans people to enter the military made public the fact that gender identity can be fluid as well.

As I was with the changes in the socialization of women over the past two or three generations, I am driven to ask what effect the openness about male sexual identity and practices has on the boy code and the guy code, particularly in the military. Surely the trend muddies the definition of masculinity traditionally embraced by the military. Again, I am raising questions I am not prepared to answer here.

These changes matter because my analysis of the snapshots in this book rests on the premise that men in an all-male friendship group will use their everyday folk practices to manage their friendships and, especially, to maintain the normative heterosexual military identity, maintaining the meaning of very close male bonding as between heterosexual men.

I could have announced in the title of this book that my ending point for the snapshots is the Vietnam War era, the last era when the vernacular photographs in my collection and in the collections of John Ibson (2002) and most other scholars interested in soldier snapshots are all on film. The feminist psychoanalytic theory about the construction of normative masculinity in the United States works perfectly fine for understanding those snapshots, but my certainty about the dynamics waivers when we get to the millennial generation of men. I solved my problem by including no digital snapshots from the Gulf War to the present. At the same time, I want to note that we still do not have a clear picture of how the social and cultural changes of the past three decades necessarily force us to reconsider some classic notions of masculinity studies, including the boy code and the guy code.

THE MEN WHO ENTER THE MILITARY

The details of the experiences of the actual men who enter the military bring us back to earth as we cautiously reconsider what we might call "orthodox" feminist psychoanalytic theory about male development. The snapshots presented in the following chapters come from military experiences across a great many years, from World War I to the Gulf War, when digital snapshots replaced film. The historian resists the temptation to treat all of the soldier snapshots as if their social, cultural, and historical contexts are identical. Ibson (2002) notes a pattern of change across decades, and much of what he says about those changes can be seen in my own collection of snapshots.

One way historians generalize about the experiences of Americans is to characterize "generations," understanding that the description of each generation grossly generalizes about a large birth cohort. Margaret Mead (1975) was interested in the particular shape of American generations and the dynamics of their interaction, and in the 1960s the increasing conflict between young people and those over the age of thirty came to be called "the generation gap." Generational analysis by historians became well known with the 1991 publication of *Generations: The History of America's Future, 1584–2069,* by William Strauss and Neil Howe. Their basic premise is that American history can be understood as an ongoing cycle of birth cohort generations, each about twenty years long. My soldier snapshots begin with World War I, the Lost Generation, roughly from 1901 to 1924. World War II was fought by the G.I. Generation, roughly from 1925 to 1945.

The postwar Baby Boomer Generation (born roughly from 1943 to 1960) fought the Vietnam War as youthful volunteers and draftees, and they were followed by a generation commonly called Generation X because of the Douglas Coupland 1991 novel of that title, though Howe and Strauss (1993) prefer the name "13th Generation" (born from 1961 to 1981) both because that birth cohort is literally the thirteenth generation of Americans since the founding and because the association of thirteen with "unlucky" seems apt. Then comes the Millennial Generation (1982–2004), only occasionally called "Generation Y" (Howe and Strauss 2000). Generation Z is commonly used to name the generation born from 2005 to the present, though I prefer Jean Twenge's (2017) invention of the term "iGen" for those young people, as they came of age when the iPhone was widely available, and Twenge sees that social communication device and social media platform as the defining feature of their lives.

The arguments by Strauss and Howe about generations and, especially, about how history repeats itself in cycles, are controversial and there is no need for me to plunge into that controversy. I raise the generation issue because generational analysis brings our attention to significant events in the lives of each generation and reminds us that the age of a person can be as important as other particular characteristics of the individual, including gender, sexual orientation, ethnicity, and social class, to name just a few.

It would be a mistake for me to assume that young men in the military in 2020 are free from the pressures of the guy code because they are from the millennial generation or, now, from the iGen (Twenge 2017). Generations matter, as norms of masculinity change a bit—but maybe just a little bit. Complicating things even more is the fact that many of the men in the military in World War I, World War II, the Korean War, and the Vietnam War were drafted (some volunteered, of course), and now we have an all-volunteer military. The men who enter the military and who show up in these snapshots are not a random sample of American men. We need to know the demographics of service members.

Those demographics matter for my analysis of masculinity as understood and performed by the soldiers because we know that ideas about masculinity vary according to the qualities listed above of a given individual—not only age, gender, sexual orientation, social class, and ethnicity, but also a list of other individual differences, including rural/urban upbringing, religious beliefs, social beliefs (prejudices, for example), and political beliefs. Drafts famously create military units overrepresented by some social classes and ethnic groups (to say nothing of segregation regulations in the US military up through World War II). But all-volunteer armies are no more a random sample of American men than are armies created by a draft. The many war memoirs I have read by veterans of the wars in Iraq and Afghanistan, for example, make it clear that many young men volunteer to serve for economic reasons.

I wrote "young men" in the previous paragraph, but yet another historical change that might have effects on the performance of masculinity by male soldiers is the increasing presence of women in the American armed services. This is a book about the men in the snapshots, but the presence of women in previously all-male friendship groups (e.g., a platoon) might change the male folk culture. My examples stop with the advent of digital snapshots, so analyzing the effects of women in the military on the performance of masculinity by the men in the vernacular photographs will have to wait for another scholar and another time.

I mentioned sexual orientation above as one of the variables affecting ideas about masculinity among men. What seems to have remained somewhat constant over the past one hundred years (World War I to the current wars) is the shape of hegemonic heterosexual masculinity, both in the public culture and in the male friendship group. What has also remained fairly constant over that century has been the presence of men in the military whose sexual identity and practices have not matched the norm of heterosexuality.

The reader might wonder why I continue to fall back upon the orthodox

feminist psychoanalytic understanding of male psychological development and its consequences for the male practices we see in the vernacular
photography. Recall that in the Introduction I invoked Clifford Geertz's
view that cultural interpretation is scientific in the same sense that clinical inference in medicine is scientific. The practitioner gathers evidence,
formulates a hypothesis about what explanation makes "best sense" of the
perceived pattern in the evidence, and "tests" that hypothesis. I turn to the
feminist psychoanalytic theory in my interpretations of these snapshots
because time and again the theory helps me make "best sense" of what
I am seeing in the snapshot, fashioning an interpretation based on what I
know from other sources of knowledge about the creation, maintenance,
and repair of American masculinities. Sometimes the snapshots, the visual
evidence, confirm what we think we know from other evidence. Sometimes the snapshot surprises us by showing something not at all obvious
in the other evidence.

3

The Concept of Play

Humans play. Everyone reading that sentence no doubt entertains a commonsense, everyday understanding of play. Playing diverts our attention from work, from unpleasantries. We play because it is "fun." We "enjoy" playing. Those words, of course, do not actually define play as a human activity. For the many moments in this book of the play captured in the soldiers' vernacular photography, I need an understanding of play that goes beyond the everyday. That understanding, which I explore here, is the "play frame" (Bateson 1955/1972).

Through the long history of ideas about play (Sutton-Smith 2001), philosophers, historians, and social scientists realized that play is a realm of experience apart from the everyday, that play provides a window into a more fantastic realm. We recognize this in children and their pretend play, their "make-believe" play, their fantasy play in which they can be anything and do anything quite apart from the taken-for-granted reality they live in. The realm of play is magical, and many scholars have recognized the play element in religion and ritual. Johan Huizinga (1949), after all, saw play as one of the foundations of the emergence of human cultures, and Brian Sutton-Smith (2017) argues that play helps us both express and manage our emotions.

The anthropologist Gregory Bateson offers what I think is the most useful understanding of play, the idea of the play frame, which he developed in the 1950s. I shall use this phrase and the idea behind it often in the chapters that follow. It is central to my understanding of how humans have meaningful communication. The sociologist Erving Goffman borrows Bateson's idea to make an even stronger argument about the play frame. Goffman (1956, 1963, 1967) bases an entire theory of social action and interaction on the similarity between theatrical stage drama (roles, scripts, props, front stage, backstage) and all everyday social reality. Goffman argues in his 1974 book *Frame Analysis,* in fact, that all of the everyday social reality we encounter is, in essence, a confidence game, with some of us acting in good faith and some of us acting in bad faith. Goffman recognizes that Bateson offered too romantic a notion of the play frame, that players in the frame do not always have the same power in the frame, nor do they always share the same motives for entering the frame. Bateson's formulation of the play frame, nonetheless, is the core idea in Goffman's dramatistic theory of social interaction.

Observing monkeys and otters playing at the Fleishhacker Zoo in San Francisco in the 1950s (he was working at the time with a team at the Veterans Administration Hospital in Palo Alto on a communications theory of schizophrenia), Bateson wondered how those mammals understood that the signals and behavior in their playfighting, for example, were not "real." Bateson realized that the mammals had exchanged the message, somehow, that they were entering a play frame, a frame distinct from their everyday interactions, including real fighting. He realized that the mammals had exchanged a "metamessage," a message about messages, and the metamessage in that case was "This is play." Once that frame was agreed to, the participants understood that the nips and bites and other displays of aggression—the nip that is not a nip, as he writes—did not mean what they meant in another frame, such as "This is a fight."

Those mammals do not have verbal language, of course, so they could not exchange the metamessage except through nonverbal means: body language, gestures, and sounds. Ethologists, those scientists who study animal behavior, have observed many sorts of signals mammals have to extend an invitation to play. Many of us have witnessed the canine "play bow" performed by our pet dogs, and when we pick up the ball the dog has placed in front of us, we have accepted the invitation to play (Mechling 1989). We humans have verbal language, of course, but it is still the case that we more often use body language, facial expression, tone of voice, and other nonverbal signals to invite someone into a play frame and to accept an invitation from others.

Bateson makes the important point that entering a play frame with others signals to the participants something about their relationship, that they trust each other to enter an interaction where messages, including actions, do not mean what they ordinarily mean. A playfight, whether verbal or physical, requires such trust, and we know trust is an important element in sustaining the bonding necessary in the military. Playing, in that sense, provides an important experience of bonding. Bateson also notes that the play frame is fragile, easily broken. The nip that is too hard can break the play frame and become a real fight. The insult that touches on a sensitive matter can turn a playful verbal duel of insults into a real fight. If the players value their relationship, in most cases they will try to repair the play frame.

Bateson notes that the play frame presents a reality in the subjunctive mood, the "What if?" mood parallel to the subjunctive mood in grammar. The play frame lets the players experience, even experiment with, a reality that does not exist outside the play frame. If the frame of everyday life features the sense-making that gives order to what is otherwise a chaotic flow of experience, then the play frame provides a "safe" space and time for nonsense. We need both sense and nonsense in our everyday lives; without nonsense, we might not fully appreciate sense (Stewart 1979). And, as Geertz (1983), shows, what we take as "common sense" is not universal; common sense is profoundly cultural.

One form of nonsense we find in the play frame is inversion—of social roles, identities, and power (Babcock 1978). In the play frame men can dress as women and women can dress as men, an inversion experienced and observed as fun because nonsensical, a violation of our usual, everyday experience of dress as a reliable signal of gender. Historically in New Orleans Mardi Gras celebrations, white men have dressed as black men, while the African Americans in Mardi Gras traditionally dress as American Indians (never as white people).

The subjunctive "What if?" mood of the play frame can be dangerous, subversive to the normal order of things. In the United States, Mardi Gras (literally "fat Tuesday" in French, a day of excess on the eve of the self-imposed asceticism set to begin the next morning in the Christian calendar, Ash Wednesday) is just one example of the playful festival Carnival, observed in many cultures, especially in Latin America and the Caribbean.

Some governments have been wary of Carnival and of the nonsense it both invites and shields. The celebration of disorder during Carnival and at other times can threaten order.

As I have mentioned already, Bateson did get one thing wrong about the play frame. He seems to see the play frame through romantic eyes, assuming that the players are there voluntarily and can exercise power equally in the play. Goffman (1974) corrected that view. Not everyone in a play frame is there voluntarily, and people often use the play frame to "mask" other motives (Sutton-Smith and Kelly-Byrne 1984).

We need one more piece of the puzzle to comprehend why an understanding of the play frame is so central to understanding the everyday cultures of the soldiers revealed in the snapshots. A combination of the Protestant ethic and the dynamics of America as a business civilization combined as long ago as the seventeenth century to create in many Americans a belief that work and play are opposite activities. Play was suspect, a "waste" of time and energy and resources. In American thought, even the idea of play as "recreation" had to have a practical goal in order for society to consider the time spent away from work as "productive," as serving work.

The accepted play/work dichotomy misdirects us. The social psychologist Mihaly Csikszentmihalyi offers a different way to look at the thoughts and feelings we associate with play. In *Beyond Boredom and Anxiety* (1975) he proposes that people could experience what he called "flow" in any number of activities, that the binary work/play is useless if you recognize that the brain surgeon and the rock climber are both experiencing a state of flow, an experiential state of engrossment in an activity, a state in which the participant loses all sense of time and place. If a task has a low degree of challenge or difficulty and the individual has a high degree of skill, then the individual experiences boredom. If, however, the task has a high degree of difficulty and the individual possesses a low level of skill to apply to that task, then the individual experiences anxiety. Neither boredom nor anxiety is fun. When skill and challenge are in a creative tension, then the individual experiences flow. To experience a state of flow is fun.

The notion of flow resembles the experiential state others identify as "ecstasy," from the Greek "ek-stasis," meaning "standing outside oneself," standing aside from the ordinary, taken-for-grated, everyday experience. When the American philosopher and psychologist William James wrote *The Varieties of Religious Experience* (1902), he explored how some religious experiences (like fasting, self-flagellation, prayer, ritual) induced in the individual a state of ecstasy, what today we might call flow.

We have, then, in the concepts of the play frame, flow, and ecstasy the ideas we need to make sense of the play of soldiers, Marines, sailors, and aviators in the military. Being in the military is a job and involves work. Recruits are given duties and work assignments in boot camp, and warriors in the combat zone have duties and work assignments making war and sometimes making peace. We now have concepts that move beyond the simple work/play model to illuminate the complex processes involved when soldiers play, but note, too, that someone can enter a state of flow while doing work.

These concepts will help make sense of particular sorts of snapshots in subsequent chapters devoted to human pyramids, cross-dressing, play-fighting, hazing, and deep play. We need to explore one more important aspect of play: how men use play to manage their emotions.

PLAY AND EMOTIONS

An important idea running through this book is that the soldier snapshots show us how men in the military use play to manage their interpersonal relationships, most importantly their friendships. In Chapter 2, I laid out a set of ideas used by scholars to understand how men construct, maintain, and repair their performance of masculinity. In Chapter 4, I explore the very complex issue of male friendship. This chapter on play lies between those two chapters because I see play as the set of practices men use to manage their male friendships. Play might not be uniquely suited for this task; some rituals also provide collective, symbolic practices and meanings for men's understanding of their friendships. Both play and ritual, two "complementary frames," as one anthropologist puts it (Handelman 1977), invoke emotional responses over rational responses. So we need to understand this final link between the performance of masculinity and the management of male friendship.

The injunctions of the boy code and the guy code generally steer boys and young men away from expressions of emotions, which are seen as feminine and weak. Unfortunately, the only emotion generally permitted in boys is anger, though adults try to channel this potentially destructive emotion (Stearns and Stearns 1986; Pollack 1998).

At a few places in this book I return to Sutton-Smith's argument in *Play for Life* (2017), his last book, published posthumously, which I find very useful in understanding what sorts of information we can glean from the snapshots. Briefly, Sutton-Smith consults the scientific research on emotions and arrives at the conclusion that a crucial function of play is the regulation of emotions. He shows how all sorts of free play and formal games muster what scientists consider the "secondary emotions" (empathy, pride, envy, embarrassment, guilt, shame) in order to control, to regulate the "primary emotions," including happiness, shock, anger, fear, and disgust (Sutton-Smith 2017, 53–54). "In short," he writes, "the primary emotions are expressed imaginatively in games; the secondary emotions, realistically in their regulation" (Sutton-Smith 2017, 71). As his subtitle says, play is essential for "emotional survival," and the bulk of his book demonstrates his thesis by showing how play and games manage the primary emotions.

I have argued that what Sutton-Smith says about play really is true of all folklore (Mechling 2019), that folk practices become the occasion to make available to ourselves and to our friends our emotions. Folklore manages and regulates our emotions, and in the male friendship groups documented by the soldier snapshots, the management of emotions is absolutely crucial to maintaining the friendships. I hope to show in subsequent chapters how we can read emotional signals in the snapshots and how the vernacular practices captured in the snapshots are part of the regulation of emotions in the male friendship group.

EXCURSUS: FORMAL GAMES

A great many snapshots taken by soldiers in camps and in the field show them playing football, baseball, and volleyball (I have seen one of American soldiers playing soccer). War and games are inextricably tangled in human history and in the language we use to talk about both realms of activity. The most famous link is made in the now-famous claim that "the Battle of Waterloo was won on the playing fields of Eton," attributed in oral lore to the Duke of Wellington but well-enough known and used to show up in other places, including George Orwell's essays in *The Lion and the Unicorn* (1941). Barbara Ehrenreich (1997) links war to the "blood sports" humans enjoy, and Alan Dundes (1978, 1997) connects the structures and meanings of sports to war. The metaphors of war pervade team sports, from the youthful game of capture the flag (Flag Wars) to American football. Peter Murphy (2001) has chapters on "sex as sport" and "sex as war and conquest" in the folk speech of men in groups. Apparently soldiers in the field relieve themselves of the stress of military life, including combat, by playing games that actually mimic violent combat.

This paradoxical relief from real combat by engaging in the stylized combat of games makes sense once one realizes the important role of "stylized" aggression and violence in the male friendship group. I explore this idea more in Chapter 10, but it is enough here to observe the therapeutic value for soldiers of team sports mimicking combat. One way of taming the fear and anxiety and stress of actual combat (including the stress of the anticipation of combat) is to engage in combat in the play frame, which is "not real" and is actually a safe space and time for exploring the anger and aggression pent-up in the warrior (Wallis and Mechling 2019). The formal game uses rules to bring order to stylized aggression.

I could reproduce here snapshots of soldiers playing team sports in their down time, but I have just made the central interpretive point about those games. Instead, I want to focus on a category of games also captured by snapshots—games of chance.

The many snapshots showing soldiers playing games of chance—notably card games and dice (craps)—should not be overlooked quickly. These are familiar pastimes, of course, but their presence in the panoply of activities helping soldiers get through otherwise boring times carries serious meanings, even more so than those represented by the recognizable contests of football, baseball, and volleyball, all games or sports well-represented in the snapshots. All games and sports involve some small measure of chance, of course, but cards and dice are closer to games of pure chance. Snapshot 3.1 has writing on the back: "crap games at ship service outing June 1 1943."

Anthropologists who have studied play and games see three basic types of games—games of skill, games of strategy, and games of chance (Roberts, Arth, and Bush 1959). Many games combine elements of all three, but the types help describe the "challenges" of most games. Anthropologists suspect that the type of games favored in a particular society might be a good indicator of the society's ideas about the relations between effort and outcome. Thus, in an achievement-oriented society like the United States, games of skill and strategy are far more common than games of pure luck. Asian societies, in contrast, tend to favor games of luck. These ideas about

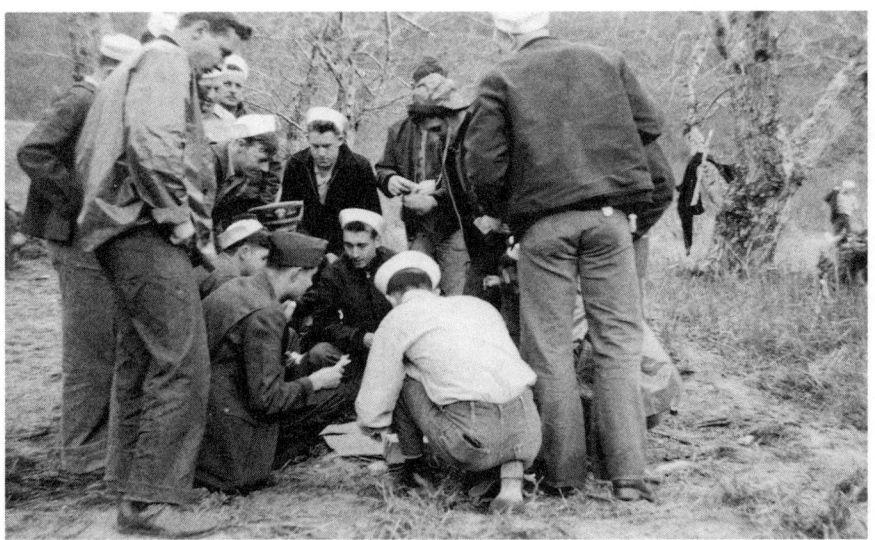

Snapshot 3.1

the correlation between the elements of games and the elements of the society playing those games are old now, and we could find many problems
with the generalizations. What we can retain from looking at this research
is the insight that some groups favor testing luck with games of chance.
Enter our soldiers.

Warriors want war to be a rational human activity, but their actual experience is of irrational chaos. Who lives and who dies seems to most combatants to be not a matter of strength, training, and strategic intelligence
but of sheer, dumb, sometimes cruel luck. Even the folk speech of warriors
reflect this experience with chance. "There it is" and "It ain't nothing"
commonly show up in war memoirs and reflect the folk speech of the warriors. Both are what I would call proverbial expressions of resignation in
the face of the irrationality of who lives and who dies in combat.

This everyday reality in the military life, especially in the combat zone,
raises the stakes of games of chance. The card games and crap games are
not mere distractions from danger; they test one's luck. This function of
the game of chance is unconscious, of course; the men are just having fun
and relaxing, and they are also bonding through the side-by-side activity
(more on this in Chapter 4).

4

Male Friendship

Of all the sorts of vernacular photography of men, photographs picturing men in more intimate poses—with their arms around each other, one sitting on the lap of another, holding hands, and so on—have received the most scholarly attention. David Deitcher's (2001) study of such photographs from 1840 to 1918 and then, the next year, John Ibson's (2002) book on such photographs from 1850 to 1950 set the standard for such study. Considering vernacular photographs well past the ending date for Deitcher's book, Ibson's collection of over five thousand images focuses more on the snapshot than on the studio portrait. The online blog by Brett and Kate McKay, the Art of Manliness, relies heavily upon Ibson, noting his important conclusion that the signs of male intimacy in the snapshots he studies reach a high point in World War II and then decline notably in the 1950s. In their most recent (2020) update of the blog, the McKays speculate a bit about the greater comfort boys raised in the millennial generation (born roughly from 1982 to 2000) have in physically expressing their affection for each other, replacing high fives and other forms of the handshake with more hugging.

Ibson's book is most important for what I have to say here, in part because his training and teaching and scholarly practices are all grounded in American studies, like mine, but also because he devotes chapters of his fine book to snapshots taken during the two world wars. Ibson's main thesis is that the images of American men with men reveal a comfort with physical intimacy between male friends, with wartime intensifying that physical intimacy, and then an abrupt decline in the intimacy in the wake of World War II.

Ibson provides examples of and discusses several of the folk events I analyze in this book, including cross-dressing theatricals (pp. 73–75), the Neptune Ceremony (pp. 87–92, 176–177), and the presentation of men in magazines and advertising. I shall not reproduce Ibson's analysis here. My collection of snapshots of men in intimate poses contains examples very much like those published by Ibson.

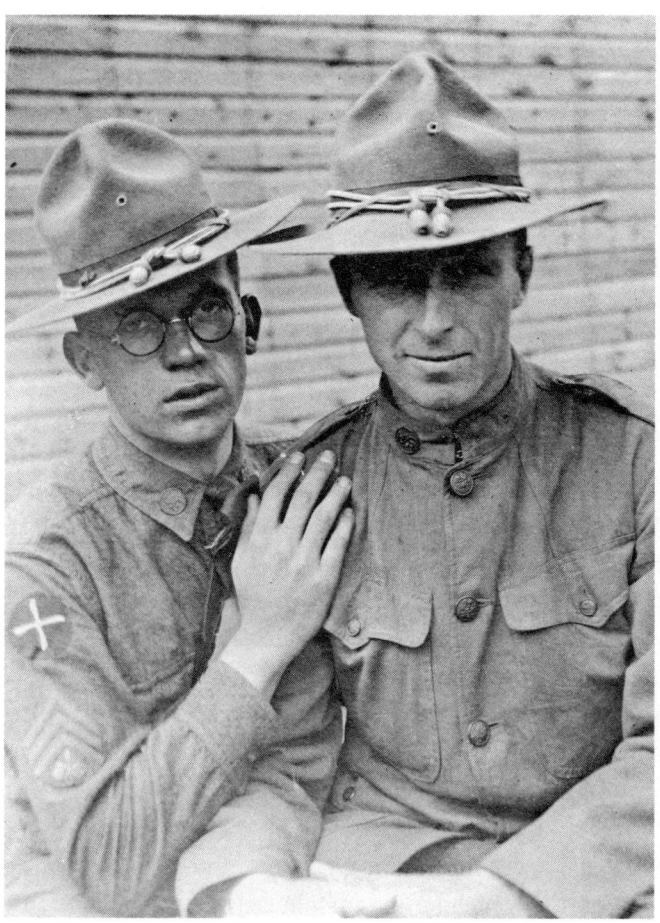

Snapshot 4.1

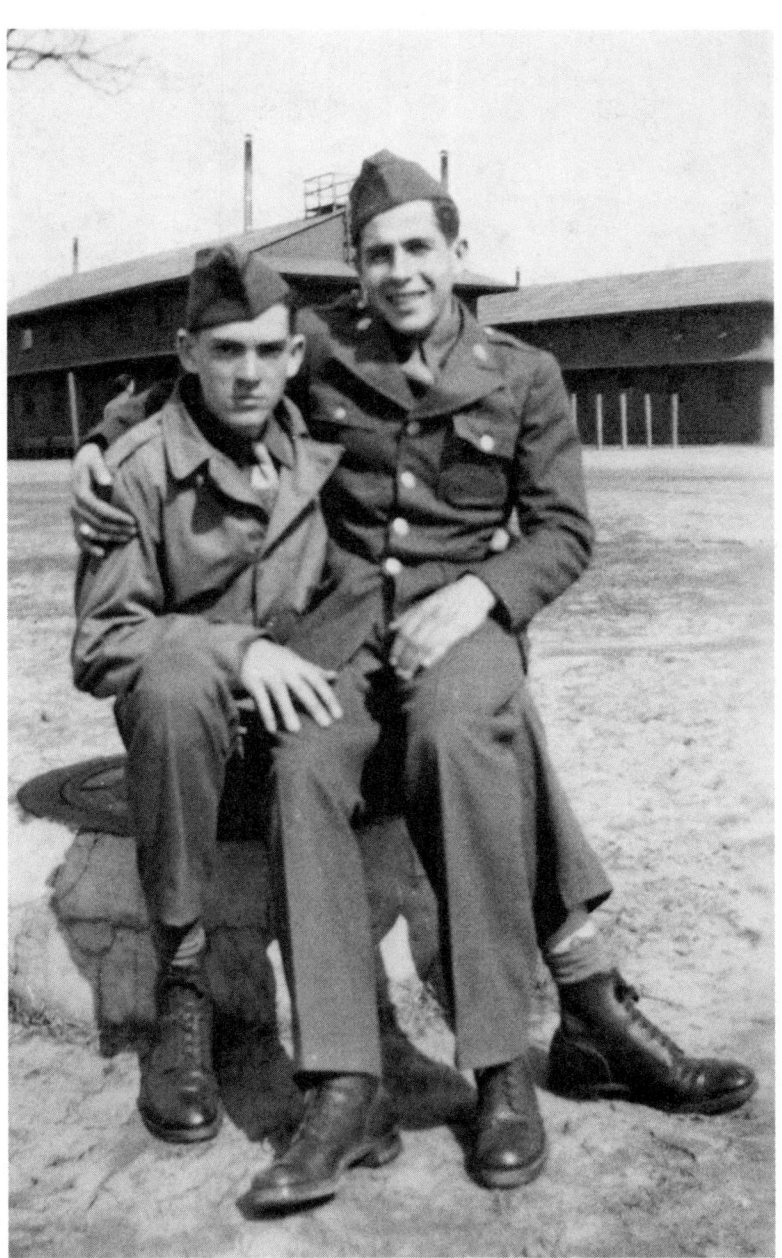

Snapshot 4.2

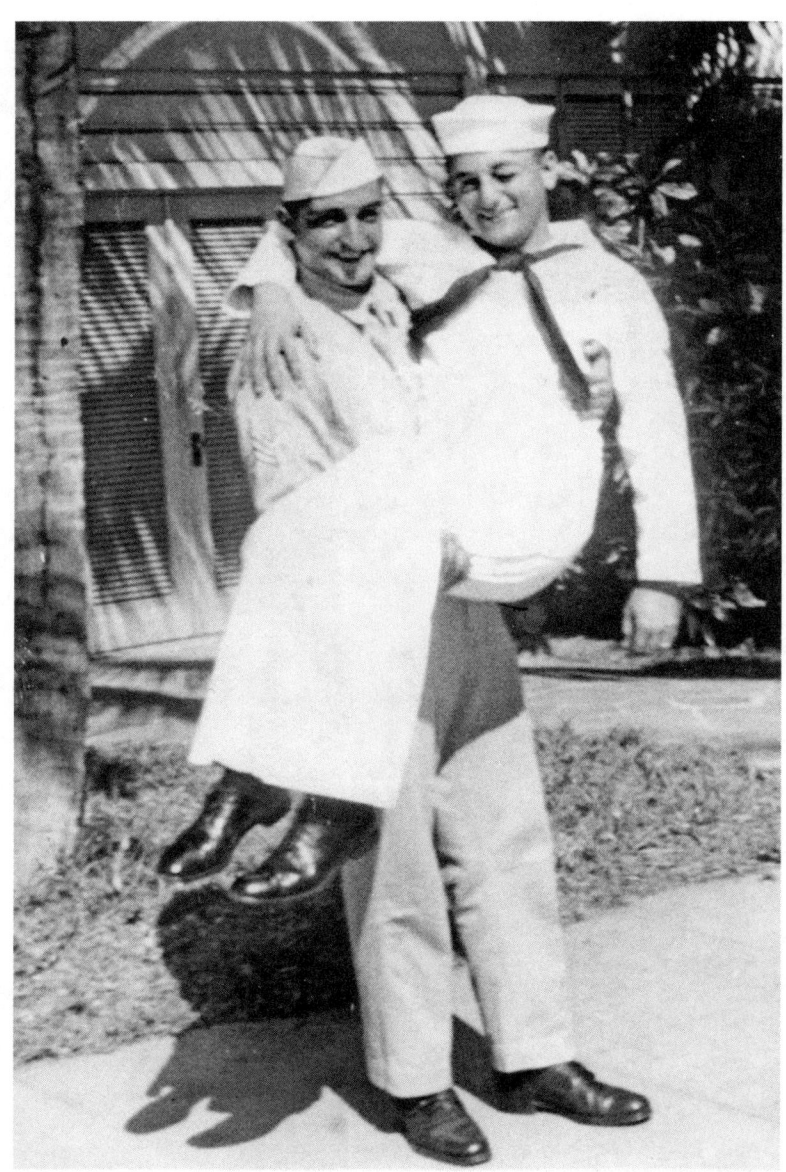

Snapshot 4.3

Snapshot 4.1 is from the World War I era, judging from the uniforms, and the other two likely date from World War II. The poses are typical of those found in the "buddy" snapshots—best friends with arms around each other, sometimes sitting on a lap (Snapshot 4.2) and sometimes even holding the other man as if he were a child or a new bride.

Other snapshots of buddies hint at stronger affection between the soldiers, as in Snapshots 4.4, 4.5, and 4.6.

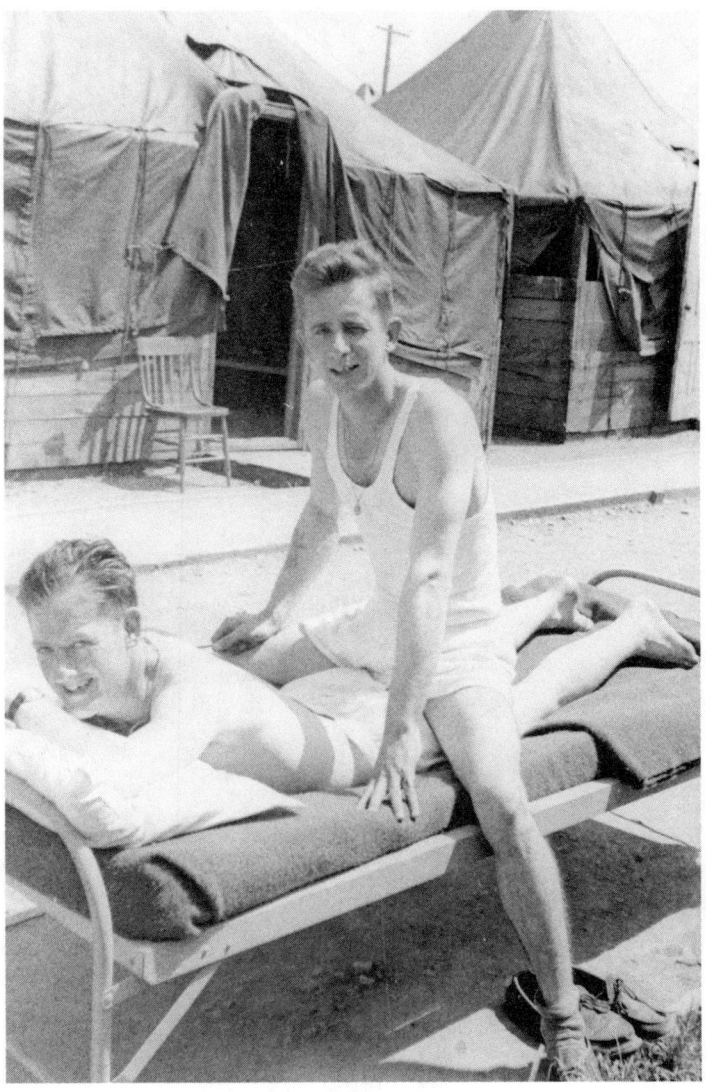

Snapshot 4.4

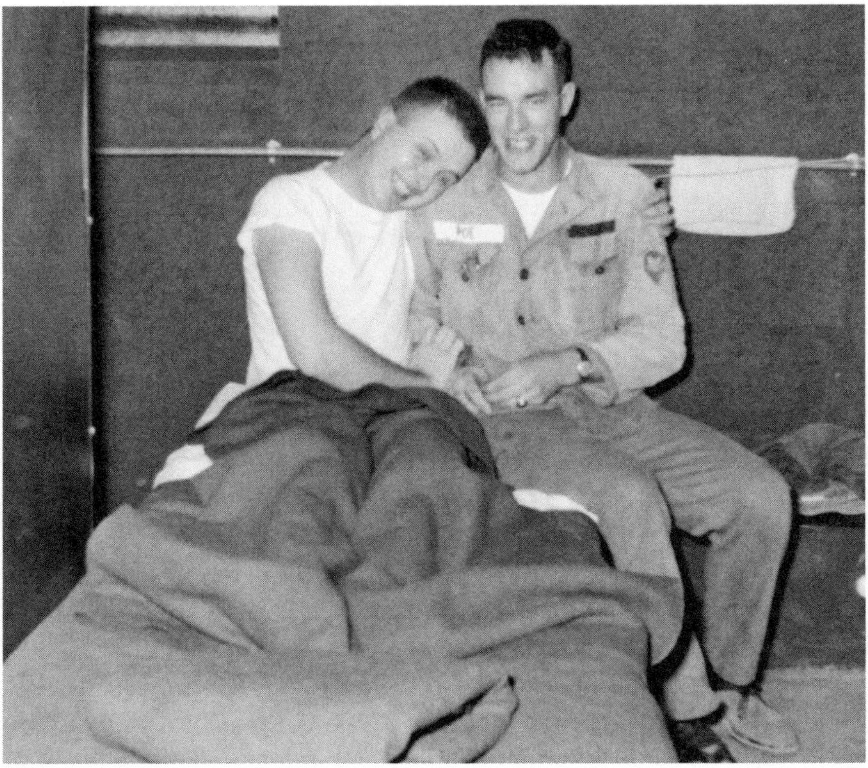

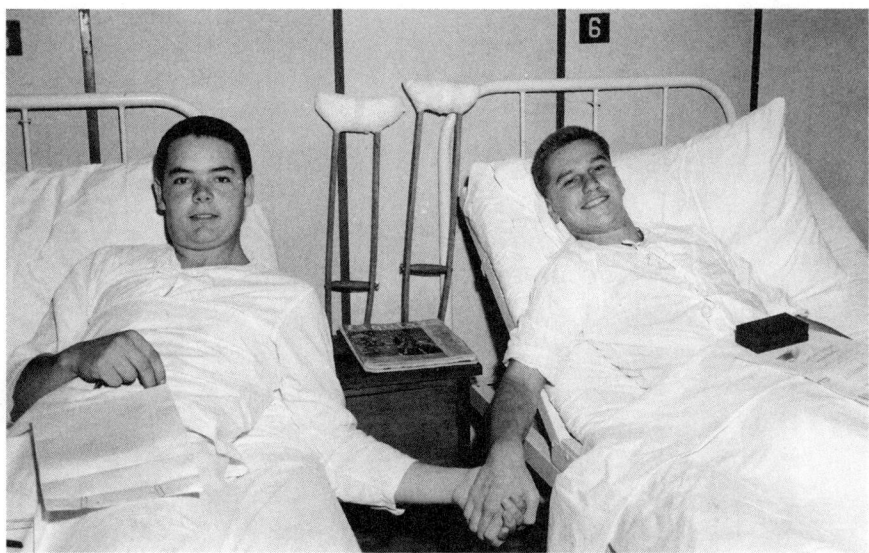

Snapshot 4.5

Snapshot 4.6

MALE FRIENDSHIP

Whenever someone writes about these buddy snapshots in the military (primarily Ibson 2002 and Hanson 2014), they make the important point that friendship bonds under fire tend to be intense. Actually, the point they make is that men forge strong, close friendships in all-male institutions, especially total institutions like the military. We know this is true even without the vernacular photography. Testimony in countless war memoirs, novels, reportage, autobiographies, and oral histories describe very close friendships in the military. Popular culture narratives—primarily film and television—spin fictional stories, some worthy of the label "mythologies" (in the sense Slotkin 1973, 1985, 1992, writes about the mythologies of the West in American popular culture), with close male friendships often at the heart of the story. Those who write about American film recognize a genre called "buddy films." Popular song lyrics often recount close male friendships. There is a reason why both Ibson (2002, 168–169) and Hanson (2014, 49) point to the song "My Buddy," extremely popular with the troops in World War II, and Ibson (2002, 169) adds that Cole Porter's "Let's Be Buddies," written by Porter for his 1942 musical, *Panama Hattie,* uses that same key term "buddies" to characterize close friendships. Finally, if we look we see strong male friendships in comic books, graphic novels, and even some video games consumed primarily by young men.

This book is about photography, and even in this narrower realm of texts we see signs of strong male friendships. Certainly it is present in certain professional war photographs, some of those images playful and happy and some painfully sad, as in the photographs of a soldier or sailor grieving for a lost friend just killed in combat. Snapshots never capture those saddest of moments, but snapshots do capture moments of the joy and pleasure men in the military take in each other's presence, and many of the snapshots through this book convey that sense of the pleasure of a man's bonding closely with other men.

Male friendship is not an easy "project" for the individual, inside or outside the military. Scholars from many fields have written about male friendship, including psychologists, folklorists, historians, sociologists, and anthropologists. Often the person writing about male friendship also looks at the research on female friendship to draw comparisons. With my own background of decades of fieldwork with Boy Scouts (aged twelve to eighteen) at summer camps in California (Mechling 2001), I especially trust the analysis of male friendship by direct observation, but all sorts of evidence about male friendship pretty much converges on a few salient features.

Generalizing about male friendships is as problematic as making any other generalizations about gender and sexual identity. Ibson (2002) addresses issues of friendship suggested by the snapshots he presents, and he relies somewhat on Peter Nardi's (1999) book, which addresses the larger issue of male friendship before moving on to the main focus of his book, friendships between gay men. Perhaps there is nothing more to say about these snapshots (and the literally hundreds of snapshots of nude army, navy and Marine buddies in Hanson 2014) and male friendship. As I said, we do not need the visual evidence to know that men in the military form strong friendships. Here, as elsewhere in this book, then, I pose the question: do the snapshots of military male friendships tell us anything we don't already know about those friendships?

Perhaps it is because so much of my own fieldwork and writing about masculinity takes boys and male teens as the subject that I find Niobe Way's book, *Deep Secrets: Boys' Friendships and the Crisis of Connection* (2011), a good place to start thinking about male friendship in these snapshots. I am not a veteran of the armed forces, so I cannot bring to this topic firsthand experience, but I have read well over one hundred war memoirs for my teaching and writing, most of the latter with my coauthor, John Paul Wallis, a Marine Corps veteran with two tours of duty in Iraq.

I would never claim that the Boy Scouts is exactly like the American military, but my extensive experience living, working, and playing with adolescent boys and men in the Boy Scouts has immersed me in an all-male culture, including experiences at the total institutions that are scout camps. I was a Cub Scout from ages eight to eleven and a Boy Scout from eleven to sixteen, and then I began my fieldwork with a California troop in 1976 and studied them on and off for many years until I finished my book in 2001. Our younger grandson entered the Boy Scouts in 2006, and I accompanied him to two different summer camps in California in five years. All told, those are lots of years of firsthand experience with male friendship in young and adult men.

Although Nardi (1999) and others writing about the history of male friendship look back at writing as early as Aristotle's, social science research on friendship really is a phenomenon of the twentieth and twenty-first centuries. In her review of social science research on boys' friendships, the earliest work Way finds is from 1902 (Bonser 1902). The concept of adolescence itself was not "invented" until G. Stanley Hall published his massive two-volume work, *Adolescence,* in 1904. For a few decades social scientific interest in young men's friendships arose, in part, out of a growing concern for (one might even say fear of) young men in cities. The Boy Scouts of America was founded in 1910, in large part a response to the adult "moral panic" about poorly socialized and uncontrollable boys (Mechling 2001, xv–xvi). The "child savers" who worked with boys in the first few decades of the twentieth century saw male friendships as both a problem and a possible solution to bringing boys under control. The street gang could be replaced by the Boy Scout patrol, the new "chums," they thought, turning natural adolescent male friendship in the direction of positive social behavior and goals.

I focus here on the patterns and meanings of friendship in young men in the twentieth and twenty-first centuries not just because I came to masculinity studies through the study of boys and adolescent males. Understanding youthful male friendship might help solve one of the nagging issues of generalizing about male friendship in the military, using these snapshots as evidence. Research on adult male friendship is a very recent phenomenon, not much older than the 1990s. That research might give us some confidence in generalizing about male friendship in the soldier snapshots from the Gulf War and the recent wars in Iraq and Afghanistan, but pushing those results back to the Vietnam era or even earlier takes some confidence that patterns of male friendship have not changed much since World War I.

The problem with this approach is that society and cultural patterns do change. Ibson (2002) certainly makes it clear that the changes in the images of male friendship in the snapshots he studies across time are in large part the result of changing cultural ideas and norms about masculinity, including changing norms about male sexual identity and orientation. Ibson's point about the movement of men away from each other's bodies in post–World War II snapshots takes note of the increasing homophobia of the postwar era, homophobia caused by a great many forces but intensified by the Cold War conflation of homosexuality with weakness in an era when the male body and male sexuality needed to convey strength and hardness in the face of communism. Ibson does not exactly put it this way, but we might say that while the male impulse toward and need for close male friendships drives the snapshots of men in close poses, social and cultural forces external to the male friendship largely determine the evidence we find in the snapshots.

What this amounts to is a return to the historian's dilemma of sorting out the impact of biology (particularly developmental psychology) from culture. If we thought the dynamics of male friendship were grounded heavily in biology, we could assume that a close male embrace in 1918 meant the same thing it did in 1943 or 1968. We know the historical contexts for those snapshots are different; do the unconscious dynamics change?

While grappling with these problems of generalizing about the meanings of male friendship in the United States across time, I find Way's (2011) analysis helpful. A developmental psychologist who has had experience as a high school counselor and as a scholar designing and executing longitudinal studies of adolescent males' friendships, Way negotiates very well the problems of generalizing about male friendships.

In my view Way's most important point for analyzing the snapshots is her discovery that boys in early and middle adolescence (American boys, but across social class and ethnic groups in her sample) actually value close male friendships where they can share secrets, feelings, insecurities, and more. The older view was that girls' friendships were more about secrets and emotions, often dyads and fragile, whereas boys' friendships were "thinner," more resilient, and more based on shared activities, such as sports. Way's research explodes that old generalization and helps us realize that adolescent boys' friendships are not that different from girls' friendships, at least around the turn of the twenty-first century.

The change comes, though, in late adolescence (ages sixteen to eighteen). Not for every boy, but for many boys several things help end the experience of very close, emotionally vulnerable friendships with other boys. Way entitles a chapter about male friendship in late adolescence "When You Grow Up, Your Heart Dies," a comment from one of her informants that captures the sense of loss and distrust reported by the young men she interviewed. Those older boys suffer the pain of loss of those close friendships, and Way attributes a range of behavior identified as the "boy crisis," from suicide to expressions of aggression and anger, to the deep sense of loss, loneliness, and isolation those boys feel in late adolescence. They experience "a dramatic decline in the richness and quality of their social relations as they enter manhood" (Way 2011, 211). Way and other social scientists she cites point to the adult "loss of social connectedness" in American culture, an idea that gained popularity with Robert Putnam's best-selling book, *Bowling Alone* (2000).

This discussion of friendships in male adolescence might seem beside the point when looking at the snapshots of adult men in military service, but I find it very useful. Men tend to enter the military at a young age, either through a draft or by volunteering. I have read enough war memoirs to know that young men often lied about their ages or gained parental permission to volunteer the service before their eighteenth birthday, which means that most young men entering the military are aged somewhere between seventeen and twenty-four (let's say).

Way's research tells us something we might not realize about this age group of young men. They are in late adolescence, and if Way is right, many of them enter the military with a deep sense of loss, isolation, loneliness, and distrust of others. They hunger for what they have lost, and the male friendship group in the military restores what they lost—the experience of close, intimate bonding with male friends. Even though a platoon is too large a group of male friends, within that group a young man can find a best friend, or two or three close friends who all provide what early and middle adolescent boys have—friends with whom they can share secrets, vulnerability, and emotions.

That young men forge such close friendships in the military is somewhat surprising, given the institution's valuing of the norms we usually associate with aggressive heterosexual masculinity. Yet young men in the military, whatever their sexual identity and orientation, are able to frame close, affectionate male friendships as heterosexual in motive and practice.

Beyond the general norm of strong, "hard" heterosexuality, with its toughness and ability to "take it like a man," there is another reason why military culture makes it difficult to forge close male friendships. Dyadic male friendships actually threaten the "good order and discipline" valued by the institution. Understanding this threat requires that we understand the distinction between "friendship" and "comradeship."

J. Glenn Gray's World War II war memoir, *The Warriors: Reflections on Men in Battle* (1959/2015), is valuable for many more insights about human nature and the violence of war than his distinction between friendship and comradeship, but that distinction is very revealing in many ways. In a chapter entitled "Love: War's Ally and Foe," Gray describes the "love we call friendship":

Friendship is thus thought to be the most unselfish form of love, since in the
pure state it devotes itself without reserve to the interests of the other. . . . What
meaning has friendship for warriors? How can a young man endure battle when
the fear of death is doubled, when not only his own life but that of his friend
is at stake? . . . Though many men never have a friend, and even the most for-
tunate of us can have few, comradeship is fortunately within reach of the vast
majority. Suffering and danger cannot create friendship, but they can make all
the difference in comradeship. (1959/2015, 89)

In short, there is "a heightened awareness of the self in friendship,"
whereas there is a "suppression of self-awareness in comradeship" (Gray
1959/2015, 90). "Friends live for each other and possess no desire what-
soever for self-sacrifice. When a man dies for his friend, he does it deliberately and not in an ecstasy of emotion. Dying for one's comrades, on the
other hand, is a phenomenon occurring in every war. . . . The impulse to
self-sacrifice is an intrinsic element in the association of organized man
in pursuit of a dangerous and difficult Goal" (Gray 1959/2015, 91). Sarah
Cole (2003, 145) also finds this distinction useful in talking about male
bonding in World War I, though she does not credit the idea to Gray but
finds the distinction made in a 1930 war novel, *Her Privates We*, by Frederic Manning.

Gray's distinction between friendship and comradeship makes the
friendships depicted in soldier snapshots even more puzzling. The military does everything it can to encourage male comradeship and discourage
male friendship. For example, the military has regulations against masturbation (Wallis and Mechling 2019, 106–117) because absorption with the
self makes it difficult to identify with the group. Close friendships can also
threaten morale, especially when a soldier is separated from his best friend
for any number of reasons, including the death of that friend. Some authors
of war memoirs actually say that the death of a close friend in combat made
them wary of ever getting that close to a friend again, a feeling that may
persist through the return to civilian life. The resulting emotional distance
the veteran sometimes practices can damage relationships with friends and
family, and is common in even mild post-traumatic stress disorder (PTSD)
in veterans.

Certainly we see comradeship in some of the snapshots, especially
the group pictures, which sometimes feature the same body language of
physical closeness as the snapshots of two "buddies." The buddy pictures,

though, confirm that, despite the efforts of the institution, strong bonds between two men cannot be extinguished.

TRUST AND FRIENDSHIP

The research on male friendship summarized by Way (2011) and her own extensive longitudinal studies of boys' friendships return again and again to the important role of trust in male friendships. Putting aside the guy code and exposing one's emotional vulnerabilities to another male requires trust. The boys interviewed in Way's study and in others she cites always named trust as a quality they valued in their close friendships. And the loss of trust, betrayal, destroys a friendship, adding to the sense of loss.

Recall that I made this point about trust in the play frame back in Chapter 3. Because the play frame opens up a possibly dangerous world of "What if?," entering a play frame requires trust. Playfighting, both verbal and physical, especially requires trust. The players trust others to follow the rules of the play frame, trust others to not use the play frame for ulterior motives.

Trust is possibly the most valuable element of a male friendship in the military. Warriors depend upon each other, and one of the greatest fears expressed in war memoirs is that the soldier would somehow not do his part. Sebastian Junger (2010) says that his greatest fear during his months at Camp Restrepo was not that he would get killed but that some mistake by him would result in the death of a comrade.

Thinking about the role of trust in male friendship leads us to a surprising conclusion about the soldier snapshots. Like other scholars, I was tempted to look at the snapshots of men, of "buddies," draping their arms around each other, downright "cuddling," sitting on each other's laps, straddling each other's bodies, and even carrying each other cradled in the strong man's arms, as visual documentation of patterns of male friendship. Certainly those images signal friendship. The paradoxical discovery, however, is that male friendship might be better displayed in snapshots of the men at play—building human pyramids, rough-and-tumble playfighting, playfighting with weapons, and caring for a pet animal with buddies. The men at play also are trusting each other.

When I began writing this chapter, I wondered if I had anything to add to the commentary and analysis by Ibson (2002) and Deitcher (2001). Way's work truly deepens our thinking about male friendship, and she articulates and gives detailed evidence for what I only vaguely understood after reading so many war memoirs. The young men in the military arrive there having experienced very close male friendships in early and middle adolescence, only to suffer a profound sense of loss in late adolescence. They show up at basic training looking to recover the male friendships they experienced as younger adolescents, looking to fill the hole left in their hearts by the loss of those friendships. They enter the military hoping to have again a male friend with whom they can be vulnerable and share secrets. The buddy snapshots do not actually show that, but the closeness discussed by Ibson (2002) in the snapshots he studies makes even more sense once we know the deep-seated need many young men have for such friendships.

And one other surprising realization is that the buddy snapshots may not be the best representations of male friendship in the military. The snapshots in later chapters might provide better testimony to the comfort and trust these men feel in each other's presence.

EXCURSUS: MUTUAL FOOT CARE AND MALE FRIENDSHIP

My collection of military snapshots, as well as those of Ibson and others, I presume, includes men touching each other in just a few ways, really. The snapshots I present here show close, in many cases affectionate touching and holding, and in other chapters we see the soldiers touching in playful ways, including playfighting.

I have in my collection, however, two images that do not quite fit the conventional snapshot of two soldiers touching. Snapshot 4.7 is a snapshot in the form of a photo postcard, taken with the "autograph" version of the Vest Pocket Kodak so popular with soldiers in World War I. With that camera an amateur could actually write on the image while negative film was still in the camera. In this case, seemingly a World War I–era image, one soldier is attending to the foot of another, and the photographer wrote "A Feat with a Foot" across the bottom of the image. Snapshot 4.8 is from an unknown period and has "Doc Wagner and Dieter" written on the image, lower right; it might be another snapshot taken with an autograph version of the Vest Pocket Kodak.

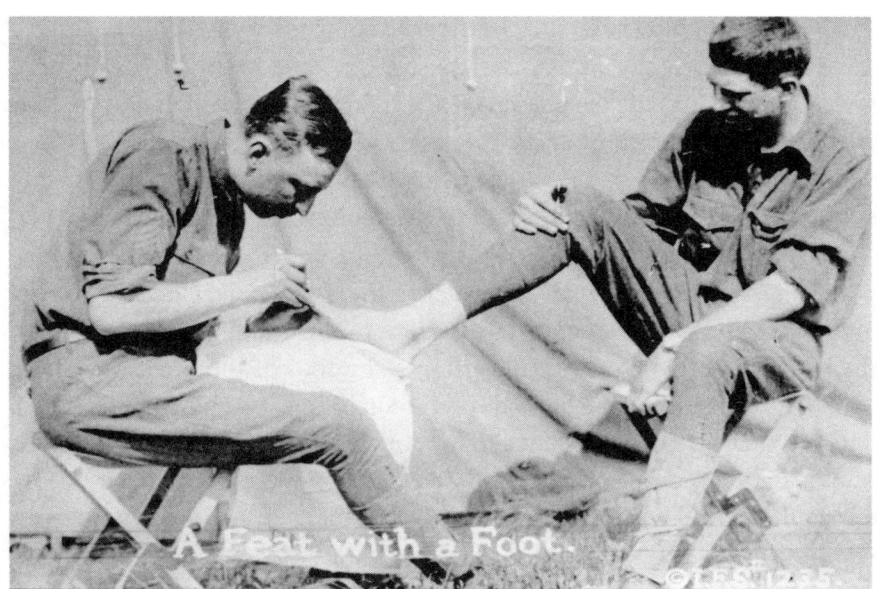

Snapshot 4.7

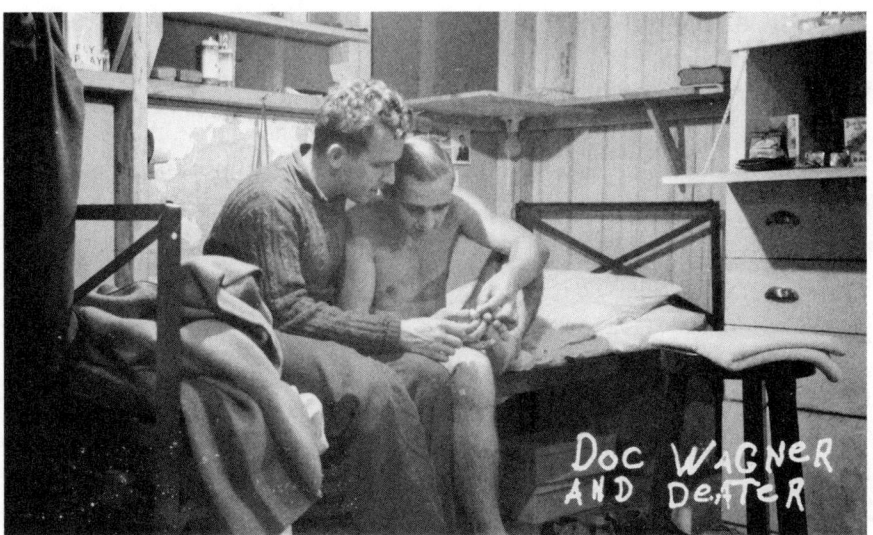

Snapshot 4.8

These seemingly trivial images deserve commentary in this chapter devoted to male friendship. An excursus on feet and male friendship may seem odd, but I think the examples are right on target for understanding friendships in all-male groups.

One day in my fieldwork with the Boy Scout troop at their summer encampment, I went back to the staff area (all open air, no cabins or tents or shelters of any sort except the canopy of pine trees) and found two older boys, members of the senior patrol, ages fifteen or sixteen, sitting in two aluminum folding lawn chairs the scoutmaster had brought and set up for the staff area. One boy was attending to the foot of the other boy. That care involved holding the other boy's foot in his lap, cleaning the foot, and applying antiseptic and a bandage to a blister that had broken. Normally scouts are not permitted in the staff area without permission from one of the adults, and the boy nursing the other explained that the scoutmaster had given him permission to do the foot care in the staff area using the staff first aid kit. I smiled and sat down on my cot to write some notes in my fieldwork notebook, which I always did away from the boys and men I was observing in my fieldwork (they knew I was writing about them), and I glanced up occasionally to check the progress of the foot care.

I was actually quite moved by the tender care the one boy was giving to the other. So much of the physical interaction I had observed between the boys at camp fit the stereotype of boys' friendly roughhousing, not just in games but even in their everyday life at the campsites, punctuating their verbal sparring with some physical aggression in keeping with their performance of the boy code. The scene I was watching involved a wholly different sort of touching, which led to a few thoughts about what I was seeing.

As I noted earlier, many masculinity scholars claim that men tend to interact with other men side by side rather than face-to-face, behavior that often puzzles women, who consider the lack of eye contact a sign of detachment, whereas men very often report the side-by-side interaction as "intimate" conversation. (We might add that men often view direct eye contact between males as an act of aggression and an invitation to fight.) The foot care, I realized, is a kind of side-by-side activity, and the intimacy experienced by the two men involved in the foot care would be intimate nonverbal communication, an expression of close friendship, male bonding.

I noted in my mention of this episode in my book that I was witnessing an example of how life in an all-male institution disrupts conventional, stereotypical ideas about the society's assignment of certain roles and activities to men and women (Mechling 2001, 179). Boys had to learn to perform duties often performed by mothers and possibly by sisters at home, duties like cooking and cleaning, but some older boys also did "emotional work" usually assigned to females. A homesick boy (usually the first-time campers, ages eleven or twelve) had to be comforted by another, older boy. I considered this a positive development in the socialization of boys.

Everything that is true of the all-male Boy Scout camp is true of the male military friendship group. Men perform a large range of roles they might think of as properly performed by women. In some cases, men touch each other tenderly. Snapshot 7.8 shows one naked sailor washing the back of another, and I would count that sort of touching as belonging to the same category as the foot care. And if the reader has any doubts about the intimacy of one person touching another person's foot, I refer the reader to the scene in Quentin Tarantino's film *Pulp Fiction* (1994), in which Vincent and Jules have a conversation about the sexual meanings of a foot massage.

It will surprise no one that care for another male's foot does not come up in war memoirs, autobiographies, and reportage. We only know about that behavior from a few snapshots. Brief reflection, though, suggests the importance of the soldier's feet. Anyone who has been in the infantry understands that an army travels on its feet and is only as healthy as its feet. World War I was notorious for the muddy conditions of the trenches and battlefields, and the malady known as "trench foot" put many soldiers on the list of disabled fighters. Instruction on care of the feet begins in basic training.

The argument I make in Chapter 7 on the cleanliness of military bodies notes that the lack of privacy and the total control of the recruit's body by the drill instructors in basic training results in what psychoanalysis would see as symptoms of a fixation on certain body parts and functions. That idea lies at the heart of the thesis Wallis and I (2020) develop about how the soldier uses his or her body as a resource for "microresistance" against the total institution of the military. The relentless attention to the cleanliness and health of the foot in basic training likely converts the feet into fetishes. The term "boot camp" and the usual reference to recruits as "boots" affirm the power of the foot as the object of intense meaning.

5

Animal Buddies

Typed on the back of Snapshot 5.1 is this caption: "'OUR MANAGERIE' (Notice the snake around one of the guys' neck)."

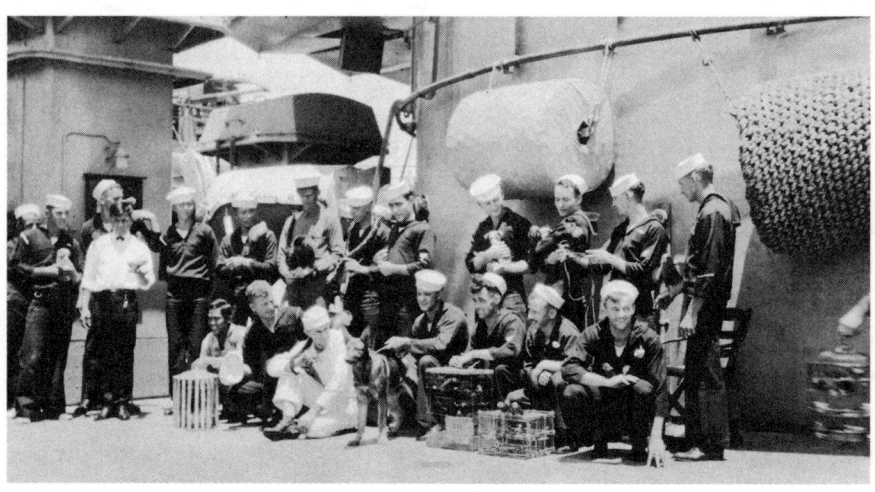

Snapshot 5.1

Taken aboard an American warship, date unknown, this vernacular photograph does, indeed, display a full menagerie of pet animals kept by these sailors. At minimum we see dogs and cats, birds, and monkeys, not counting a few animals not fully visible in the cages or peeking from pockets (possibly pet mice?). Other snapshots in my collection show soldiers with raccoons and kangaroos. Monkeys show up frequently as pets in snapshots taken in the Pacific theater during World War II.

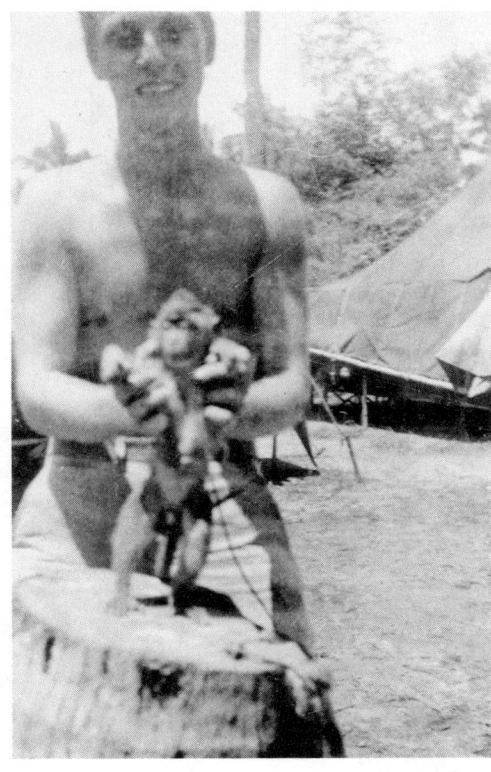

Snapshot 5.2

Some species of animals make better pets in the field than others, but the more familiar pets—dogs and cats—show up repeatedly in the snapshots.

Arnold Arluke and Lauren Rolfe's (2013) book, *The Photographed Cat,* devotes an entire chapter to the maritime practice of keeping cats on ships. This custom has a practical side, of course: keeping the mouse and rat populations under control. It is clear from the photographic evidence consulted by Arluke and Rolfe and in many of the snapshots in my collection that the sailors treated the cats as true pets. Those authors "read" the photographs of cats for "sentimentality signs," and the faces of the sailors in Snapshot 5.3 suggest the affection those sailors have for the cat and the kitten in the photo. (What we are to make of the fact that the rat is on a string leash held

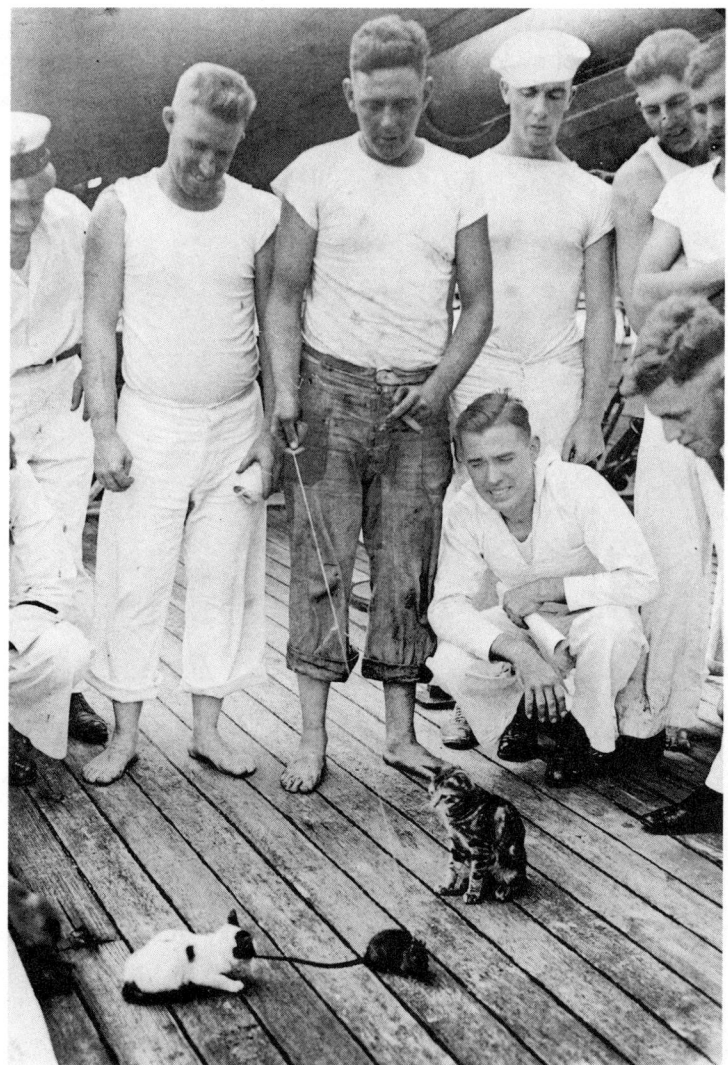

Snapshot 5.3

by one of the sailors must remain a mystery.) Soldiers also kept cats and kittens as pets in camp and in the field, as in Snapshot 5.4, taken in 1918 in El Paso, Texas. Judging from the uniform, Snapshot 5.5 is also of World War I vintage.

Snapshots of family pets, mainly of dogs and cats, are common, and it is not news that pet-keeping has a long history in American culture (Grier 2006) or that a great many Americans consider their dogs and cats to be members of the family, treated quite often as adults treat their children.

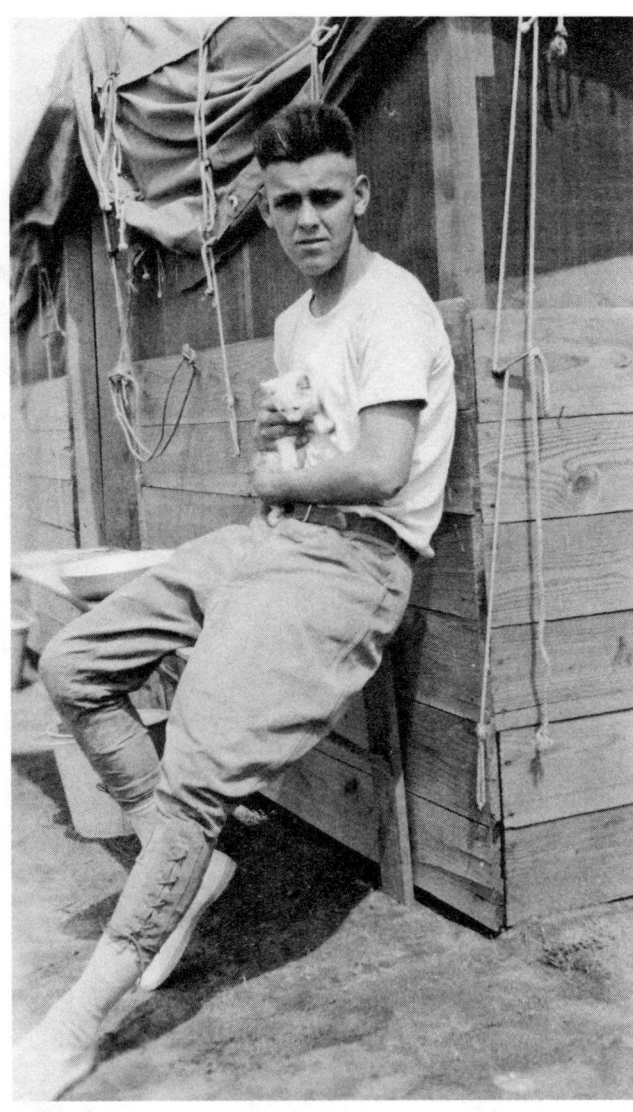

Snapshot 5.4

Pet-keeping might seem unremarkable, not worthy of its own chapter in this book, but I have titled the chapter "Animal Buddies" for a reason. For male warriors, animal buddies serve emotional functions similar to those served by friendships with other male warriors. "This is my buddy" could be the caption of snapshots of two soldiers or of a soldier and his dog.

John Paul Wallis and I (2019, 55–66) explore at length the use of dogs in formal therapy with veterans suffering from symptoms of post-traumatic stress disorder, making the important point that the warriors themselves

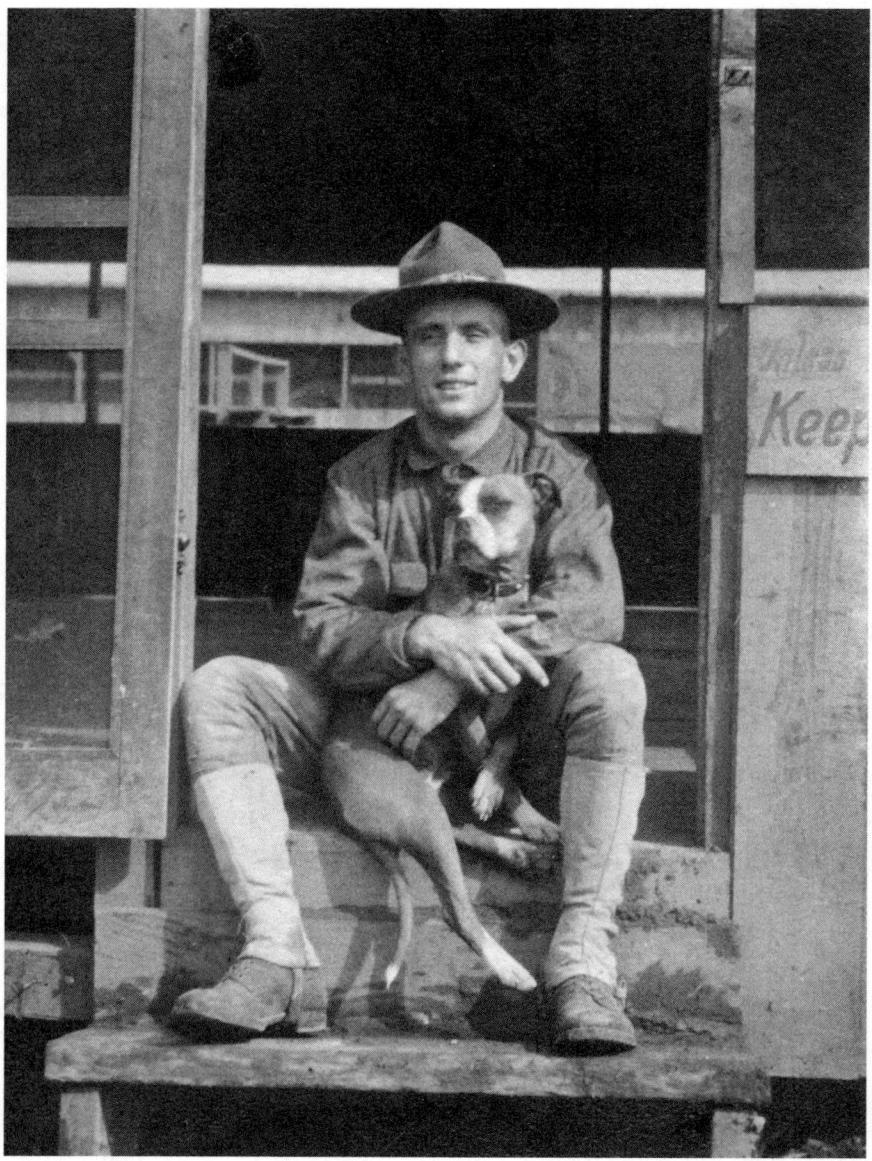

Snapshot 5.5

have discovered the more immediate therapeutic value of adopting dogs
in the combat zone. That chapter in our 2019 book offers Wallis's own
testimony about his platoon's adoption of a stray dog during one of his two
tours as a Marine in Iraq, and he relates his own distress at abandoning the
adopted dog when his unit had to move on. Military regulations forbid the

practice of adopting stray dogs, though officers often look the other way as long as they can. Still, it takes great effort and resources to actually bring an adopted dog back to the United States, and most of the dogs adopted by American military units in Iraq and Afghanistan are abandoned or even destroyed. The PTSD experienced by a warrior can be intensified when the temporary pet-keeping is terminated by abandonment or even the destruction of the dog.

I will not reproduce the entire story in the chapter on animal companions in *PTSD and Folk Therapy* (Wallis and Mechling 2019), but I want to use the plethora of snapshots in my collection of soldiers with animals to explore here what animal adoptions do for the warriors such that they want to capture the memory of the animals in the snapshots.

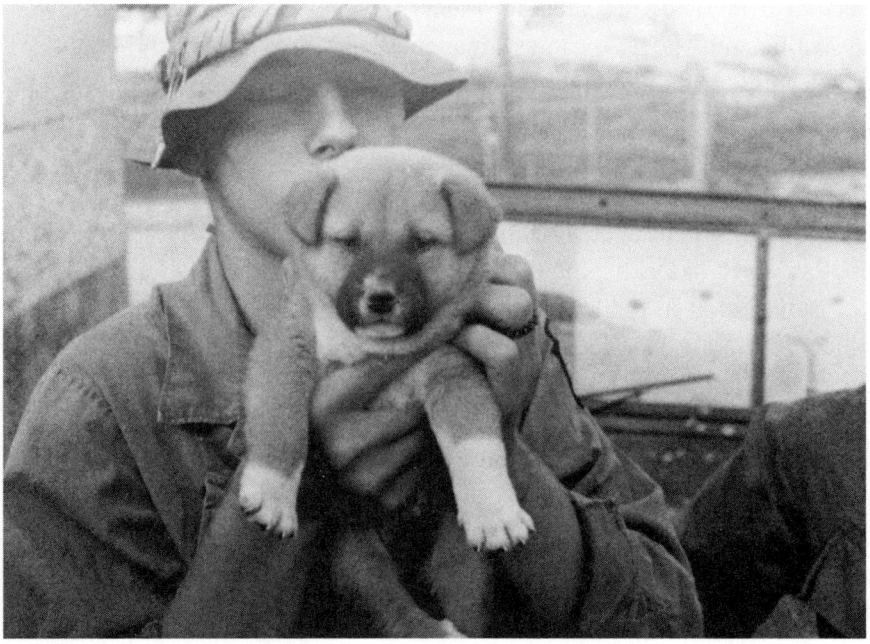

Snapshot 5.6

Snapshot 5.6 is one of two that I bought together in an online auction, both taken in Vietnam (guessing from the clothing and from the fact that the images are 35 mm color prints) and each showing an American soldier with a different dog. The dog in Snapshot 5.6 is a puppy and the solider is kissing it, closing his eyes as he might when kissing a romantic partner. It is possible that he was just blinking at the moment the shutter clicked, but I think his tenderness in holding the puppy (which is unquestionably cute) favors the interpretation that he is kissing the puppy. He loves that puppy, and we humans use kissing as a signal of love. Anthropologists find kissing as a practice in 90 percent or more of human cultures, and nonhuman primates use kissing as a gesture of bonding (Thompson 2018). Just like humans, bonobo apes, the primates closest to humans, "kiss and make up" after a fight (Kirshenbaum 2011). Kissing "stimulates the brain hormones, dopamine and oxytocin—both of which promote bonding and attachment in human beings" (Thompson 2018; see also Steenhuysen 2009).

This brief excursion into evolutionary psychology and endocrinology may seem to be a strange detour from the simple observation that the soldier in Snapshot 5.6 is kissing a puppy, but the kiss adds something to the general benefits of pet-keeping. Plenty of research, some of it reviewed by Wallis and I (2019), shows the mental and physical health benefits of pet-keeping. Human infants develop attachments to caregivers, and youths and adults can develop similar attachments to animal companions (Rockett and Carr 2014). The soldier kissing the puppy in Snapshot 5.6 reminds me that there are some military snapshots of one soldier kissing another.

What the scientific research on kissing tells us is that one man kissing another likely serves some combination of signaling affection, bonding, and submission in the hierarchy. In American culture men can kiss each other without the kiss carrying any romantic or erotic meanings so long as the frame for the kiss makes clear its nonsexual meaning.

Many of the psychological and medical benefits of pet-keeping flow from caretaking. Snapshot 5.7 shows a soldier gently caring for a new litter of puppies, and Snapshot 5.8 shows (as the writing on the back indicates) "some of the crew washing . . . the ship's mascot." Whereas Snapshot 5.7 shows a single soldier caring for the puppies (at least at that moment), Snapshot 5.8 shows a group of men participating in one way or another in the care of the ship's mascot, a dog.

In the study of American men's behavior in groups, social scientists make the important point that men often experience male bonding by doing something side by side. Fathers and sons, for example, can experience that close bonding by working on a physical project together, such as repairing a car or building something in the garage or backyard. Boys and men playing a video game, sitting side by side, can bond in that activity while never engaging in eye contact.

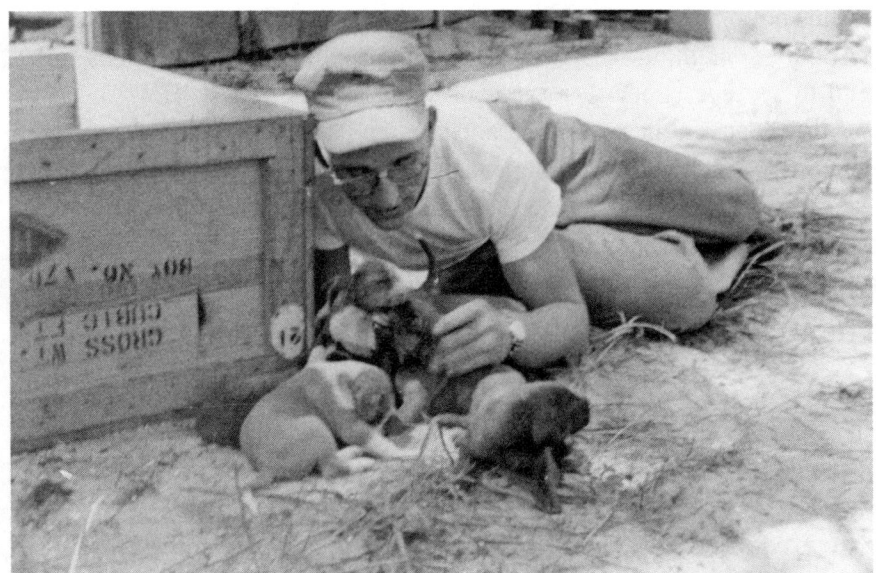

Snapshot 5.7

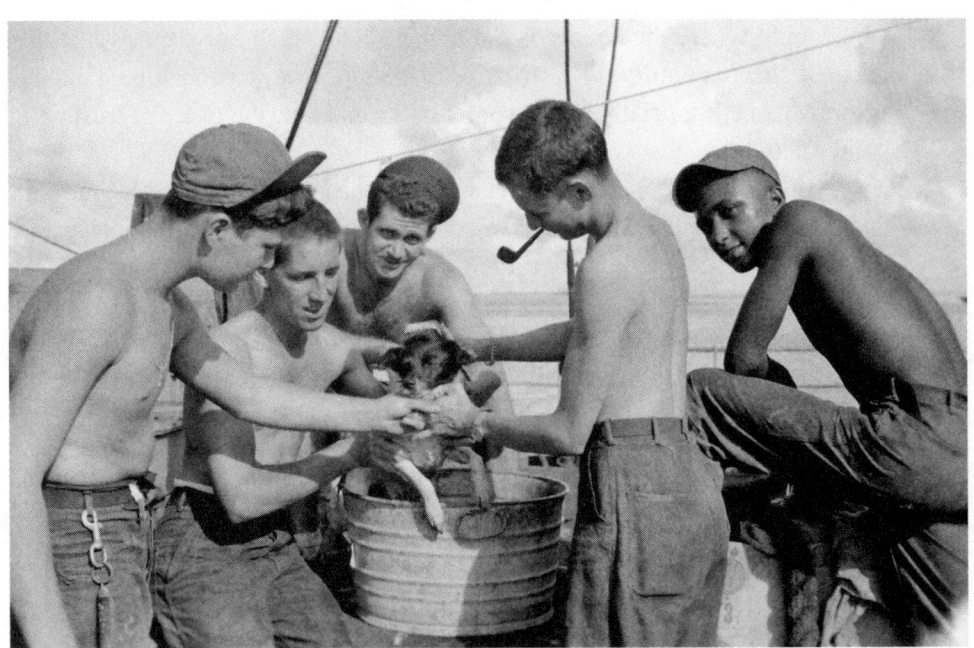

Snapshot 5.8

This notion that men can bond not by looking each other in the face but by doing something side by side genuinely puzzles many women, who tend to see eye contact as a signal of bonding and trust. How much of this difference in the ways men and women prefer to communicate (Tannen 2007) is based in evolutionary psychology and how much is cultural (learned) is not a question to be tackled here. What we do know about men is that eye contact can be a strong signal of aggression and plays a role in the hierarchy of males in primate groups. Put differently, American men learn to avoid eye contact with other men unless their intention is aggressive. Male bonding generally does not require eye contact; hence the experience of bonding by engaging in an activity side by side. The men in Snapshot 5.8 are experiencing male bonding through their collective care of the dog.

A key term here is trust. The dozens of war memoirs Wallis and I read for our book on PTSD and "folk therapy" in the combat zone testify time and again to the role of trust in the camaraderie of the combat unit. Warriors must trust each other. They might and often do mistrust the military hierarchy. They tend to mistrust the civilians around them, now that wars are fought where the enemy is not a uniformed force but dressed like the rest of the population. The trust relationship with a pet adopted in the combat zone, especially a dog, sometimes must take the place of trust with other people.

In the previous chapter I discussed trust in relation to Way's study of adolescent male friendships, how trust is so important to boys in early and middle adolescence, but often their experience in late adolescence is one of betrayal, loss of trust. The young men in these soldier snapshots often found in the military a return to the close bonding and trust they felt in early and middle adolescence. The loss of a buddy, human or canine, in the combat zone brings the young soldier back to that grief of loss.

PART III
The Male Body in the Military

6

The Male Body

The snapshots in this book are filled with male bodies, and not just with any male bodies but with the bodies of men in the American military. The male bodies in these snapshots help create the meanings of the pictures, both the meanings for those taking the snapshots, for those in them, and for those of us gazing at the strangers in the orphan snapshots.

The work of anthropologist Mary Douglas (1966, 1970) guides my thinking about the male body as a symbolic text to be read and interpreted. She is not the only scholar to focus on the male body, but her ideas are a good place to start. As we shall see in subsequent chapters and snapshots, the male body plays a large role in the everyday lives of soldiers.

Douglas points out that the human body is the perfect symbol for society. The body has a clear boundary separating the inside from the outside. Douglas adds the binary clean/dirty to this basic insight of the body as metaphor for society. "Dirt" is "matter out of place." Culture is our primary way of creating order and meaning in our lives. Order is *nomos,* but everyday life brings "anomalies," events and objects that threaten order.

Anomalies, therefore, are dangerous, so cultures devise strategies for dealing with the danger. As Barbara Babcock-Abrahams (1975) says, drawing on Douglas's ideas, sometimes a culture tames an anomaly, takes away its power, by ignoring it. Sometimes a culture tames an anomaly by actively repressing it, even destroying it. Sometimes, though, a culture seeks to take away the power of an anomaly by drawing attention to it, by making it the symbolic center of a ritual. Clifford Geertz's example of how cultures deal with the anomaly of the birth of an "intersexual," an infant born with the genitals of both sexes, in his essay on "Common Sense as a Cultural System" (1983, 81–84), covers all of these strategies, from "correcting" nature's error (the American response) through surgery and hormonal treatments, to the Navajo response that the intersexual individual is "divinely blessed" and the proper object of "wonder and awe," to the Pokot (an East African tribe) response seeing the intersexual infants as errors to be discarded, either ignored or even killed.

As we shall see in later chapters, one of the strategies cultures (and groups in cultures) devise for taming the threat of anomaly is to put the anomaly at the center of play and ritual. As I hope to make clear, one of the anomalies the men in the snapshots must deal with is the anomaly of very close bonding, the feeling of emotions strongly related to love, while needing to define those feelings as those between not lovers but heterosexual male friends.

Interpretive anthropologists and folklorists now commonly look at the meanings of "dirt" that crosses the body's boundaries and the ways cultures devise ideas and rituals to deal with the danger of the "pollution" caused by dirt, as Douglas puts it. For example, to one extent or another cultures create practices (taboos) around materials that cross the boundary between outside the body and inside the body, including food, drink, and air. Cultures also create taboos dealing with substances that exit the body, including urine, feces, blood, menstrual blood, semen, pus, saliva, tears, and sweat. Not every culture treats every bodily excretion as dangerous, but across cultures you will find attention to each of these.

Military examples abound. I own and have seen plenty of snapshots of soldiers preparing and consuming food and drink—mostly beer—but I don't learn much from the snapshots about the soldiers' practices and attitudes about the food and drink. For that we have oral evidence and some material evidence. It seems each generation of soldiers has its own rumors and legends about substances the military puts in the food to control the soldier's body, from saltpeter to suppress sexual drive, rumored during the Korean and Vietnam Wars, or laxatives in chewing gum to deliberately incapacitate soldiers, according to soldiers in Iraq and Afghanistan (Wallis and Mechling 2020).

"Germs" hold their own special place in the history of how cultures deal with threats to the body. In her two books on cancer and HIV/AIDS, Susan Sontag (1978, 1989) deftly shows how the vocabulary of disease moves back and forth between the individual body and the society. She shows how the metaphors "bleed" into one another: sometimes the body becomes the symbol of society, and sometimes the society is talked about as if it were a body. Sociolinguists have also noted the importance of the body as a symbol. George Lakoff and Mark Johnson (1980; see also Lakoff 1987) discuss all the ways we commonly use the body as a metaphor.

Of special interest for understanding the everyday male culture un-packed by soldier snapshots is the folk speech of soldiers about their bod-ies. Peter Murphy's 2001 analysis of the everyday speech of men when talking about their bodies and about sex points to a few key ideas, the most important of which is that, while women tend to identify with their bodies, men tend to maintain a separation between self and body and think of their bodies as something they own (Murphy 2001, 32). The folk speech betrays this attitude, from metaphors of the male body as a machine to the penis as a "tool."

The feminist critic Susan Bordo begins her 1999 book on the male body with "Prologue: My Father's Body," and she includes snapshots of her fa-ther from his youth to his old age (1999, 3–11). The prologue permits her both to describe her feelings about the first male body she knew growing up as a female and to foreshadow themes she takes up in the book, such as male power in the patriarchy. I shall return to Bordo's analysis of the male body when considering the role and meanings of male nudity in the mili-tary snapshots, especially the penis, which is not the phallus (the symbol of male authority). Bordo has much to say about the penis "in hiding and on display" (the title of her first chapter), as we shall see. For now, however, it is enough to note that Bordo begins with the premise that male bodies are not just the bodies of males, they are cultural forms with meaning (1999, 26). This theme of "male embodiment," of how "men's lives are impacted by their embodied experiences and their perceptions of their own bodies" (MacMullan 2002, 1), runs throughout masculinity studies, showing up in feminist writing by women and by pro-feminist writing by men.

Refining our focus even more, let us look at what scholars say about the male body at war.

HARD BODIES AT WAR

If clean/dirty is a common, meaningful binary describing a male body, strong/weak is a binary used just as often. The metaphorical uses of strong/weak move back and forth between the individual body and the body as nation. George Mosse (1998) and other scholars tell some of the history of the use of body metaphors in discourse about the nation. The male ideal is a hard, strong body. Scholarly studies of the male body at war often focus on the use of the male body in propaganda (e.g., Paret, Lewis, and Paret 1992). In both World War I and World War II, German propaganda used images of the ideal German male body to rally the population in proud support of the war (Theweleit 1989), but we find the same use of the strong, hard male body in American war propaganda and advertising.

Christine Jarvis's 2004 book, *The Male Body at War,* analyzes American mass-media images of the male body in World War II, sometimes comparing the use of the body in American propaganda with German practices, but what she writes about those images also applies to wars before and after that one. Anyone who has ever seen a poster or magazine illustration from the war understands immediately when she argues that the government and commercial institutions "shaped the male body both figuratively and physically in an effort to communicate impressions of national strength to U.S. citizens and to other nations" (Jarvis 2004, 5).

Jarvis's analysis of what she calls the American visual "rhetoric of muscles" (2004, 48) shows how the juxtaposition of servicemen's bodies with killing machines of iron and steel communicates strength and "hardness." Hard bodies are the goal. The rhetoric of male muscled bodies also required visual images of nude or partially nude warriors, for example, the famous series of homoerotic magazine ads featuring partially nude soldiers bathing and using Cannon towels (Ibson 2002, 169–172; Hanson 2014, 64–67).

Jarvis's book on the American male body at war is best paired with George Roeder's *The Censored War: American Visual Experience during World War Two* (1993), since the latter book looks at war documentary photography. Roeder shows how the government's rules against showing the wounded and dead bodies of American soldiers relaxed and how such images became common in American newspapers and magazines, up through and including the wars of the early twenty-first century.

The use of images of hard male bodies at war is clear from all this scholarship and more. The subject of the present book, however, is the meaning of the snapshots capturing the everyday lives of soldiers, not the more public uses of the hard body in propagandistic accounts of war.

The presence of propaganda in the popular culture consumed by the soldiers in the snapshots, such as *Life* magazine pictorial coverage of World War II, makes them "shadow texts" (Brummett 1991, 2004) known to the men in the snapshots. But let me back up a minute. Jarvis devotes the chapter "Classified Bodies" to the process the military used to build and "sculpt" the bodies of the men showing up for service (2004, 56–85). First, those bodies were screened via the medical examination at induction, and then they were built into the strong, hard, male bodies the military needed through physical training in boot camp and beyond. Every soldier in my snapshots went through this process of screening and training.

Enduring the physical training in boot camp, where the drill instructors tell the recruits that "pain is weakness leaving the body," the young men being made strong and hard also have in their mind's eye the many popular culture images of the ideal male body. The popular culture images consumed by the young men who fought in World War I did not feature the partial nudity and "muscle rhetoric" Jarvis found in World War II images, but it is worth noting that the comic books so popular in the 1930s began carrying ads for Charles Atlas's plan for making "weakling" young men into muscled heroes (Black 2009). Most young men internalized that ideal they found in magazines, comic book heroes, and advertisements.

The pose we see in Snapshot 6.1 reflects the typical boy's or young man's sense that his masculinity resides in his muscled body.

Also consider Snapshot 6.2.

Taken in Vietnam on January 25, 1967, this photograph displays the male warrior's body. The soldier pictured sent this posed snapshot home to his mother with the inscription "To Mom, Love always, Your Son, Donald." He is proud of his body, and we can imagine that he carries with him the attitude Murphy (2001) writes about—namely, that his body is a machine, a tool, not really separate from the tools of war adorning his body, including the rifle, the bandoliers of cartridges, and the hand grenade. He is standing outside the heavily sandbagged bunker, showing no fear and poised at the ready. His sweet message to his mother seems to contradict the hard-body strength and potential aggression and violence in the snapshot, but surely he sent that snapshot and wrote those loving words on it to assure his mother that he could take care of himself and come home safely.

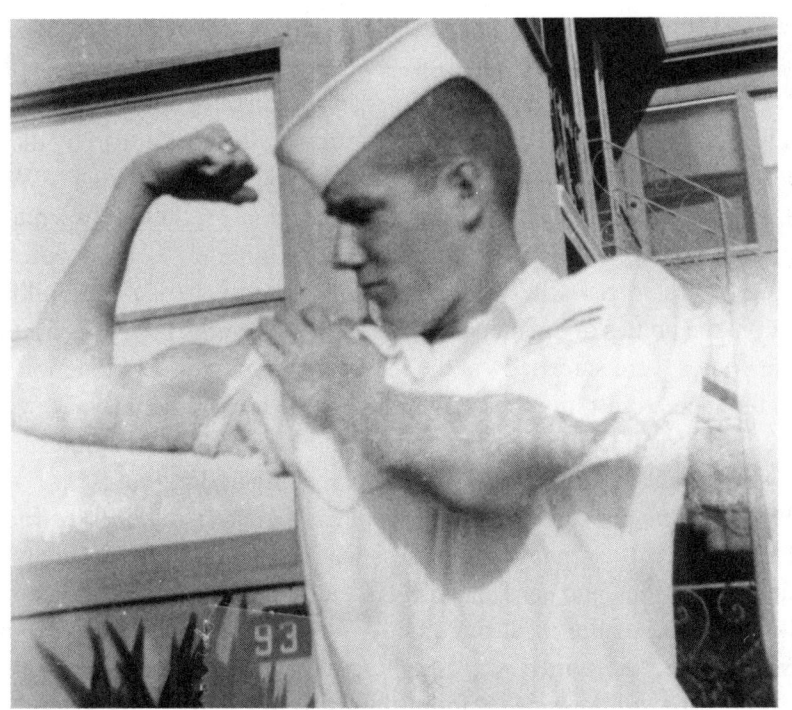

Snapshot 6.1

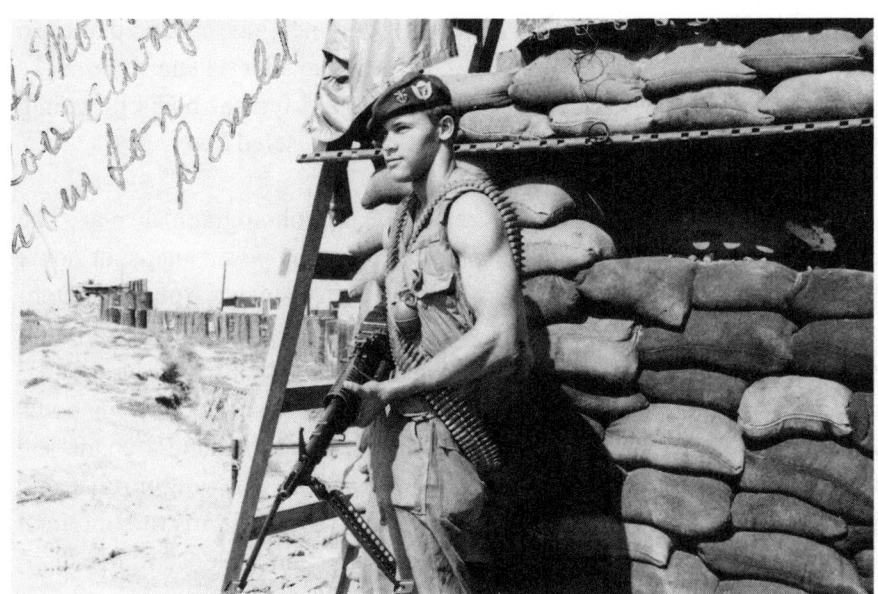

Snapshot 6.2

THE WOUNDED BODY

Continuing her examination of the embodied masculinity of the American soldier in World War II, Jarvis titles a chapter "Representing Wounded Bodies" (2004, 86–118). While Jarvis mainly uses verbal evidence to show the great fear soldiers have expressed at being wounded, especially the fear of literal emasculation by wounds to the genitals, we could extend her perspective to think about the visual representations of wounded soldiers in war photography. Paradoxically, surviving a wound can be a sign of strong masculinity, of the ability "to take it like a man." Jarvis taps Elaine Scarry's ideas in *The Body in Pain* (1985), and in the realm of photography we can add Susan Sontag's *Regarding the Pain of Others* (2003), posing in her usual way the question: why do we take any pleasure in viewing war photographs of soldiers and civilians in pain?

The wounded male body actually is a common motif in mythology and other narratives about male initiation. The mythopoetic men's movement of the 1980s and 1990s took as one of its founding statements the book *Iron John: A Book about Men* (1990) by the poet Robert Bly, which is based on a story collected by the Brothers Grimm about a boy maturing into adulthood with a wild man as his mentor (Mechling and Mechling 1994). Bly invokes a Jungian interpretation of the thigh wound experienced by the Prince, the boy in the story. Bly also knew the work of Bruno Bettelheim, the child psychiatrist whose book *Symbolic Wounds: Puberty Rites and the Envious Male* (1954) discusses experiencing a wound (notably circumcision) as a rite of passage from boy to man.

I do not own in my collection, nor have I ever seen, any snapshots of soldiers freshly wounded, though there are plenty of professional war photographs of wounded warriors. The closest I have is Snapshot 4.6 of two buddies in hospital beds, their crutches behind them, holding hands and smiling. Freshly wounded warriors are not the proper subject for snapshots, it seems; nor are snapshots of dead fighters, with a few exceptions, one of which I reproduce here as Snapshot 6.3.

THE DEAD BODY

Encountering a dead body is, for most people, a deeply disturbing experience. Many people report that their first experience seeing a dead human

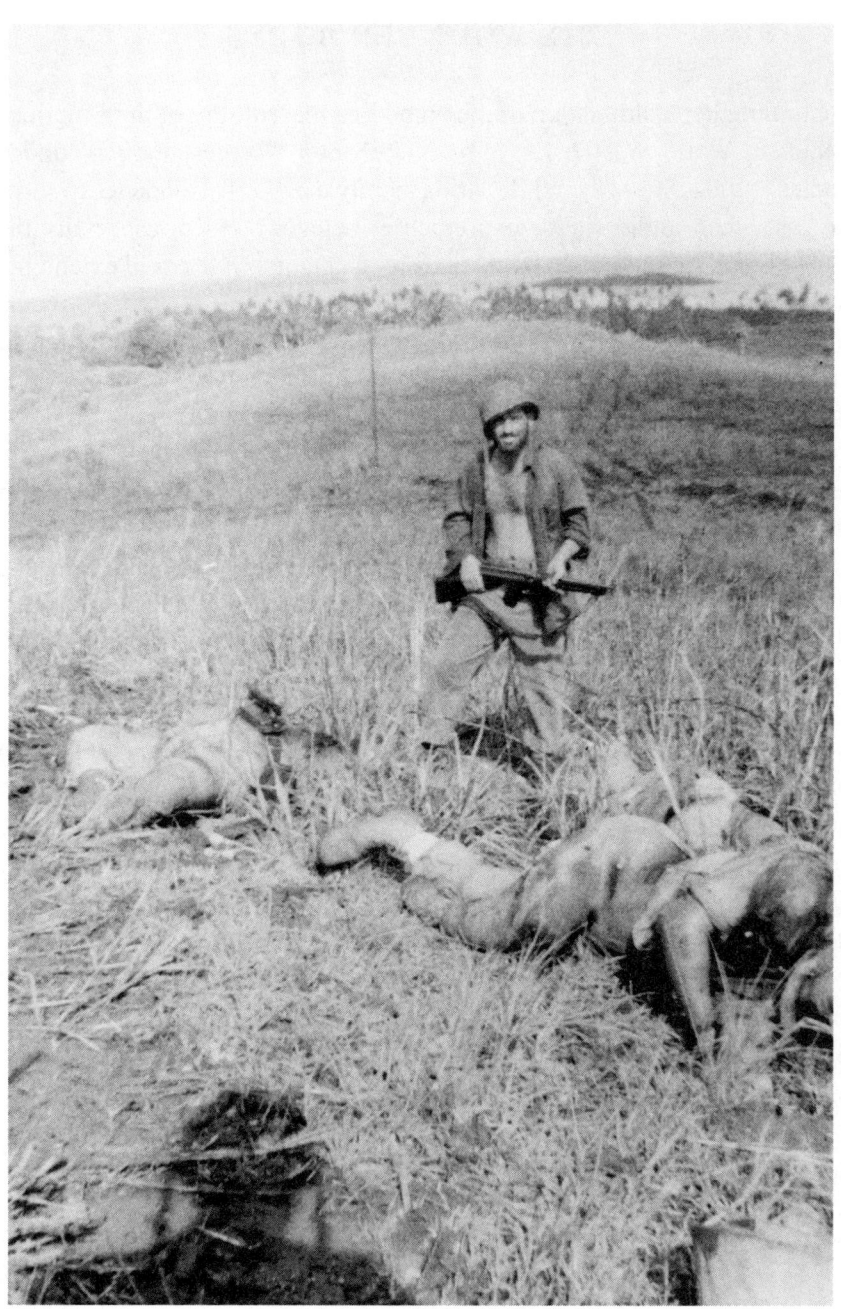

Snapshot 6.3

body close up is something they never forget, not only the sight but also, especially, the smell. First responders (police, firefighters, emergency medical technicians) and professional medical providers have to get over that initial reaction to do their duty. Combatants in the military must do the same. The military trains soldiers to overcome their natural reluctance to kill other humans, but does not train them well to deal with the death of others. There are procedures and rituals in the military for coping with the death of comrades, but the closer the living soldier was to the dead friend, the less satisfying the rituals are. The war memoirs written by veterans testify to the indelible memories of death in the combat zone.

Professional photography taken in the aftermath of combat often includes images of the dead, sometimes mutilated, bodies of combatants and civilians. Photographs of immediate death in the heat and chaos of battle was not possible for many decades, so long as the technology required bulky equipment and long exposures. The widespread use of handheld 35 mm cameras as early as World War I made possible the occasional professional photograph in the heat of battle, but by far the most common photographs of the victims of a battle are taken in the aftermath (Tucker et al. 2012).

The American Civil War (1861–1865) was the first war to provide extensive photographic documentation of battlefields littered with the dead bodies of soldiers and, in some cases, army horses. At first the federal government censored images of the dead from Civil War battles, but President Abraham Lincoln decided that American civilians should realize what a terrible war what happening far from their homes. In images taken at the Battle of Antietam (1862) and later, we can see changes in the representation of the dead as photographed by Matthew Brady (1822–1896), his colleagues, and other professional photographers (Tucker et al. 2012, 85). Brady's photographs of the dead in the aftermath of the Battle of Gettysburg achieved the propaganda purpose Lincoln intended.

In World War II the government initially forbade its own professional photographers and those combat photojournalists working for newspapers, magazines, and photography collectives like Magnum from making public images of dead American soldiers. Images of dead enemy soldiers were permitted. Like Lincoln before him, though, President Franklin D. Roosevelt decided that the American public needed to see the terrible cost of war, so in 1943 the government gave *Life* magazine permission to print George Strock's photograph showing American Marines dead on Buna

Beach, New Guinea (Tucker at al. 2012, 201). As shocking as that photo is and was then to the readers of *Life*, the photo does not show the faces of the dead Americans, a tradition that continued to be honored in later wars.

Vernacular photographs of dead combatants and civilians are far more rare, in my experience. Historians of war photography consider a photograph of a dead German sharpshooter slumped in a tree in World War I as the first such snapshot (Tucker et al. 2012, 201). In my own collection of vintage soldier snapshots, I have just one example: Snapshot 6.3. Many vintage snapshots in my collection have PASSED BY THE CENSOR stamped on the back, but this one does not, and I have no idea how it got past the censors. Several elements assure us that this is an amateur photograph. The figures are not framed symmetrically, and we see in the lower left the shadow of the soldier (likely a Marine) taking the snapshot. The landscape and ocean suggest it was taken on an island in the Pacific theater in World War II, and the Marine near the center of the snapshot is carrying a weapon common in that war, the Thompson submachine gun.

The two (or possibly three) dead bodies in the snapshot are difficult to see in detail. Their clothing suggests they might be Japanese soldiers, but even that is uncertain. The body most fully shown is in a state of rigor, muscles frozen as if he is trying to push himself up, which adds to the grotesque nature of the scene. Almost certainly these are not American dead, not just because of the strong norm against portraying dead American soldiers, but more because of the pose of the standing Marine. This snapshot strongly resembles those taken by hunters standing over their dead prey (Mechling 2004), a disrespectful pose a Marine would be unlikely to take if the dead in the snapshot were Americans. Like those snapshots, this snapshot is a souvenir of the hunter with his trophies.

I have introduced a range of ideas here about "embodied masculinity" because every experience a recruit has from his first physical examination reminds him that he has a body, that the body is a machine, and that the recruit's body actually belongs to the military. The recruit can never stop thinking about his body and about the bodies of his buddies. The recruit and then the soldier understand firsthand that his body is both real flesh and blood and a symbol to be owned and manipulated. No wonder so many of the snapshots we encounter in the remaining chapters are "about" the male body.

7

Clean and Dirty

Combat is dirty business. One historian wrote an entire book on the role of mud in the history of military combat (Wood 2006). Battles have been won and lost over centuries in mud, sometimes mud so treacherous that it swallows up men, as happens to Kiowa, the Native American in O'Brien's well-known novel of the Vietnam War, *The Things They Carried* (1990). World War I memoirs and reportage, including war photography, mention muddy trenches and fields as a constant source of discomfort, difficulty, disease (trench foot), pain, and even death. Mud runs are a feature of basic training, and even in civilian life mud runs have become a competitive game. One assumes from the fun (i.e., the smiles in the snapshots) associated with military training in mud that it must have meaning and pleasures beyond mere readiness for battle. Rough-and-tumble playfighting in mud is an old and common form of play, and it is a frequent element in college "class scraps" (Bronner 2012, 118–134). The male pleasure in playing with mud has many levels of meaning, some unconscious (Mechling 2016b).

In Chapter 6 we encountered Mary Douglas's foundational work on the body as symbol, carrying personal meaning, both within the male group and for the larger society. Her binary clean/dirty is useful for understanding a series of snapshots I present in this chapter.

John Paul Wallis and I (2020) show how basic training (boot camp) in the military can create fixations on body parts and bodily functions that provide the unconscious drive for using the body to make small gestures of "microresistance" against the military. Basic training is a military experience precisely matching Erving Goffman's (1961) description of a "total institution," such as the military and prisons and mental hospitals, where the entire experience of the "inmate" or "resident" is controlled by others. The experience of basic training infantilizes the recruit, changing his appearance (shaving his head, making him wear uniform clothing), giving him a nickname, and totally controlling his bodily functions, telling him when and where to sleep, what and when and how to eat, and when he can shit and piss. (I adopt here the folk speech for defecating and urinating, just as I did for my essay on the connection between urination/pissing and masculinity—see Mechling 2014.) Furthermore, there is absolutely no privacy for bodily functions in basic training. Recruits must piss and shit openly in each other's presence, often against a background of the drill instructor's counting out the seconds each recruit is expected to spend executing those functions in a stall without a door.

Wallis and I (2020) argue that the infantilizing total control of the recruit's primary body systems fetishizes those activities so that the soldier is continually hyper-aware of his body and of the materials that cross the boundary between the inside and the outside of the body (back to Douglas). The anxiety about the body created in basic training surfaces in the folk practices of the male friendship group in the military. The power of these unconscious anxieties and fetishes involving the body shows up in the snapshots.

There are a great many snapshots capturing two activities that reflect anxiety about male bodies—photos of men on latrines and of men bathing. Both of them invoke the symbolic power of clean/dirty. Both involve the naked or partially naked male body and invite interpretation about the comfort these men take being naked in each other's presence.

ON THE LATRINE

The reader might be surprised to know how many snapshots soldiers take of each other on latrines of all sorts, from indoor ones, as in Snapshot 7.1, to outdoor wooden ones, as in Snapshot 7.2, to rustic ones consisting simply of a lashed construction of a log over a trench. The men on the

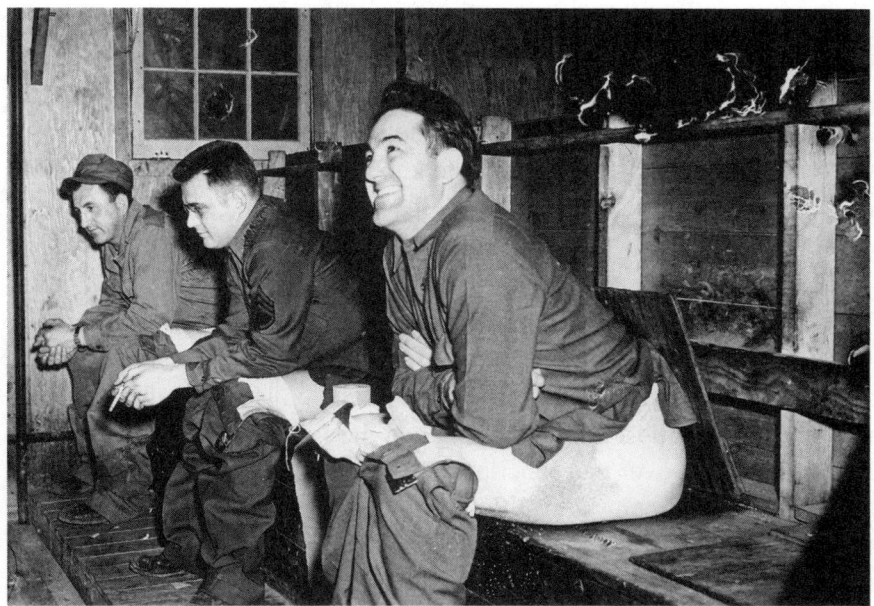

Snapshot 7.1

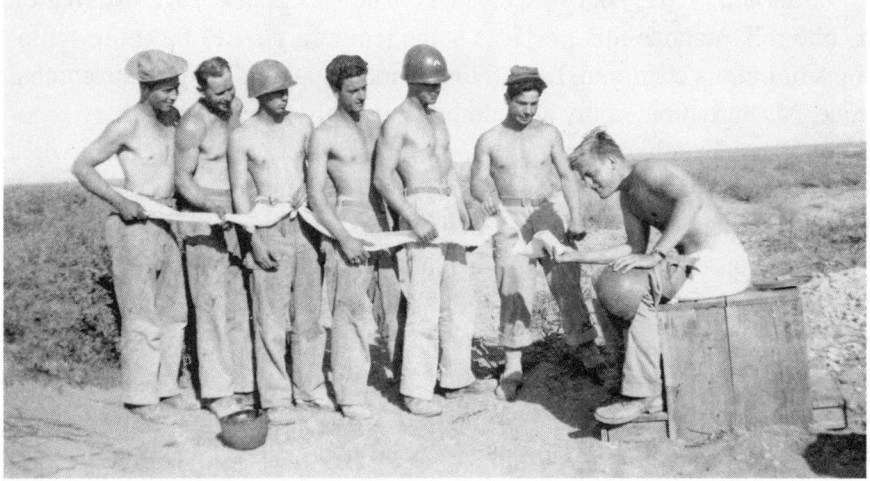

Snapshot 7.2

latrines are usually smiling for the camera, though in a few they are reading something and not focused on the camera. But even those snapshots do not seem to be taken in secret. Those being photographed know it and think it is funny. The soldiers in Snapshot 7.2 are even having fun, lining up for the latrine and holding a long piece of toilet paper. All smiling.

Again, the behavior of soldiers "taking a shit" is not a subject talked about much, except in those war memoirs that recount the memory of the smell of being on "shitter duty," which involves pulling out from under the seating a half-barrel of feces, pouring motor fuel over the contents, setting fire to it, and stirring it with a long stick to make sure it all burns. Soldiers and veterans never forget that smell. Snapshots do not capture that smell, of course, though I have seen some digital snapshots of soldiers engaged in shitter duty. The snapshots truly capture some sort of pleasure at the latrine, so this is one of the cultural puzzles we would not even know about were it not for snapshots.

Surely the plenitude of snapshots of soldiers on latrines reflects a fixation created initially in basic training and the fact that the drill instructor had total control over that function. That the function took place without any privacy at all helps create the anxiety that cements the fixation. Parents, teachers, and society work very hard to teach the boy that toilet functions are private matters. In fact, the entire history of toilets and the design of bathrooms in Western societies reflects the move toward privacy. Still, the lack of privacy does more for the military group.

Wallis and I (2019) devote a chapter ("The Jack Shack") to masturbation as one folk practice that provides some temporary relief from the symptoms of trauma stemming from living working, and fighting in the combat zone. Masturbation, oddly and almost laughably, is against military regulations, though soldiers are rarely punished for masturbating except when caught masturbating while on guard duty. The connection to the issue of privacy in performing bodily functions lies in the unstated reason why masturbation is against military regulations. Consulting Thomas Laquer's (2003) history of masturbation, Wallis and I (2019, 112–113) note that the reasons for the condemnation of masturbation in the early eighteenth century moved from moral objections (Onanism in the Bible) to ethical and even political objections. Put simply, the secrecy and "excess" of masturbation violated emerging Enlightenment norms. The Enlightenment values "*self*-governance and *self*-control" (Laquer 2003, 277). But from the 1960s to the present, the focus has been upon individual freedom of expression, including an openness about masturbation.

If the military institution's official policy about masturbation really is about keeping the focus on the group rather than the individual, we can see how privacy in the toilet overvalues the individual. In many ways the notion of privacy is about individualism and autonomy, both anathema to the military's values of comradeship, group cohesion, and good order and discipline (as the regulations put it). This suggests that the lack of privacy in bodily functions aims at conveying the message that there is no room for privacy or individualism in the military unit. That lack of expectation of privacy continues in the field.

And note that in these snapshots and in every other one I have seen, the soldiers are shitting beside others. Shitting beside another soldier paradoxically reinforces male bonding. The lack of privacy, as we have seen, values the group over the individual, but since male nudity is involved, the ease of being naked in front of other soldiers reinforces the message that the men do not see each other as potential sexual objects of desire. We see this elsewhere in the snapshots in this book, as playfighting and other activities (e.g., the bathing in the next section) take place in the nude.

I should add one further point, not about the military but about anther male organization and the possible direction of privacy in the military. I visited the annual summer encampment of the Boy Scout troop I studied (Mechling 2001) for over two decades. Until the 1990s the camp latrine was a "two-seater," a wooden one not unlike that in Snapshot 7.2, over a trench. The camp latrine, called the KYBO (Keep Your Bowels Open) in camp lingo, was located away from camp but out in the open, screened only a bit by some low bushes. The boys and men at camp thought nothing of sharing the latrine, enjoying the beautiful mountain scenery, and chatting about camp.

By the 1990s cases of sexual molestation of boys in the Boy Scouts led to new rules in the organization in general and at this troop's camp specifically. Certainly a boy and an adult man could no longer be on the KYBO at the same time (when approaching the KYBO, you had to ask whether anyone else was there), but the rule also extended to two boys. Later, as I attended two different California Boy Scout camps with my younger grandson, I saw that they were moving from gang showers to individual shower stalls for both the men and the boys. This made me wonder whether the trend in the military, especially with the integration of women into previously all-male groups, was toward individual privacy in bodily functions. Certainly the Porta Potty, or similar enclosed, single-seat latrines used in the wars in Iraq and Afghanistan, seem to have replaced the open latrines we see in the snapshots. Perhaps the snapshots have recorded a custom no longer practiced, though the individual and group psychological need is still there.

I see one more, unconscious process at work in the soldier's fixation on shitting. Think of this as an anal fixation, which leads to the following thoughts.

When I was trying to make sense of the plentiful equation of feces and food in the folk speech of the adolescent boys at the troop summer encampment high in the Sierra Nevada mountains of California, I finally landed on a psychoanalytic understanding of the anal fixation in the boys' everyday conversations (Mechling 2001, 200–205). In *From the History of an Infantile Neurosis* (1918/1955), Sigmund Freud describes a patient nicknamed the Wolf Man for his dreams about white wolves in trees, and solves the puzzle of the patient's symptoms of gastrointestinal distress by seeing the symptoms as the result of the young man's repression of his feminine side. The anal fixation resulting in the snapshots of soldiers on a latrine likely comes from the same dynamic process. The agenda of the military is to create the normative, heterosexual male, which requires the rejection of the feminine—reflected in the misogyny and homophobia in the folklore—and requires that the male repress his feminine side. The result is the anal fixation we find in so many all-male groups, especially those in total institutions.

BATHING

As I wrote at the beginning of this chapter, being a soldier is dirty work. Many war memoirs testify that one of the pleasures of coming in from the field and back to base camp is the opportunity to wash off all the dust and dirt—sometimes a week's worth or more. It is not surprising, then, that soldiers find a great deal of pleasure in bathing, and that pleasure seems to be captured quite often in snapshots. There are so many snapshots of bathing soldiers that the act must have been very important to them, and since the bathing snapshots are of the male body, we might take the theories about the meanings of male bodies to make "best sense" of these snapshots.

The soldiers are wrapped in towels in many of the snapshots I have in my collection, as in Snapshot 7.3. The soldiers abandon that modesty in other snapshots of bathing.

In more permanent bases in the field, the soldiers construct something like a shower system outdoors, with a wooden platform to keep their feet from getting muddy. Soldiers regularly took such snapshots, and in most

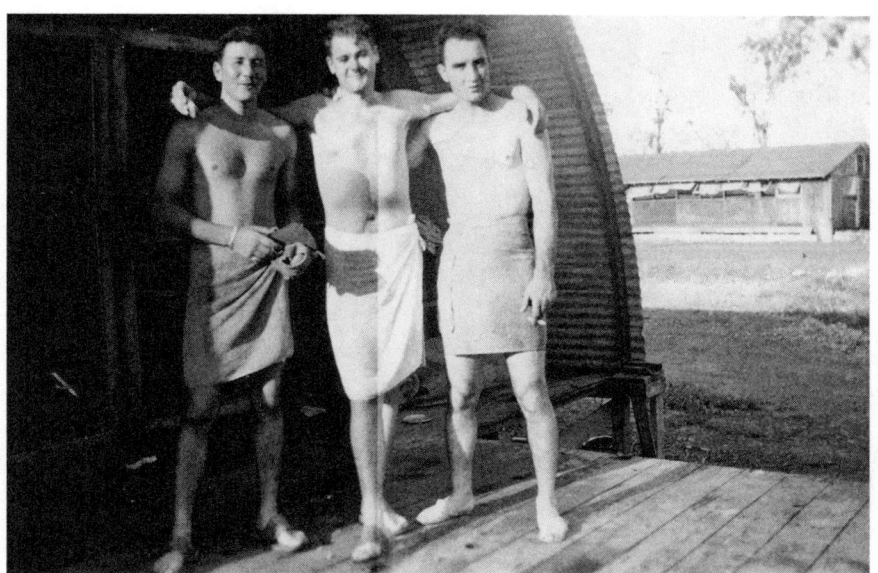

Snapshot 7.3

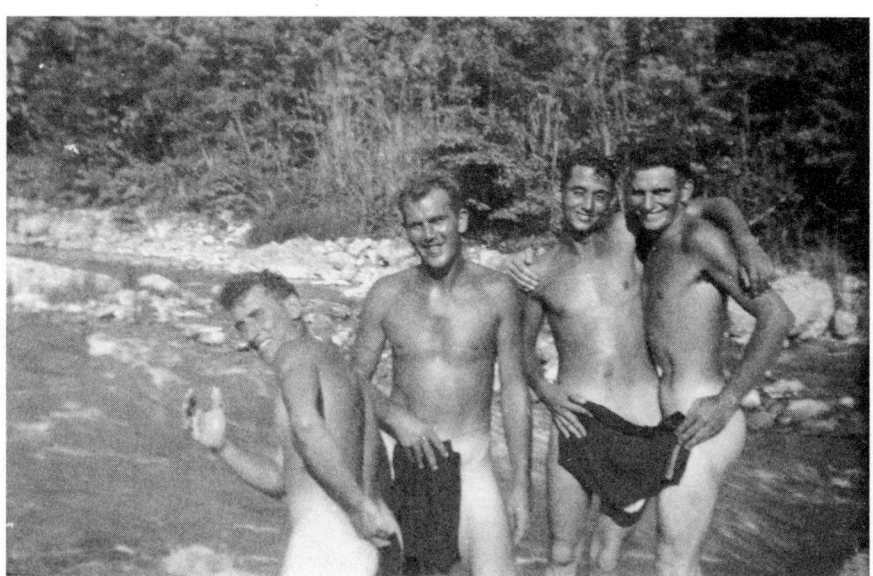

Snapshot 7.4

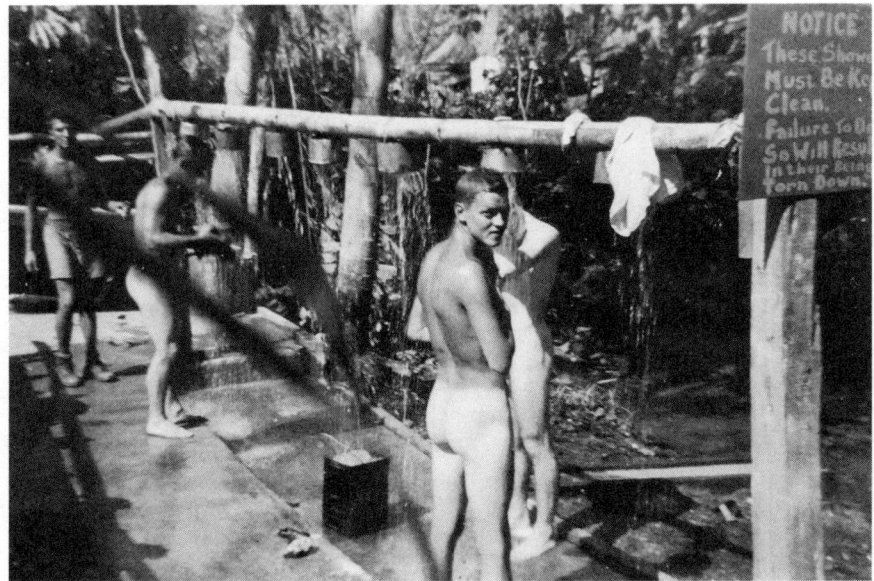

Snapshot 7.5

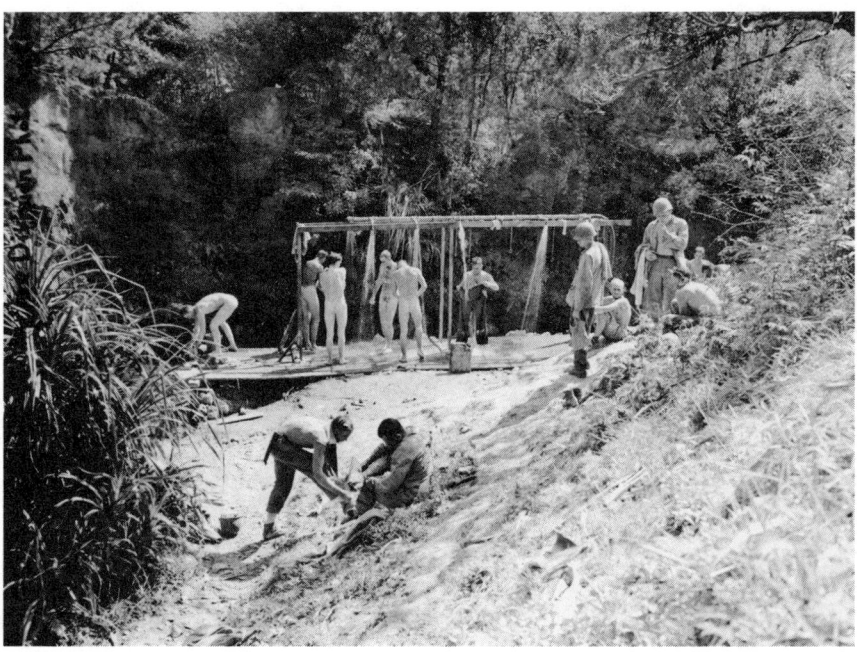

Snapshot 7.6

cases the men showering appear to know they are being photographed; often they are smiling in the direction of the photographer, as in Snapshot 7.5.

On board ships and submarines, the preferred method of "showering" was standing on deck and pouring buckets of water over each other or improvising outdoor showers, as in Snapshots 7.7 and 7.8. Again, the photographer takes the snapshot from behind the bathers. Note how one submariner is washing the back of the second submariner in Snapshot 7.8.

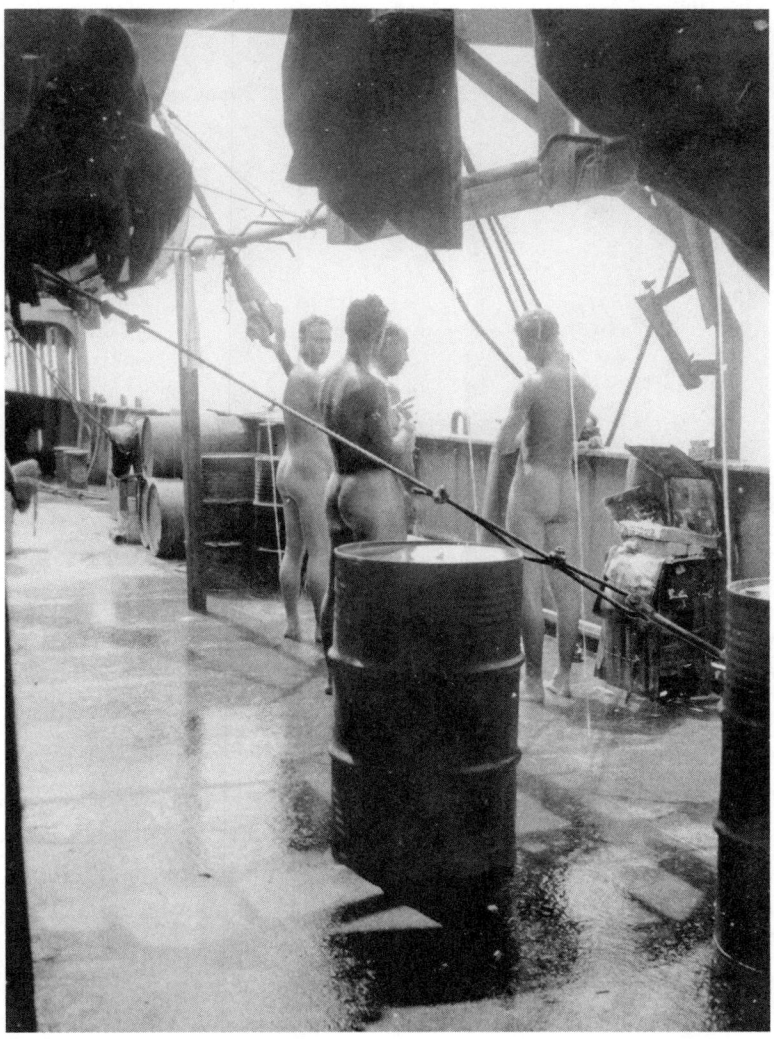

Snapshot 7.7

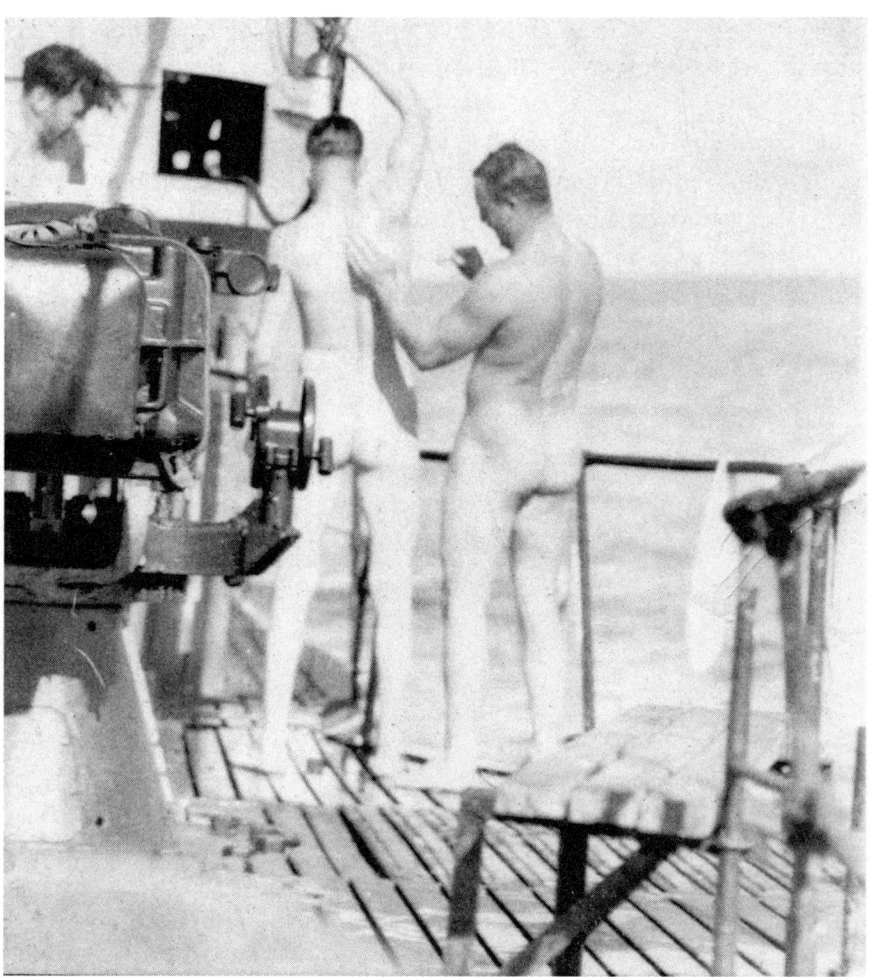

Snapshot 7.8

During World War II the bare butts of soldiers bathing that we see in so many snapshots began to show up in official military photography published in magazines (like *Life*) and newspapers. The Naval Aviation Photographic Unit, led by the famous modernist art photographer Edward Steichen (Phillips 1981; Faram 2009), produced hundreds of photographs documenting everyday life among sailors and Marines. A large number of these official photographs are of the sailors bathing—on board ships and on Pacific beaches. Evan Bachner's (2004, 2007) two books of photographs he gleaned from the archives of the Naval Aviation Photographic Unit contain dozens of images of the bare butts of sailors and Marines. In fact, in his introduction to the 2004 book, Bachner says that visiting the Brooklyn Museum of Art in 1997, and seeing Horace Bristol's famous photograph of a naked gunner in a PBY Air-Sea rescue plane picking up a ditched pilot, piqued his interest in the trove of photographs from the Steichen photographers (Bachner 2004, 5, 17). That airman's naked butt might be the most famous picture in the body of work by Steichen's unit.

Dian Hanson's book, *My Buddy: World War II Laid Bare* (2014), assembles the snapshots collected by Michael Stokes, all featuring the sort of nudity and male camaraderie I see in the snapshots in my much smaller collection. Hanson also includes commercial photographs from magazines and pulp fiction novel covers; there are no frontal nudes, but some fall into the genre of the Cannon towel magazine advertisements from the war era (Hanson 2014, 65–67). Hanson and some of the other guest commentators in the volume acknowledge the paradoxical male bonding created by the nudity, and unlike the official photographs published by Bachner, many of the snapshots presented by Hanson show male genitalia.

Hanson's is mainly a book of snapshots and commercial images, with little analysis. One World War II veteran's commentary assures the viewer that all the nudity and demonstration of affection did not signal homosexual desire or even practices, insisting that the conditions of combat create strong bonds of affection between men, affection without any sexual meanings.

Men bathing and swimming nude ("skinny-dipping" in folk usage) has a long history, including representations in Western art. The invention of photography in 1839 added to the body of artistic images of men skinny-dipping, and a few artists—notably the American Thomas Eakins (1844–1916)—worked in both paint and photography. In 1844, Eakins photographed his art students (all young men) swimming nude in the river in Philadelphia and then used that photograph to paint one of his most famous paintings, "The Swimming Hole" (1884–1885). Eakins's photographs count as art photography, of course, but the advent of the snapshot, when cameras became smaller and lighter than the equipment Eakins used, led to many vernacular photographs of boys and men skinny-dipping. Popular, mass-mediated culture in magazines and advertisements long ago normalized and celebrated male skinny-dipping as a wholesome part of growing up male in America. In popular culture, images of boys skinny-dipping appeared in commercial stereoviews, in postcards, and on the covers of the *Saturday Evening Post*—namely, the painting by J. C.

Leyendecker (1874–1951) in the August 19, 1911, edition, and the painting by Norman Rockwell (1894–1978) published on June 21, 1921. One of the Cannon towel advertisements from World War II (all featuring mostly naked soldiers in various settings) is a skinny-dipping scene. The illustrator who painted those images must have had firsthand experience or at least have seen photographs of soldiers and Marines bathing nude in rivers, lakes, and the ocean (Hanson 2014).

THE MALE BUTT AND MASCULINITY

The snapshots of soldiers' bathing I have presented so far present the nude or partially nude male body, the nudity consisting of views of the male buttocks (the "butt," in folk speech). In the next section I shall deal with the more scarce snapshots showing male genitalia. But I need to pause here to consider the place of the naked male butt as an icon of American masculinity and strength.

The naked butts of soldiers, sailors, aviators, and Marines appear in both private snapshots and in more public, professional photographs. The prevalence of the male butt in military photography begs explanation. Certainly part of the explanation is that showing male genitalia was viewed as more "obscene," so the naked male body often turned away from the camera with the butt blocking a view of the penis. But that explanation ignores the symbolism of the male butt.

Art historian Patricia Lee Rubin (2018) has written a large volume on the male "view from behind" in Renaissance art. As an art historian she is interested in the conventions, the rhetoric of showing the male butt in paintings and sculptures, and she argues that "rear views of well-formed men could . . . be objects of admiration and were used to characterize the heroic, the stalwart, and the brave" (2018, 9). Rubin pays close attention to the body language in the paintings and sculptures she studies, with special attention to the way the male figures stand. "In the rhetoric of representation," she writes, "the V-legged stance stood for virility and strength" (2018, 118). Apparently, military snapshots and documentary photography of the male butt are part of a long tradition in the history of art of seeing a man's backside as a symbol of strength.

Much of the cultural analysis of the male body focuses on the penis as a representation of the cultural phallus, symbol of male power. I shall get to a discussion of the penis in these soldier snapshots in the next section, but for now I have to puzzle out an explanation for the obvious pleasure soldiers take in photographing their buddies' butts and for the buddies taking pleasure in showing their butts to the camera.

The butt is so common in military photographs that its meaning must be more than just "not the penis." It is likely that the muscled male butt represents strength, not just in the individual soldier but in the nation as well. Nazi visual propaganda frequently featured the naked male body, especially the butt, and in the United States we see the same wartime use of the male butt to represent the strength of the nation in the fight. How else can we account for all the nude male bodies in magazine advertising (Cannon towels and other products) and in the propaganda photography by Steichen's Naval Aviation Photographic Unit? The naked, muscular male torso works as well for the message of American strength.

I do not think the everyday soldier or sailor was picturing the butts of naked buddies with the message of national strength in mind. Rather, the naked butts in their everyday lives served a few functions probably unconsciously condensed in the snapshots. The nudity in the snapshots conveys the easy comfort the men had being naked in each other's presence. Paradoxically, the nudity reinforces the heterosexual norm, even though the assumption that all the men are exclusively heterosexual is mistaken. We know from histories like Allan Bérubé's (1990) and from novels like James Jones's *The Thin Red Line* (1962) that the sexual orientation of the soldiers has always been more diverse and fluid than the heterosexual norm.

Probably even deeper in the unconscious of those taking the snapshots and of those being photographed are the elements that create a fetish of the butt for these soldiers. As I indicated earlier, the conditions experienced in basic training—the nudity and the strict control of bodily functions (food crossing the body's boundary to the inside, urine and feces crossing the boundary of the body to the outside)—create psychological fetishes expressed as physical symptoms long after basic training. These body fetishes, which amount to heavily energized attention to bodily functions, provide some of the energy and power for what Wallis and I (2020) call the use of the military body for microresistance against the institution.

In this energized system, the male butt comes to symbolize two things. First is the necessary repression of the feminine in the male soldier, a point made above when I offered an interpretation of the snapshots of men on latrines. As Nancy Chodorow (1978) and other theorists of masculinity put it (e.g., Frosh 1994), masculinity has to be defined as "not female." The repression of the feminine element in the young man results in an unconscious preoccupation with the butt.

There is a second symbolic meaning of the male butt in the male group. In my article on the custom of paddling the butt in male hazing rituals, especially in college fraternities (Mechling 2008b), I argue that the male butt represents the target for the feminization of the man. In the binary scheme of gender and sexual relationships, the male penetrates the female. The folklorist Alan Dundes points out that the folk speech and acts in many contests between men, from ritual oral insults to the game of football, feature "putting down" the opposing male, putting that dominated male in the "down" position of the female in customary sexual intercourse (Dundes, Leach, and Özkök 1970; Dundes 1978). The rectum is the site of potential penetration and, accordingly, the site of the potential feminization of the male. Even folk speech about the female genitals makes the connection, such as calling a woman "a piece of ass." Clearly the folk consider the male butt the site for the potential feminization of a male.

The important point I make in that paddling essay is that, while the paddle represents the penis, the important thing to note is that the fraternity brothers paddling the initiate attack the butt but do not penetrate it. The potential penetration never happens (though in some notorious cases of male hazing, especially in sports teams, the rectum is actually penetrated by an object, which destroys the symbolic value of paddling the butt).

I know that the interpretation of the imagery of the male soldier's butt in professional and amateur photography relies heavily on the psychoanalytic theory of masculinity, and I know that some will dismiss these meanings out of a general aversion to psychoanalytic theory or, for that matter, to explanations from depth psychology altogether. In the tradition of adopting the method of clinical inference for cultural interpretation (Geertz 1973b), I would say to the skeptic that there must be some explanation for the ubiquity of the male butt in military photography.

EXCURSUS: THE MARINE'S BUTT; OR, BOHICA

The near-obsession of Marines with the male butt deserves its own excursus before I move on to the appearance of the male genitals in the soldier snapshots.

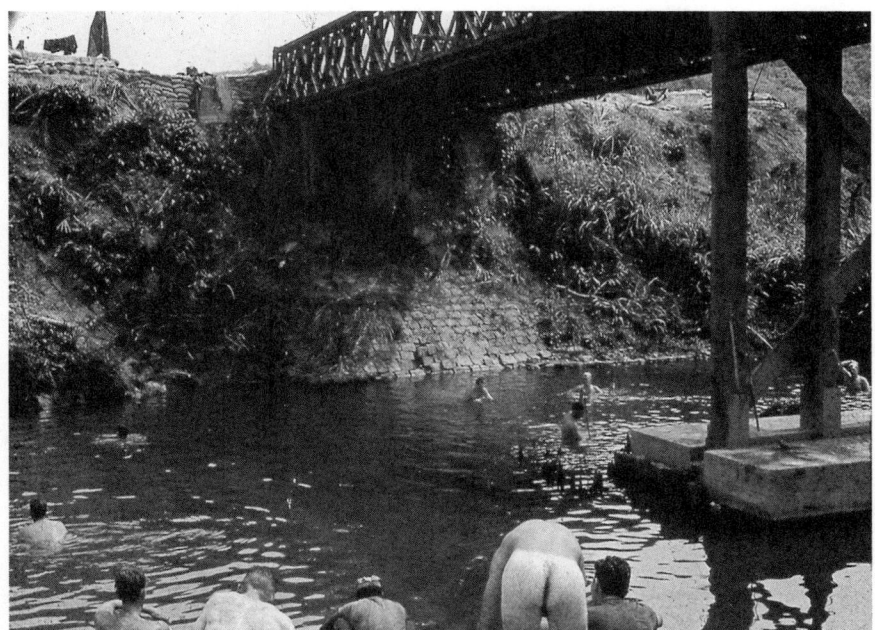

Snapshot 7.9

Snapshot 7.9 is a slide (smaller than 35 mm, possibly from a "half-frame" 35 mm camera or 126 or 127 slide film) with APRIL 68 printed on its cardboard frame. It is set in Vietnam (April 1968 would have been a "hot" moment in the war), and it captures some Marines skinny-dipping in a river. I am guessing that they are Marines because of their prominent role in the jungle fighting in Vietnam, but also because the Marines seem to fixate on the male butt.

Both official war photography from World War II and snapshots feature the butt. A famous photograph by Karl Thayer Soule, "Wash Day at Guadalcanal," of many naked Marines washing their clothes in the Lunga River, was made available to newspapers and magazines by the Associated Press in December 1942 (it was published in *Life* magazine). A similar photograph by Ralph Morse is in the book, *Life Goes to War* (Scherman 1977, 133). Bachner (2007, 126–127) shows similar photos by Sergeant Robert R. Brenner, a Marine Corps photographer. By 1942, it seems, the American readers of *Life* magazine were seeing tasteful photographs of half-naked Marines, the butt-naked half.

Snapshot 7.10, also from World War II, is a vernacular version of that Associated Press photo.

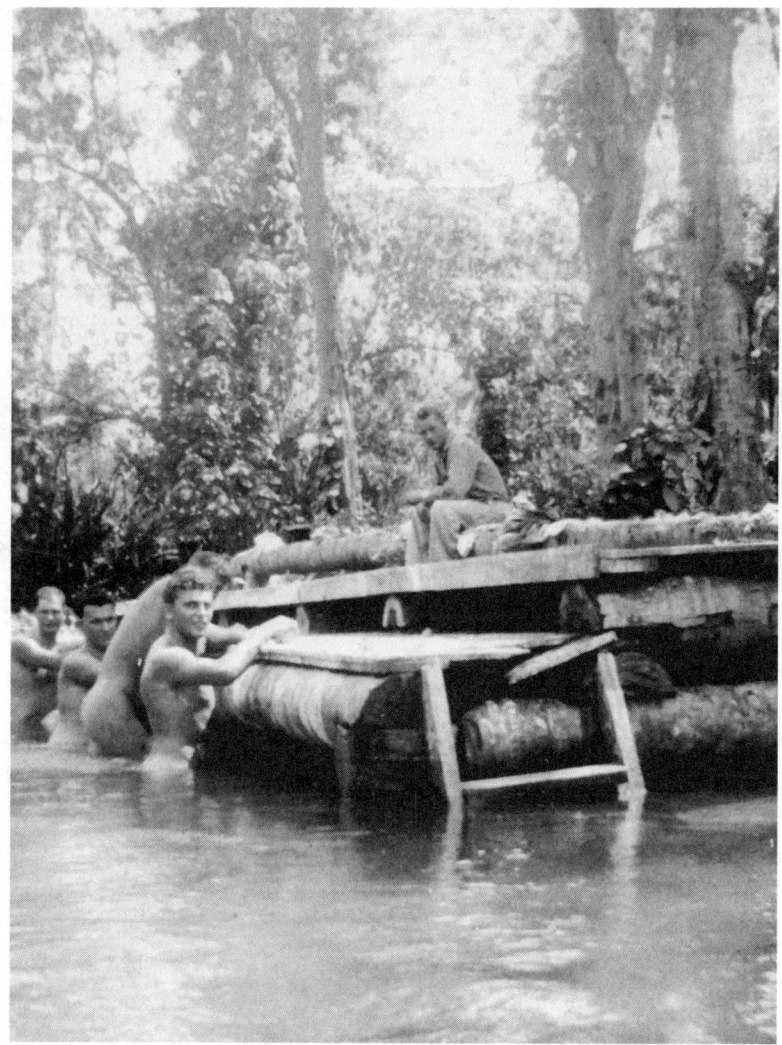

Snapshot 7.10

The American military folk term BOHICA, standing for "Bend Over, Here It Comes Again," purportedly originated with the Marines in World War II, and it became common among Marines in Vietnam. Marines use it to announce that something bad is coming, either from the enemy or from the US military establishment itself—in the case of Marines, "the Corps." The image the term evokes is of a Marine bending over to expose his backside to the bad thing that is going to happen—metaphorically, something penetrating his butt, an act of male rape. The folk speech for this would be,

"We're about to get fucked." BOHICA is the way Marines say that, finding humor (gallows humor) in that phrase.

Many veterans have commented on the seeming fixation Marines have with the butt (e.g., Zeeland 1996). Maximilian Uriarte is a Marine veteran of the Iraq War and has drawn and written a very popular comic strip, *Terminal Lance*, well-known among Marine Corps veterans. For years Uriarte's strip circulated on the Internet (from his blog). His graphic novel, *The White Donkey* (2016) and his compilation of comic strips, *Terminal Lance: Ultimate Omnibus* (2018), have made him popular beyond the loyal corps of Marines who follow his strip.

Uriarte knows the Marines well and is one of those commentators who observe their obsession with the butt and the "Green Weenie," which is Marine slang for the Marine Corps (a metaphorical green penis). For example, an early 2010 strip reproduced in his *Omnibus* (2018, 22) and titled "It's Already Gay" illustrates the "oil check" practical joke of one Marine pushing his finger onto the butt of another Marine, through his underwear. In his commentary on that strip, Uriarte notes the irony in the fact that "so many Marines are against gays and lesbians serving in the military, but are guilty of doing gayer shit than the average gay man on a daily basis" (2018, 22). With the strip and its title, Uriarte was trying to draw attention (before the change from Don't Ask, Don't Tell to a policy allowing LGBTQ people to serve openly, in 2011) to the foolishness of the homophobic, heterosexist attitude held by many Marines. These themes appear quite often in the strip over the years (Uriarte 2018, 45, 75, 84, 136).

The Marine fascination with the butt and penetration by the Green Weenie signals a complex layer of meanings. The butt is the symbolic site of the feminization of a man, which is represented by passive penetration, a point made by Dundes (1978) about the symbolism in male contests and by me when writing about the paddle used in fraternity and other male group hazing (Mechling 2008b). The Marine attacking with an oil check finger poked at another's anus (in the joking frame, as far as the attacker is concerned) is the symbolic male feminizing the other Marine. But that Marine, the "butt" of the joke, cannot be "all butt hurt" (a phrase I learned from my Marine coauthor, John Paul Wallis) as the victim of the joke; he must show that he can "take it like a man," take the joke, and deliver one in retaliation (if he is not intimidated by the bullying). The additional complication when we try to sort out the meanings and persistence of this fixation is that the oil check is always performed for an audience of fellow Marines, never in private, where the play frame would be absent, suggesting either full-on bullying or even a clumsy sexual advance. The public performance seems to be enjoyed by the audience, who most often laugh at the play. My best guess is that the audience simultaneously identifies with both the aggressor and the victim, a complicated reaction made possible only because of the paradoxical nature of play and its ability to signal unconscious wishes. The Marine Corps can be "the gayest" group a man might join (Uriarte 2018, 22), but the "play with gay" among men who consider themselves heterosexual is made possible by the play frame, which also covers the act of photographing the naked bodies and bare butts of fellow Marines.

I now move on to the few snapshots in my collection that show the soldiers as full frontal nudes. My analysis continues to be speculative, relying heavily on feminist psychoanalytic theory and critical practice.

SOLDIERS' GENITALS ON VIEW

Not only are the soldiers in Fig. 7.11, 7.12, and 7.13 nude, but these snapshots show the men's genitals with no sign of modesty. Such snapshots are rarer than the snapshots of nude soldiers showing only naked butts. Certainly the more public, professional photography of naked and near-naked soldiers and sailors never shows the penis, a taboo that apparently outlasted the ban on photographs showing the dead bodies of American warriors (Roeder 1993).

The snapshots show what the more public photography does not show, the everyday experience of soldiers being fully naked in each other's presence. As I note constantly throughout this analysis, the ability to be fully naked in each other's presence signals a lack of interest in the male body as the object of sexual desire. The female body is the "proper" object of the heterosexual male gaze. Some men do gaze upon the male body as an object of sexual desire, but until recently that motive and that gaze were deeply closeted, repressed, dangerous to express. The comfort of full frontal nudity in the snapshots, vernacular photographs not subject to the public standards of good taste in magazines and government propaganda, confirms for us the necessity of the soldier's taking-for-granted the naked bodies of his buddies. That began with the lack of privacy in basic training and recurred in the conditions of being posted in the field.

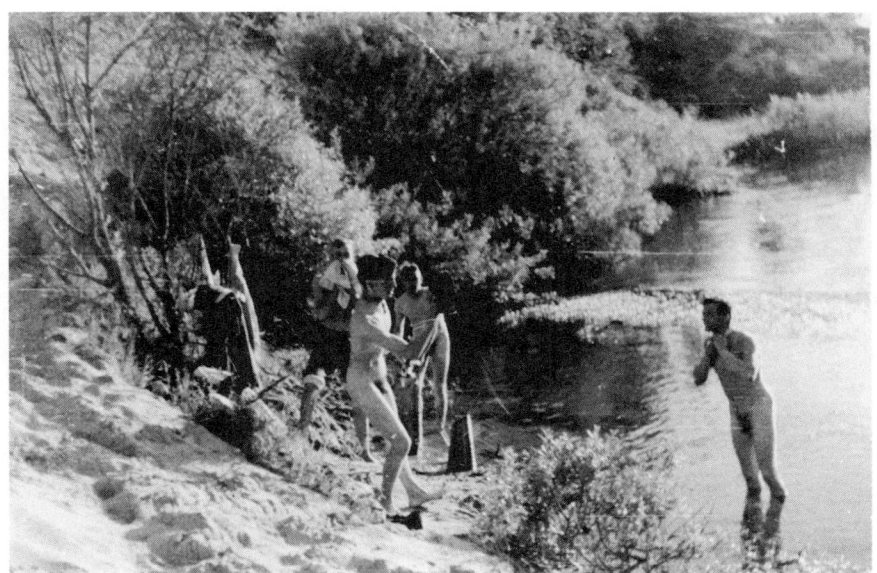

Snapshot 7.11

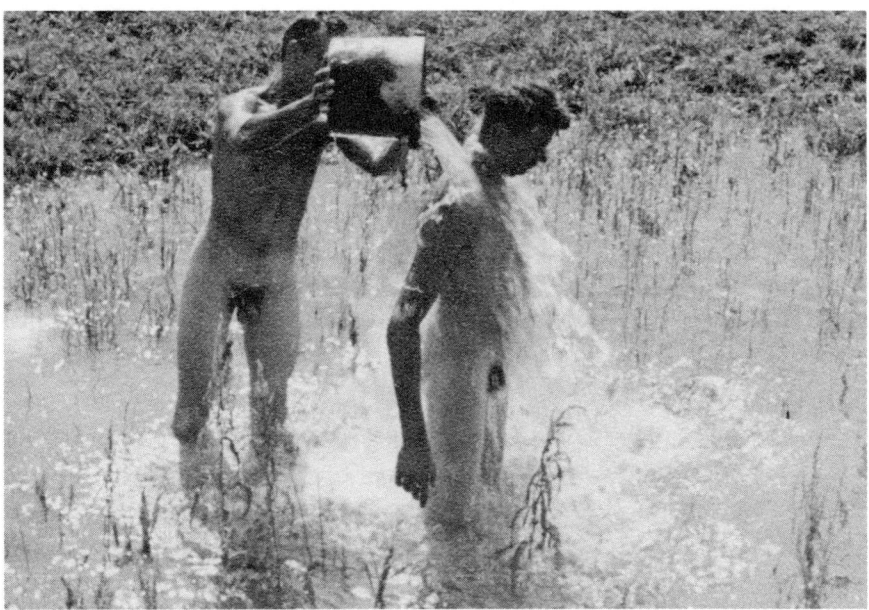

Snapshot 7.12

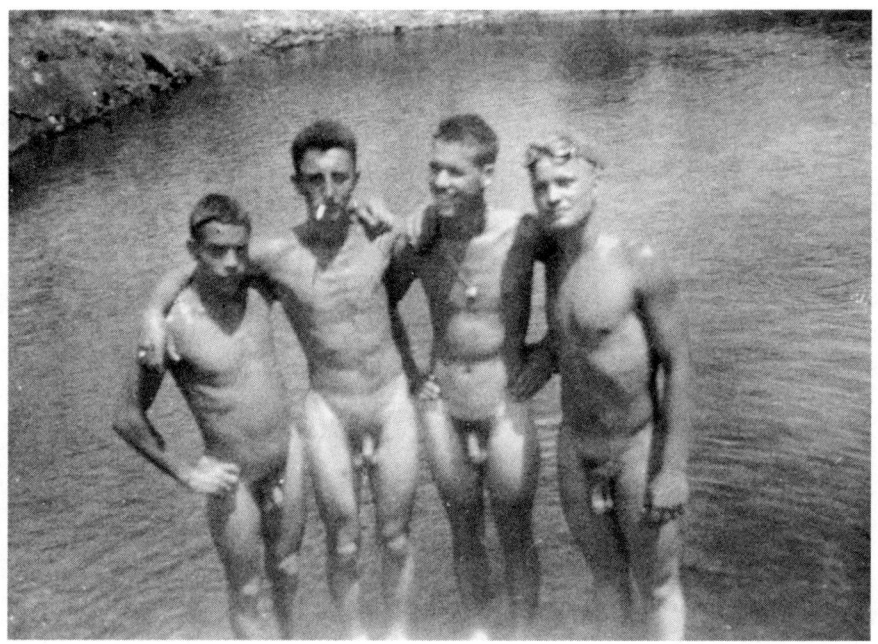

Snapshot 7.13

Snapshot 7.4 and the three above (7.11, 7.12, 7.13) capture moments where the young men are skinny-dipping, and that mainly male custom deserves a brief mention here. For most of the twentieth century young men more often than not experienced swimming with friends as something you did naked. Rural boys certainly went skinny-dipping, but even urban boys swam nude with other boys and adolescents at school pools, YMCA pools, and Boys' Club pools, and the tradition of nude swimming in pools extended to college and universities and ended relatively late in the twentieth century. Summer camps for boys also featured nude swimming in lakes, as some autobiographical testimony and home movies document (e.g., Camp Hawthorne in the 1940s).

Thus, many young men reporting for basic training (boot camp), up to the late twentieth century, had experience swimming naked with other boys and men, and the lack of privacy at boot camp probably extinguished any lingering modesty a young recruit might have. Certainly among the hundreds of snapshots of naked soldiers in Hanson (2014), many are of soldiers skinny-dipping in streams, rivers, lakes, and the ocean.

The photographs confirm that the soldiers are comfortable being naked in front of each other, and already I have made the point that one unconscious function of the casual nudity is the message that the men do not see each other as potential objects of sexual desire. In Gregory Bateson's language, we should really say that there is a metamessage establishing the frame: "This is bathing." That frame, set aside from everyday life (since the men do not go about their everyday lives naked), establishes the nonsexual meanings of bathing naked, not just the visual messages, but also some playful touching. Soldiers use the phrase "grab-ass" to describe the play-fighting focused on the butt, clothed or naked, but playing grab-ass naked inevitably draws attention to the penis, as well.

All this suggests the casual, taken-for-granted and even playful nature of the full nudity in group bathing. The penis, though, is not just a biological organ (Mechling 2008a). In the study of masculinity, especially the study informed by feminist psychoanalysis, the penis carries heavy symbolic meaning. None of the soldiers in these and other snapshots showing the penis (many in Hanson 2014) would be likely to or even able to consciously link the display of their penises in carefully framed situations (primarily play and bathing frames), their gaze at friends' penises, and the penis as a cultural symbol. However, most of the men in these snapshots were raised in American culture, and if the cultural analysts are correct, the men in the snapshots grew up in a culture permeated with messages about the meanings of the penis. For that reason it is worth a brief look here at what feminist scholars say about the penis.

Susan Bordo (1993, 1999) is one of the scholars who have articulated in clear terms what some philosophers and theorists (e.g., Michel Foucault and Jacques Lacan) have written (MacMullan 2002). Lacan is responsible for the most (and most dense) theorizing about the penis as phallus (elaborating on Freud's view), as a cultural construct signifying power, privilege, and dominance. Bordo does not disagree with Lacan and others about the phallus as a cultural signifier, but she is more interested in the actual penis and the ways in which it is hidden and revealed in everyday life and in popular culture. As Bordo famously says, "The phallus . . . haunts the penis," by which she means that the actual penis does not always perform the phallic ideal (Bordo 1999, 95). The phallus as public signifier suggests to men that their manhood, their masculinity, depends upon their penis, and the cultural ideal is that a penis be large, strong, and hard (Bordo 2002).

If, as Chodorow and other feminist psychoanalysts say, the necessity of breaking the male child's identity away from the mother means that masculinity is defined in our culture as a negative, as "not female," then this dynamic makes even more important the visible penis, the most dramatic sign of "not female." In a chapter devoted to "Hard and Soft" (elaborated on in a chapter, "Does Size Matter?" in Tuana et al. 2002), Bordo surveys all the ways men seek to have a penis that measures up to the ideal of the phallus. Men's documented dissatisfaction with the size of their penises is part of the "muscle dysphoria" common in young men, the male parallel with female anorexia (Bordo 1999, 221; Bordo 2002). Young men generally do not feel they are big enough or strong enough to prove their masculinity. They might feel shame about their bodies, including shame about their penises.

The penises in the snapshots here and in the larger collection published in Hanson (2014), for example, are all soft, as are the few penises that show up in the documentary photography found in Bachner's two volumes (2004, 2007). The soft penis signals what we observed earlier—namely, that these men can be naked in each other's presence because they do not see each other as appropriate targets of sexual desire. Of course, it is likely that there are gay men and bisexual men in the group, but they must also embrace the rules of the play frame or the bathing frame. An erection would seriously break the frame.

EXCURSUS: A SOLDIER PISSING

I begin my scholarly article "Pissing and Masculinity" (Mechling 2014) using the word "urination," but briefly into the discussion and analysis I change to the folk term "pissing" to describe that bodily function, since that folk word really conveys the power of urination in the performance of masculinity. I shall adopt the same term here. While I have in my collection a dozen or so snapshots showing the penis of the man or men in the snapshot, Snapshot 7.14 is the only one I have of a soldier actually pissing. I know that there are others that have been taken and that have survived all the events and choices that can cause a snapshot to be lost, discarded, or destroyed (e.g., Hanson 2014, 194–195, has several). A single snapshot or even a few do not amount to a pattern, so it would be possible to discard this snapshot from analysis as an aberration signaling nothing of importance in the social construction, maintenance, and repair of military masculinity. There is a pattern, however, in the role of pissing in performing

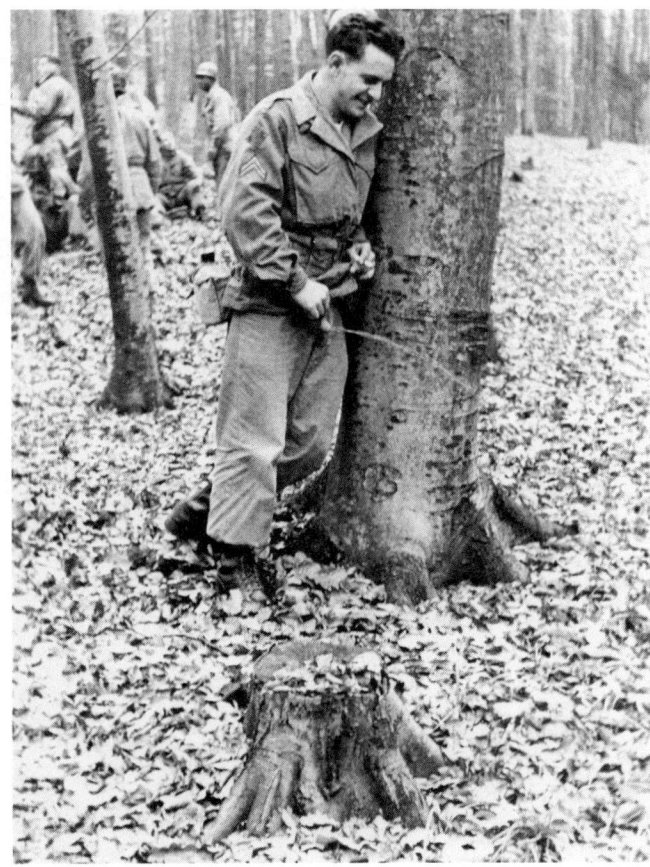

Snapshot 7.14

masculinity, so this snapshot actually stands for others and for men's judgment that pissing together is a form of bonding.

In fact, there is a notorious photograph—a cellphone video, actually—from 2012 in the Helmand Province of Afghanistan taken by a Marine of a circle of his Marine buddies urinating on the dead bodies of Taliban fighters they had just killed in a firefight. The leak of the video to the public created a furor, of course, but in truth there is a long history of American soldiers' pissing on the dead bodies of enemy soldiers as a show of contempt and other strong emotions felt by the soldiers in those moments (Wallis and Mechling 2019, 130–131).

Snapshot 7.14 is not in that genre of aggression toward the enemy; rather, it reflects the ease military men have in each other's presence. And it is not just being nude in each other's presence. The numerous snapshots of men on latrines suggest a fixation begun in basic training, where the basic bodily functions are not private and an authority figure has total control over the "when" and "where" of those functions. Those conditions likely create the same sort of fixation with pissing. Someone, the soldier taking Snapshot 7.14 or the soldier in the snapshot, wrote on the back: "Just one of those pictures that anyone can have by just coming in the army." Someone was sent this snapshot and message.

The soldier in Snapshot 7.14 has sought a little privacy pissing behind a tree trunk, though the photography negates that privacy. Actually, men often take pleasure in pissing side by side, often commenting on the power or distance of the stream, and even joking about penis size (Mechling 2014). Most of the scholarly discussions of men's bonding side by side do not include pissing, but many men experience that as a strong form of bonding.

8

Human Pyramids

Snapshots of men and women, usually men, climbing on each other into the form of a human pyramid seem to be a popular way to commemorate a gathering. Boys of all ages seem to like building such pyramids; men often form human pyramids when visiting a beach (Mechling 2016b), and my collection of military snapshots has plenty of examples of soldiers and sailors poised in these human constructions. Human pyramids are one of those occasions seemingly created just for the sake of a photograph. I doubt many gatherings of people build a human pyramid unless there is someone present with a camera to document the achievement.

The visual and even documentary histories of gymnastics and dance suggest that humans have enjoyed climbing on each other across history and cultures. As for many traditional customs I analyze in these pages, it simply is not enough to say men in the military build and record human pyramids because it is "fun." It is that, doubtless, but a thick interpretation of the human pyramid as a tool in the performance of masculinity in the all-male friendship group demands more.

Let me begin with evolutionary psychology and the need for touch (Montagu 1986). Primatologists see firsthand how much primates seek and enjoy the touch of others (Sapolsky 1997). The research on the need for humans to touch each other is well-enough known that I assume I do not need to review that literature here. Children touch each other comfortably, including the rough-and-tumble playfighting I discuss later in Chapter 10.

American culture at times interrupts the natural pattern of men touching other men. The comfort American men have touching each other varies across time and other factors, like ethnicity. Photography captures this history in ways no written documents can, and the books by David Deitcher (2001) and John Ibson (2002, 2007, 2018) document the changes. Ibson (2002) uses the snapshots of men-with-men in the twentieth century to make an argument that the intimacy of body language between men we see in photography intensifies during World War II and then virtually disappears from the vernacular photography of men together in the late 1940s and into the 1950s.

As we saw in Chapter 4, buddy pictures are plentiful among the soldier snapshots from twentieth-century wars and persist even into this century, confirming Ibson's thesis. Putting your arm around a buddy or two for a snapshot in the military seems natural; the human pyramid expands the opportunity for touch.

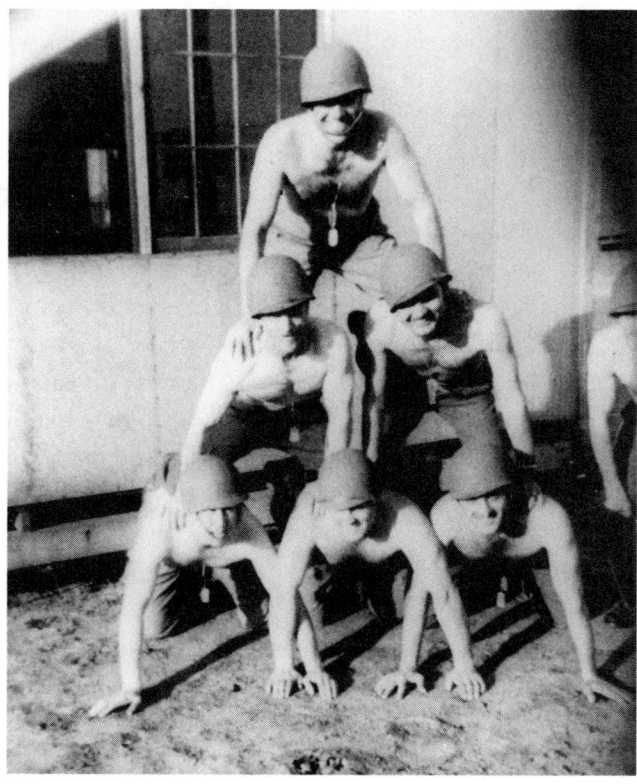

Snapshot 8.1

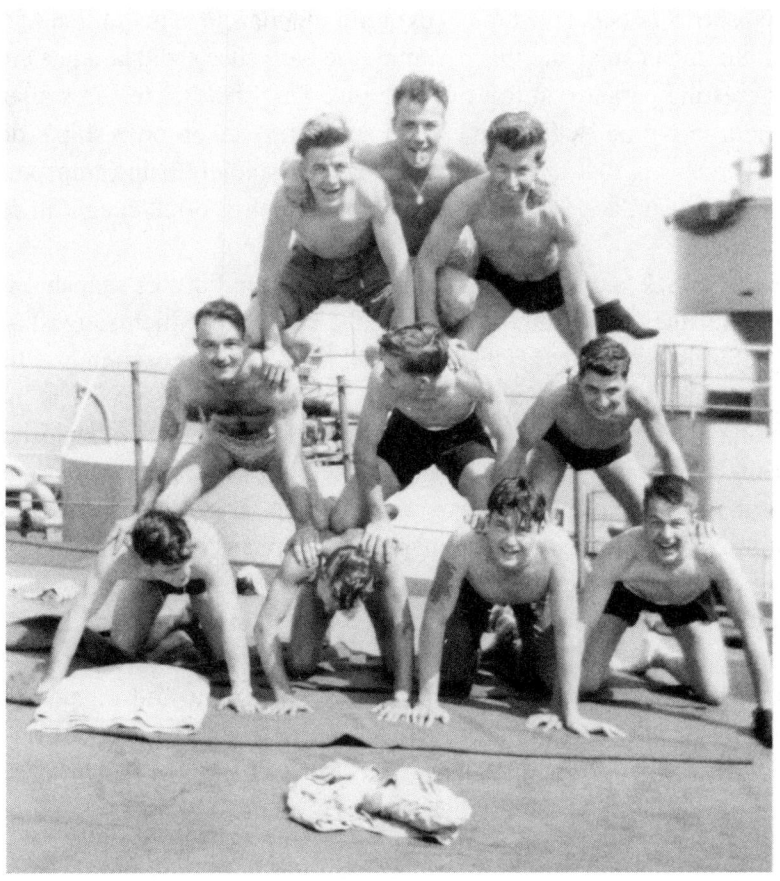

Snapshot 8.2

The human pyramid has several features relevant for a discussion of the social construction of normative heterosexual identity in the military male friendship group. The first feature is the way a pyramid literalizes the hierarchy within the male group. Male friendship groups, like other male primate groups, tend to form and respect a hierarchy of power within the group. Physical strength and size often are the basis for the placement of a particular male in the group hierarchy, though there can be other factors as well, such as intelligence, skill at humor, and even wealth. The human pyramid literalizes the hierarchy of strength in the male group, the larger and stronger males forming the first row (which will bear the most weight) with each successive row formed by increasingly smaller and lighter men, until one (usually the smallest and lightest) perches on the top.

Snapshot 8.1 shows the typical pyramid found in so many military snapshots. Six men can create this pyramid (the bare chests and helmets create an interesting paradox in this photograph). Snapshot 8.2 features a larger pyramid, this time with ten men and apparently taken on a ship's deck. A good guess is that they are not sailors but soldiers being transported, and they are on deck for some sunbathing, which is often caught in other snapshots.

Snapshot 8.3 features a six-man pyramid again, but this snapshot is of interest for the group gathered and for the uniforms, which suggest a period before World War II. The men could have just all posed in two lines, but six decided to create a pyramid for the photo. Snapshot 8.4 is in the form of a real photo postcard, not a commercial card but a true snapshot in a format some cameras made possible. There are eight men in that figure, but note the man in front of the pyramid flexing his biceps. Boys and men alike often flex this muscle for snapshots, emphasizing the link between physical strength and masculinity.

In the snapshots reproduced here we see pyramids with varying numbers of men and in different settings. Men perched on the shoulders of buddies do not constitute a true pyramid, though I would include these snapshots because of the male touching framed as play.

Male strength is highlighted here; in Snapshot 8.5 one man alone is bearing the weight of three others, and in Snapshot 8.6 we see all three men flexing their biceps.

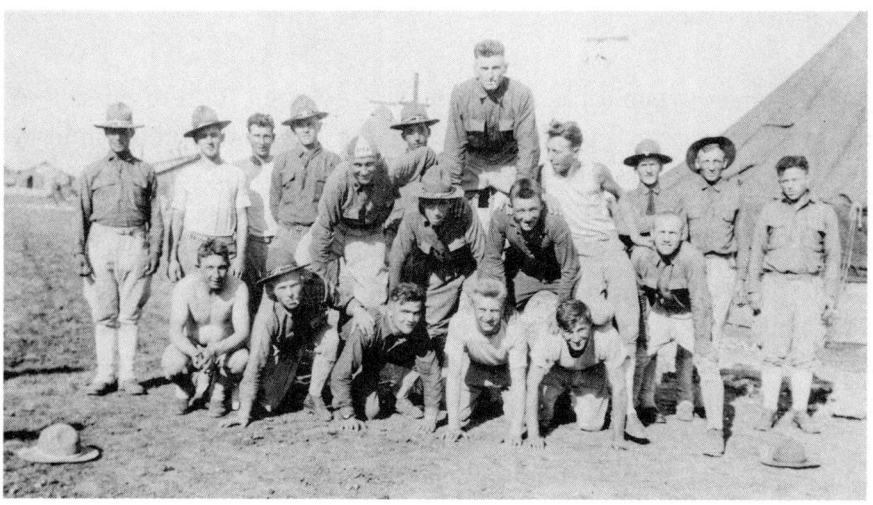

Snapshot 8.3

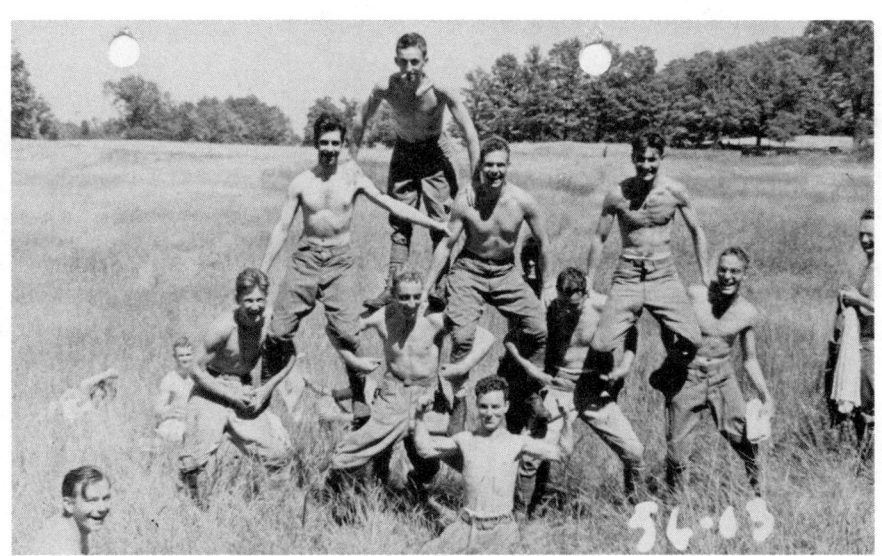

Snapshot 8.4

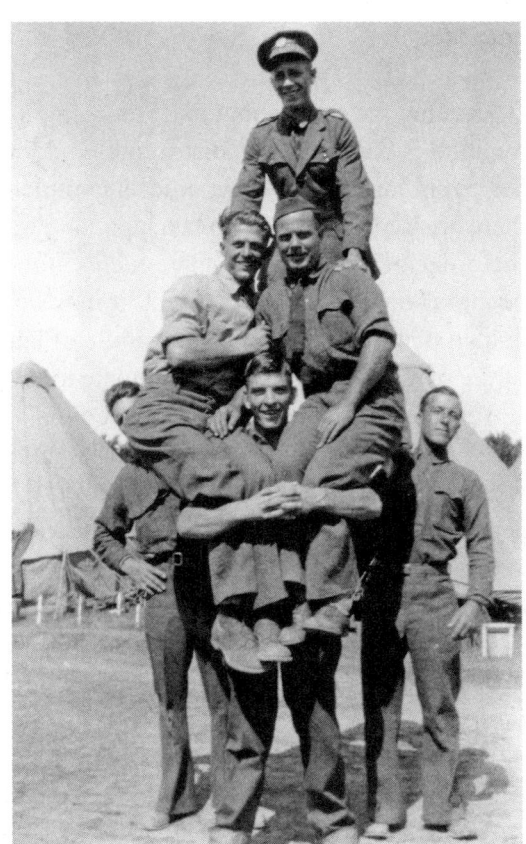

Snapshot 8.5

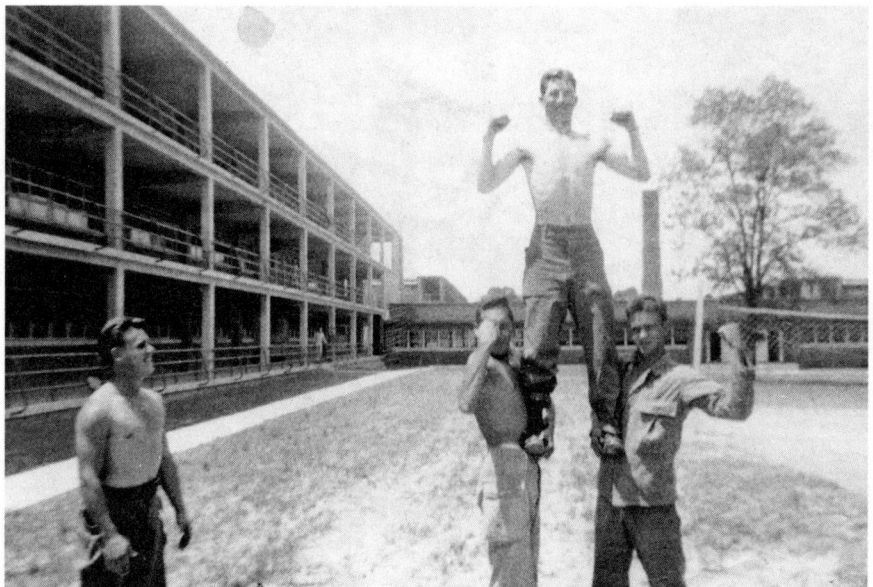

Snapshot 8.6

Keeping the point about male touching in mind, consider how a human pyramid is built and then disassembled. Men climb on each other to build the pyramid. Once the pyramid is complete and the photographs taken, there are two basic ways to take apart a pyramid. One is to slowly reverse the order of building and have men climb down one by one from their positions on the pyramid. I think it may be more common, though, for a human pyramid to collapse into a pile of laughing bodies. The play frame of the pyramid provides safe, intimate touching by men in groups.

Yet more is happening in this seemingly simple play with bodies and weight and balance, which are the elements of some circus acts, like high-wire and trapeze acts. Paul Bouissac's (1976) semiotic analysis of circus acts makes a relevant point here that the audience's engrossment with those acts relies upon the fact that the performers are defying gravity, that they are using their bodies to stop themselves from falling. Falling, however, is also an element of the fun. Roger Caillois (1961) describes four basic forms of play and the pleasure of play, including the one relevant here, *ilinx,* the pleasurable feeling of vertigo, from simple spinning to games involving falling. So the two pleasures lie in the tension of defying gravity when the pyramid is finished, and then the pleasure of falling.

A soft surface like the sand of a beach is not required for the fun of

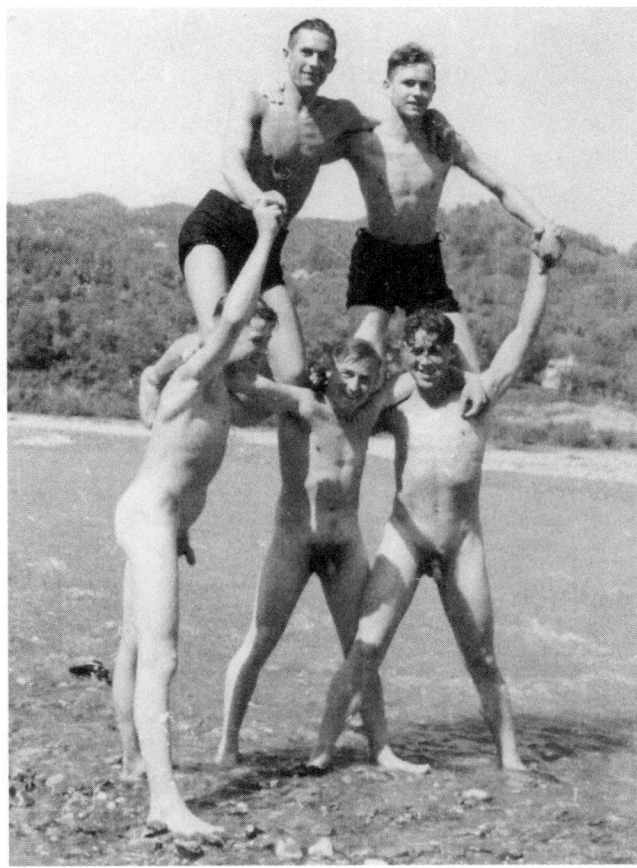

Snapshot 8.7

building a human pyramid, but many of these snapshots are taken at beaches, some even in the water. Snapshot 8.7 signals that sometimes men in groups build these structures while naked, often while skinny-dipping.

The case of human pyramids is clearly a case of military male bodies at play, but in a sense even the latrine snapshots and the snapshots of bathing make sense only if we understand that the men in the snapshots are experiencing their activities as playful. The nudity is not serious, and the comfort of the nude men is possible mainly because they have adopted a play frame where messages (the nudity, the touching) do not mean what they would mean in other frames. This is why Chapter 3's discussion of play is so crucial to understanding the chapters in Part III, "The Male Body in the Military." Each successive chapter in this section probes deeper and deeper into the ways the play frame makes possible folk practices men use to manage their friendships and their emotions in the male group.

9

Cross-Dressing

Anyone who has seen the Rodgers and Hammerstein musical *South Pacific* on the stage (1949) or on film (1958) saw something quite entertaining because of its nonsensical reversal of gender dress—namely, manly sailors dressed as women. The photographic evidence suggests that such cross-dressing was no invention of the play's authors and lyricist but actually was quite common in the American military. The vernacular photographs of male soldiers, sailors, and Marines dressing as women record the practices in three different settings—all-male theatricals, Crossing the Line (Neptune) Festivals on ships, and everyday, informal, playful cross-dressing for no particular formal event.

Males cross-dressing as females is one of those folk practices we do not read about in the usual war memoirs and war reportage. Instead, photography reveals this common tradition. In some cases the photography is by professionals reporting on the theatricals and on the Crossing the Line Festivals. Often official ship photographers record the latter, though there are plenty of amateur, vernacular snapshots also capturing the festive play. At first glance the snapshots of males cross-dressing in each of these three settings seem simply silly and fun. Those terms mask, however, more serious gender maintenance taking place within the "safe" play time and space.

The following analysis will assume the normative heterosexual identification of the men dressing as women and of the male audience for the formal and informal performances. For some people, cross-dressing excites sexual pleasure and might even play a part in sexual play. Even before puberty, some boys are attracted to wearing their sisters' or mothers' clothing. I have no access to the inner states and motives of the men in these snapshots who elect to dress as women, and I recognize that even using the word "elect" might suggest a level of voluntariness not really present in the event. As we saw in the initial exploration of the play frame in Chapter 3, some people may be participating reluctantly, giving into peer pressure to join the play. And, as we saw in the case of people who use play to "mask" other motives (Sutton-Smith and Kelly-Byrne 1984), it is possible (probably even likely) that some men who elect to dress as a woman for the playful "fun" of theatricals, festivals, and everyday play might actually experience sexual pleasure in the performance.

I write "performance" to remind us that gender identity is largely constituted through performance (Butler 2006, 2011). Males in the military friendship group understand that the social construction, maintenance, and (if necessary) repair of their performances of normative heterosexual masculinity are just that, performances, and usually the male group enforces the norms of performance. They have learned the boy code (Pollack 1998) and the guy code (Kimmel 2008), at least for public performances of manhood. The male group often uses teasing to keep performances in line with the stereotypes of the heterosexual norm, so a man who deviates at all from expected male dress will be subject to the pressures of teasing and sometimes worse.

Except in carefully constructed play frames, like those that follow.

ALL-MALE THEATRICALS

Historians and anthropologists show us the historical depth and cultural range of the phenomenon of males dressing as females (e.g., Garber 1992; Senelick 2000). Marjorie Garber (1992, 16) notes that the "transvestite" (another term for cross-dressers of both sexes) creates a temporary cultural crisis of categories. Male and female are the binary cultural categories for sorting people, but sometimes an anomaly—a disordering event or object—disrupts these categories. For example, Clifford Geertz (1983, 80–84) notes that the occasional birth of a true hermaphrodite (an intersex person), a child with both male and female genitals, poses a crisis of categories. Anthropologists observe that although some cultures can absorb such anomalies, others employ an assortment of strategies for dealing with the anomaly, including "fixing it" (the medical approach in the United States), ignoring it, or putting it at the center of some sort of cultural performance (Babcock-Abrahams 1975). In most cases the anomaly is seen as dangerous, as "liminal," existing between the comfortable cultural categories.

Cross-dressing is common enough across human history and cultures that we might view it as a safe cultural strategy for dealing with the dangerous anomaly in the system of signaling gender with clothing. Cross-dressing in public is safe so long as takes place in the play frame, a temporary, subjunctive ("What if?") reality where things do not mean what they would mean outside the play frame, in the world of common sense where men dress as men. In the play frame the sense gets inverted, creating nonsense. In the play frame the incongruity of a male dressing as a female is humorous. The more manly (muscles, body hair, etc.) the male cross-dresser, the more humorous is the performance. The tradition in some high schools of "powderpuff football," staging a playful game in which the female cheerleaders dress in football uniforms to play ball while the male football players dress as cheerleaders, is good fun for the teenagers who are nervous anyway about their sexual and gender identities.

The theatrical performance in the all-male group is the most "dramatic" version of cross-dressing as play. It is well-known that boys played the female roles in Renaissance theater, but the modern practice of young American men dressing as young women in college theatricals began at Harvard in 1844 (British schools had been doing that for decades), and the practice spread to other Ivy League colleges (Garber 1992, 60; Senelick 2000, 356–358). In fact, any all-male school mounting theatrical productions put boys in girls' clothing to play those parts.

Boy Scout camps and other all-male summer camps also need boys to dress as girls for camp theatricals. The Boy Scout troop summer encampment I studied for many years (Mechling 2001) developed a tradition of cross-dressing for theatrical performances in two settings. One was the campfire skit, which sometimes required a boy to play a female part, and the other—one far more elaborately costumed and performed—entertained the younger boys (ages eleven to thirteen) when the older boys (the senior scouts, ages fourteen to seventeen) "themed" a day of fun and contests on an island in the lake around popular films or television series. The first I saw was *Gilligan's Island,* a very popular television show featuring two women (Ginger and Mary Ann); another summer the seniors themed the day of fun around *Austin Powers,* a popular comedy film with two sexy female characters (one named "Alotta Fagina"); and yet another summer the seniors chose *Star Wars* as a theme. In each case one or two boys would dress as the female characters and work hard at "acting female," which usually involved what they saw as the body language of girls. The audience of younger boys clearly enjoyed the performance of an older boy as a female character.

Boys the ages of these scouts (eleven to seventeen) are going through pubertal body changes that are puzzling and troubling enough in their everyday lives. They are literally in transition from boy to man, but some boys dressing as girls does not threaten their categories because everyone involved understands that these performances are in the play frame, where nonsense prevails and things do not mean what they would mean outside the play frame (Stewart 1979). What was true in these Boy Scout camp theatrical performances is true of any theatrical performance in an all-male school. All-male schools are becoming rarer, as are all-male units in the American military, which might mean that the formal cross-dressing theatricals will fade away. The needs met by the cross-dressing are unlikely to disappear, however, so the informal versions of cross-dressing in male groups seem likely to endure.

Allan Bérubé's (1990) history of gay men and women serving in the armed forces during World War II reconstructs the prevalence of cross-dressing in the theatricals by male soldiers, a phenomenon long overlooked because of attention given to the United Service Organization (USO) shows that actually had female performers. Although World War II is the time period of Bérubé's book, he notes that cross-dressing in theatricals in the US Army began in World War I as a Progressive Era strategy to protect American soldiers "from liquor, gambling, prostitution, and venereal disease by organizing programs of wholesome and uplifting recreation in their camps" (Bérubé 1990, 75).

Bérubé notes that many closeted gay men in the military were able to find "temporary refuge" in their impersonation of women in the theatricals (1990, 67–68), but heterosexual men were also dressing for female parts. Under pressure to improve troop morale, the military actually endorsed and promoted theatricals involving female impersonation, and in 1942 the Office of Special Services concluded that it was good for morale to create "within the military a version of the civilian theatre world," so the office wrote and distributed scripts and instructions for constructing costumes (Bérubé 1990, 68–69).

The theatrical frame relied for its meanings on one key feature of all play frames, that of paradox, where things in the frame do not mean what they would mean outside the frame. Thus, argues Bérubé, because "female impersonation seemed so vital to the war effort . . . soldier-entertainers and military officials, with the help of the press, found ways to use drag entertainment for the duration while walking a fine line between its homosexual and heterosexual meanings" (Bérubé 1990, 68). It is precisely the confusion of category that makes the cross-dressing male soldier in these theatricals a valuable icon for the audience of men, whether heterosexual, bisexual, or gay. The cross-dressing male soldier paradoxically reinforces the heterosexual norm. In the play frame the process of inversion, where sense becomes nonsense, relies on the audience's knowing what is "normal." The fun of watching a male soldier "perform" as a female depends upon the audience's knowledge that they are watching a man, and in most performances the cross-dressing man is performing a stylized, exaggerated version of the female. That is the paradox of cross-dressing in the play frame—the performance validates and reinforces normative heterosexual masculinity.

CROSSING THE LINE FESTIVALS

Festivals provide another play setting for cross-dressing. Folklorists, historians, anthropologists, and sociologists give us a broad understanding of the functions of festivals in cultures (e.g., Abrahams 1982, 2005; Abrahams and Bauman 1978). There are world-famous festivals, like Mardi Gras (the American version of Carnival) and Halloween, but there are countless other calendrical festivals, some religious and some secular. Ethnic groups in cities organize festivals celebrating their cultures, usually with food and dress and music, and even small communities celebrate local festivals.

Crossing the Line is probably the best-known military festival. This is an old festival (also called a Neptune Festival, after the Roman god of the sea) and is celebrated on both military and merchant ships when they cross the equator. Crossing the equator is one of those liminal times and places "betwixt and between" cultural categories, in this case two hemispheric categories, but the crossing also becomes the occasion for the hazing and initiation of sailors, of the "Pollywogs" experiencing their first time "crossing the line," by the Shellbacks, the experienced sailors who have crossed the line before and had their own initiation into the brotherhood of those who have crossed the line.

Bronner (2006) offers a detailed and persuasive analysis of the meanings of all the traditions involved in the Crossing the Line Ceremony, showing how the ceremony follows structures and symbolic actions anthropologists and folklorists find across time and space. I shall not reproduce Bronner's astute analysis here. He does illustrate his book with several snapshots, some featuring the cross-dressing (e.g., Bronner 2006, 21) that is a part of the festival. In fact, many Crossing the Line Festivals have been photographed over the years, by both professional shipboard photographers and by amateur photographers. Snapshots 9.1 and 9.2 are both from Crossing the Line Festivals.

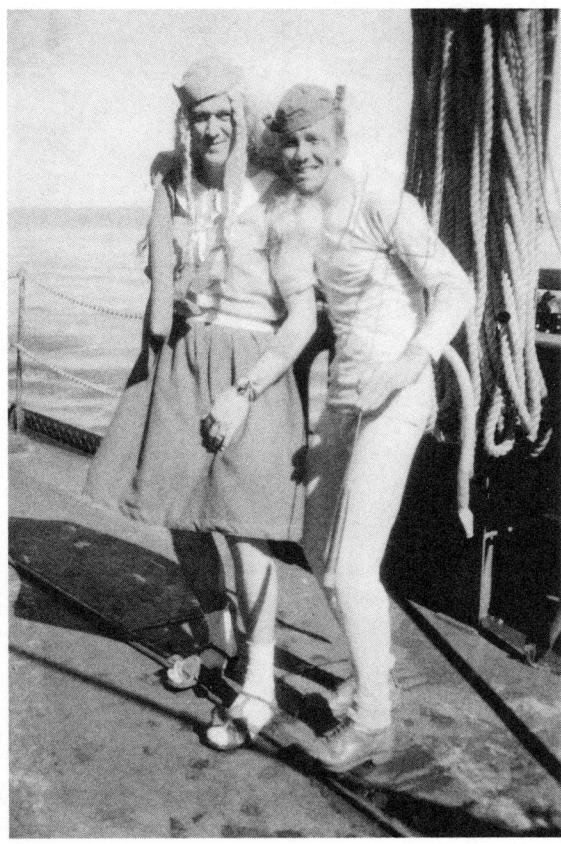

Snapshot 9.1

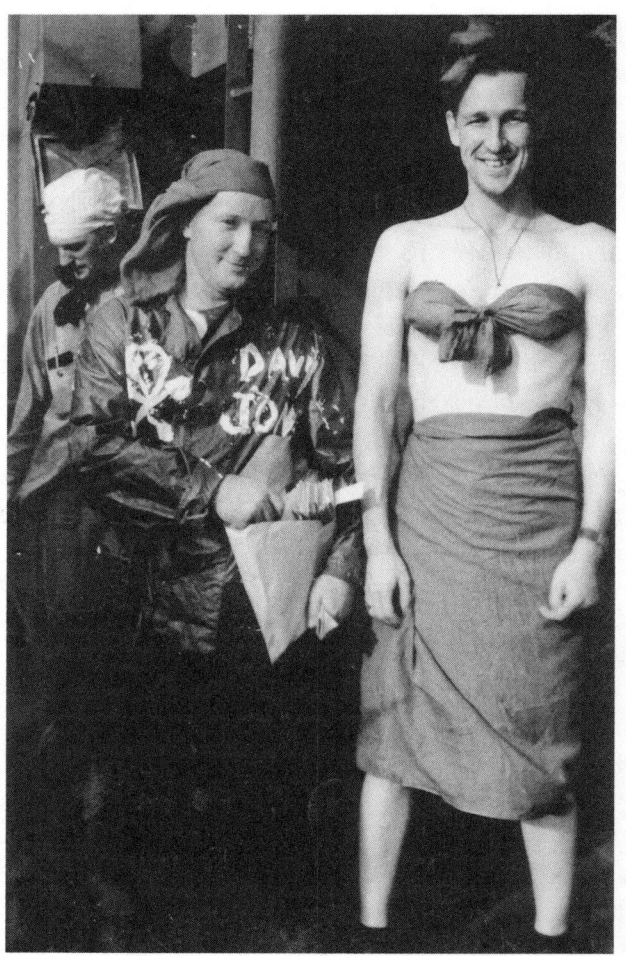

Snapshot 9.2

INFORMAL CROSS-DRESSING

The first two settings for male cross-dressing in the military are more formal, safe time and spaces for a male's pretending to be a female. The third occasion, everyday life at a camp or base or in the field or on a ship, still invokes a play frame but does not have the "safety" of a formal theatrical or a formulaic festival. The play frame in these instances is still in the subjunctive, "What if?" mood, and the play frame in these spontaneous, informal instances still takes its energy from the paradox of things not meaning what they would mean outside of the play frame.

The snapshots of playful, informal cross-dressing by men in the military are all the more intriguing precisely because there is not a formal event "masking" the motives for the play. Certainly, in both the theatricals and the festivals the men who cross-dress choose those roles somewhat voluntarily, though status in the male friendship hierarchy may mean that some men are assigned the female role by a more powerful member of the male group. The informal cross-dressing seems fully voluntary, and the smiles affirm the playful pleasure of the performance.

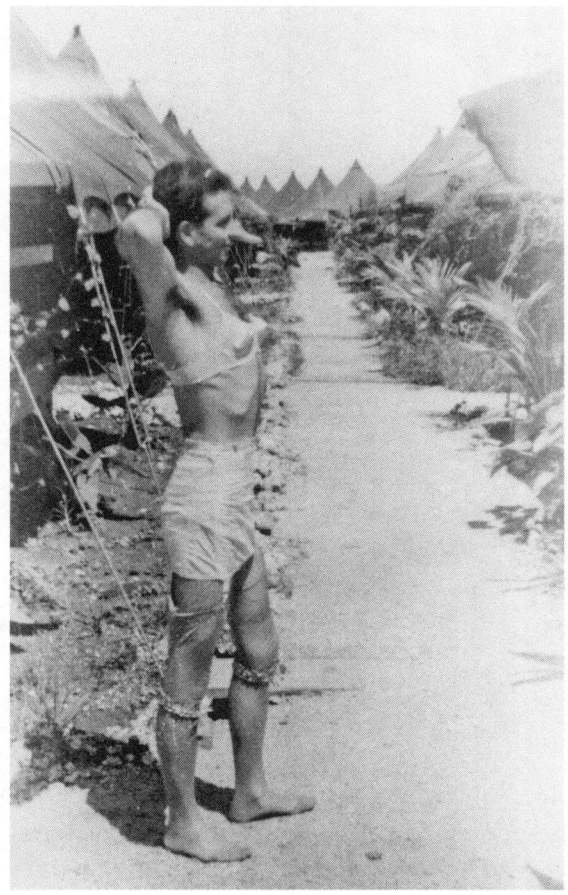

Snapshot 9.3

Snapshots 9.3 and 9.4 of single men are just two of many I could reproduce here, and they feature two different strategies for dressing as a woman. In Snapshot 9.3 the soldier (in the Pacific Theater during World War II is a good guess) has obtained a bra, panties with garters, and hosiery (possibly from a cooperative member of the Women's Army Corps, or

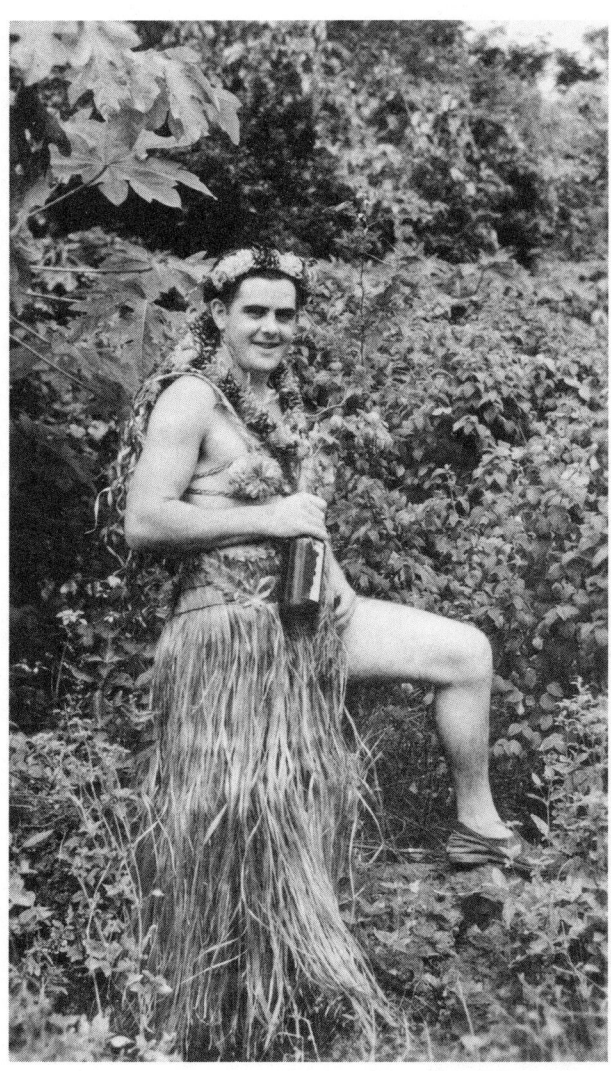

Snapshot 9.4

Women Accepted for Volunteer Emergency Service, or a nurse). His pose, with his hands behind his head, mimics the iconic female pinup pictures these soldiers doubtless have on their walls (Gabor 1972; Collins 2000).

The soldier in Snapshot 9.4 adopts a Polynesian costume for his cross-dressing adventure, and in this case we have his writing on the back of the snapshot: "What do you think of that? I'd say pretty hot stuff. Acting a damn fool one day & that is the result. Taken on Saipan August of '45. I didn't take the skirt off of a gal but would have if I could find one—ha ha." The writing obviously is a message to the person to whom he is sending the snapshot, most likely a male friend or relative because of the "joke" about taking the skirt off a woman. The writing assures that the person viewing the snapshot has no doubt that the subject of the snapshot is a heterosexual man just having fun ("acting a damn fool"); once more the play frame provides a safe time and space for a brief excursion into nonsense.

That Polynesian costume in Snapshot 9.4 actually shows up in many snapshots of cross-dressing men from the Pacific theater. The snapshots of a cross-dressing soldier alone are interesting enough (he is not alone, after all—there is a friend taking the snapshot), but more interesting for our understanding of the functions of cross-dressing in the male friendship group are the snapshots of a cross-dressing soldier with one or more buddies who are dressed as men.

Snapshot 9.5, for example, appears to have been taken on a ship's deck. These might be soldiers being transported (see the uniform of the figure in the back, watching the tableau) and not sailors, but in any case we are viewing one soldier dressed in a Polynesian costume (bra, lei, and grass skirt) and sitting on the lap of another soldier. The body language of the two men says a lot. The cross-dressing man is using his posture to perform

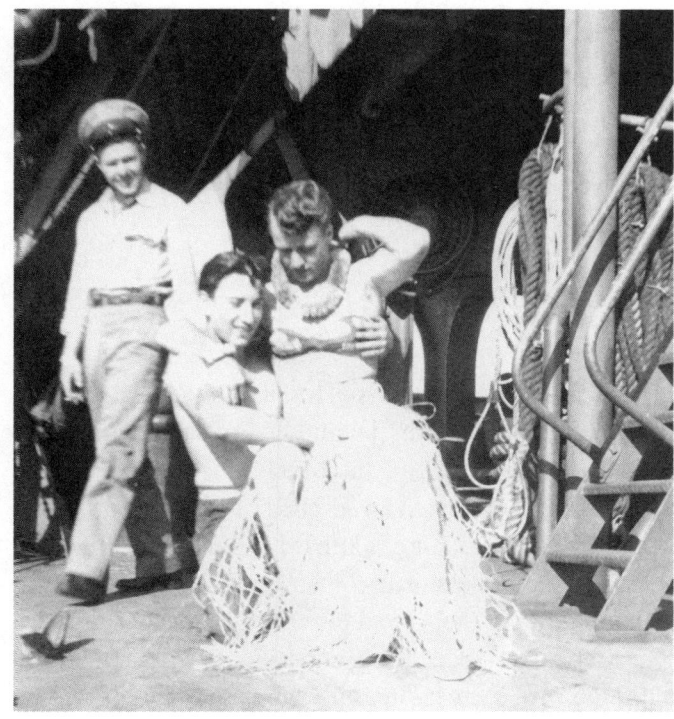

Snapshot 9.5

the female role, sitting on the other man's lap, with one arm around his neck and one bent behind his head as in a female pinup (see Snapshot 9.3). The soldier holding "her" has his left hand on the fake breast, while his other hand is placed over what would be the female's genitals. I shall have more to say about this, but first let us examine Snapshots 9.6 and 9.7.

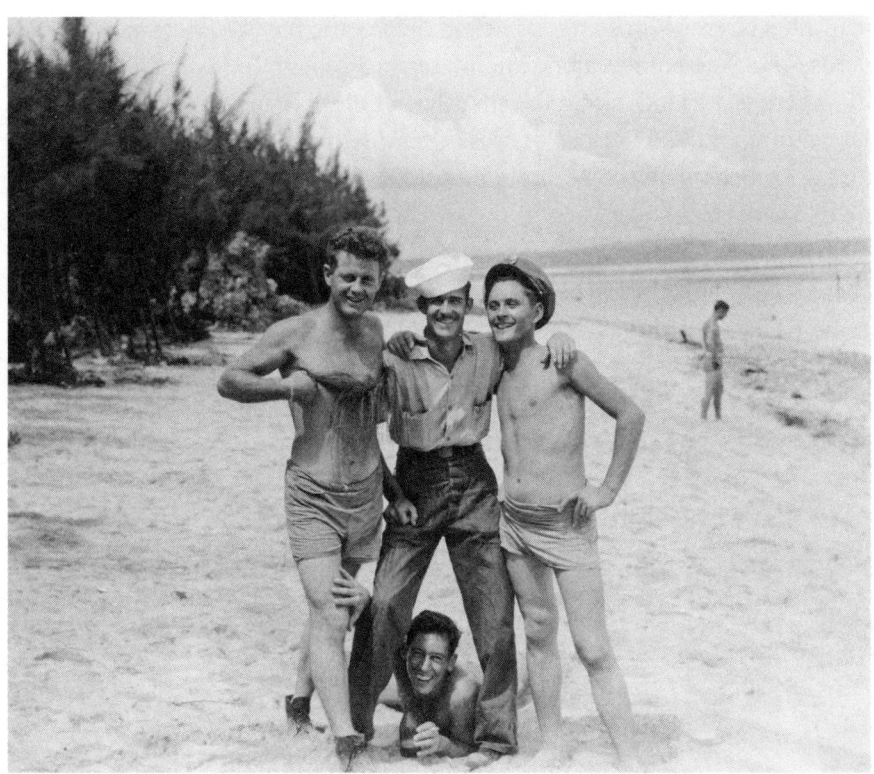

Snapshot 9.6

In Snapshot 9.6 four friends, perhaps all sailors, are having fun on the beach; certainly the fully dressed figure in the middle is a sailor. On either side of him are shirtless men in shorts for the beach; but the man to the right of the sailor in the center has created an ad-hoc bra of some sort difficult to discern. (Is it made of seaweed or of cloth?) In some ways the most interesting of the four figures is the shirtless man lying on the sand and looking out at the camera through the spread legs of the dressed sailor. In his left hand the prone man holds a beer bottle and a cigarette, but his right hand is touching the thigh of the cross-dressing sailor near the knee. He

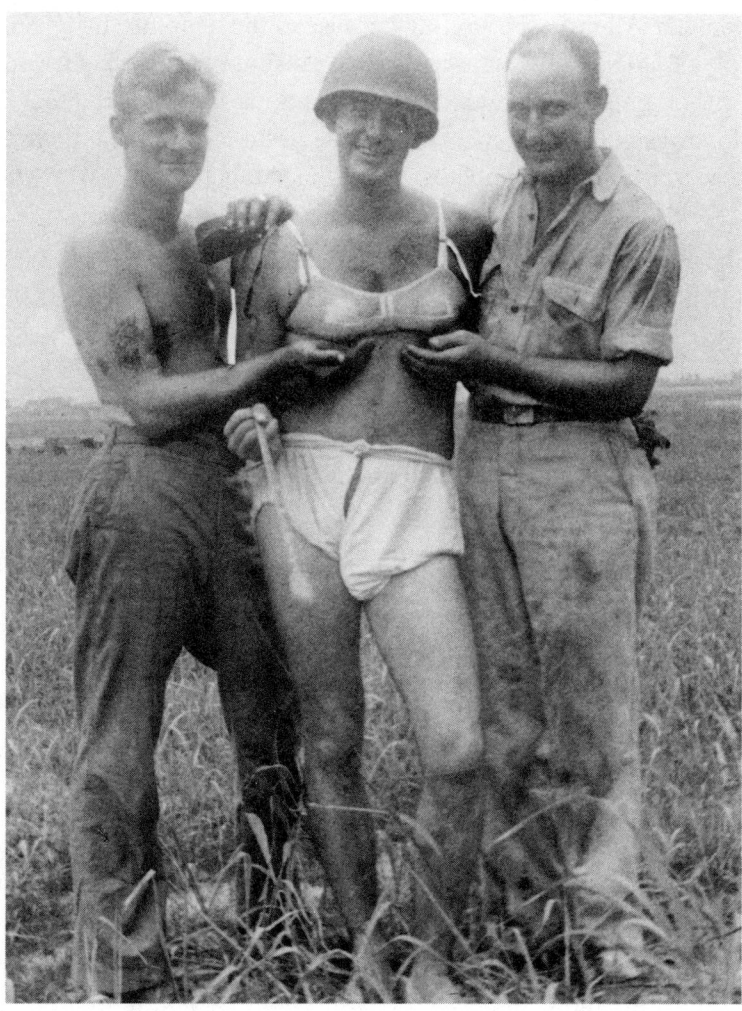

Snapshot 9.7

could have put that hand anywhere, but he chose to touch the cross-dress-ing sailor as if "stealing" a feel of a female thigh or knee, an erotic gesture.

In Snapshot 9.7 the erotic gesture by the two men flanking the cross-dressing soldier is aimed at the fake breasts. This gesture is not unique to this snapshot, and I have seen other snapshots of soldiers and sailors squeezing the fake breasts of cross-dressing friends in everyday play. The cross-dressing soldier in the middle perfectly represents the par-adox of the performance. The helmet signals the masculine soldier, and the improvised female "panties" barely disguise what appear to be large male genitals. All three are smiling because of the nonsense being enacted in the play frame. In this snapshot, as in Snapshot 9.6, the male friends are keeping their bodies close and draping their arms around each other in the ways John Ibson (2002) documents, in the gestures of male intimacy that disappear from vernacular photographs of men together after World War II and into the 1950s (Ibson 2002, 2018).

THE PLEASURES OF CROSS-DRESSING

A cultural analysis of cross-dressing in the military needs to consider both the psychological and sociological aspects of traditional practices in the all-male friendship group. As Bérubé and others note, military authorities recognized as early as World War I that formal theatricals featuring cross-dressing men improved the morale of the troops, and naval authorities recognize the same function of the Crossing the Line Festivals, another formal frame in which cross-dressing is expected and enjoyed. "Morale" has both psychological and social dimensions.

In my analysis here, as I indicated earlier, I am not able to speculate on the motives of the men who choose to cross-dress in the formal and informal play frames. Doubtless the men who dressed as women in these snapshots identified themselves, in their own minds if not in public, as primarily heterosexual, bisexual, or homosexual, though even these categories too simply describe the complexity of sexual identity and practices among young men. Moreover, many seventeen- and eighteen-year-old men have not yet settled on a comfortable understanding of their sexual identity, made all the more anxiety-producing by participating in an all-male organization valuing normative heterosexual qualities and behavior. In the military, sex between putatively heterosexual men can be very "contextual" (Ward 2015; Zeeland 1993, 1995, 1996, 1999; Savin-Williams 2017). With masturbation as their primary sexual outlet, heterosexual young men fighting the wars in the twentieth century created in their minds and on their barracks walls covered with female pinups the idealized, imagined female sex object. Gay American soldiers fighting in twentieth-century wars had to mask their real sexual identity, in most cases joining the male banter among friends about women and sex.

Guessing about the motives and reactions of the soldiers watching the cross-dressing performances by other men is as risky as speculating about the motives of the volunteer cross-dressing men, but the psychologists and anthropologists who have thought and written about male cross-dressing provide a few insights. The psychological writing about cross-dressing tends to focus on the cross-dressers themselves and the pleasures of cross-dressing, whereas I am interested here in the psychology of the watchers who take pleasure in observing the cross-dressing performance by a friend.

The discussion above about the play frame and the pleasures of nonsense as a break from oppressive sense-making in the everyday world points us to one sort of understanding of the pleasure experienced by watching a male friend dress as a woman. One well-established theory of humor is incongruity theory, which fits well the image of a male soldier dressing as a woman (Oring 2016). Cross-dressing is fun for both the performer and the audience because it is humorous. That analysis seems too simple, though.

In some respects the question "What is the pleasure experienced by the men watching a buddy dress as a woman?" amounts to "Why would men in the military find pleasure in watching an unmasking of the fixity of gender?" Again, we return to the paradoxical features of the play frame. Play opens up another reality for the brief time and space of the play frame event. Everyday life, including in the military, affirms normative gender distinctions and the uses of dress, as Laurence Senelick puts it (2000, 2) to "render the gender of the wearer discernable at a glance." The cross-dressing buddy totally disrupts that order of things and creates an attention-getting bit of disorder (nomos versus anomaly, sense versus nonsense). Senelick (2000, 1–2) uses the work "magical" to describe the transformation achieved when a person dresses as the opposite sex would. The cross-dressing buddy opens up a reality where gender is not a fixed quality of the self, where the "true self" and the "performed self" are seen as possibly different, a world in which gender and perhaps sexuality are fluid. This play frame peek into an alternative reality is safe because of the fundamental paradox of play, and it is safe because it is confined to a play space and time. It usually does not last long enough to truly upend the accepted norms of gender display and sexuality.

It is worth asking if a man observing a male friend's cross-dressing performance can experience ecstasy or flow in the act of watching. That depends on the setting, of course. Observing cross-dressing males in both theatricals and formal festivals (like Crossing the Line) likely can transport an observer into the state of flow experienced by audience members watching a performance. Interestingly, secular festivals like Crossing the Line resemble religious festivals in many ways, and we might expect that participants in Crossing the Line play would experience the ecstasy religious festivals sometimes evoke. An element of flow is total engrossment, a loss of the sense of time and place during the experience. There is no reason not to expect that, given the right circumstances, a male watching his buddy cross-dress might experience ecstasy or flow.

Finally, we should not overlook the possibility that some of the men watching a buddy cross-dress are sexually excited by the performance. Exploring this possibility would be highly speculative without personal testimony, of which there is none, but some of the snapshots provide clues that for some men present, both performers and audience, sexual desire might fuel the energy of the performance and the pleasure of watching the performance. The snapshots of informal examples of cross-dressing provide most of these clues.

We saw in Snapshots 9.5, 9.6, and 9.7 men in groups of two, three, and four having fun with one of them cross-dressing. The body language of the men, in particular the ways the men not in women's clothing touch the cross-dressing man, reproduce the more intimate ways men touch women in public. Most striking is Snapshot 9.7, in which the buddies on both sides of the very masculine cross-dressing soldier in the middle cup his fake breasts with their hands. This snapshot is not an unusual one.

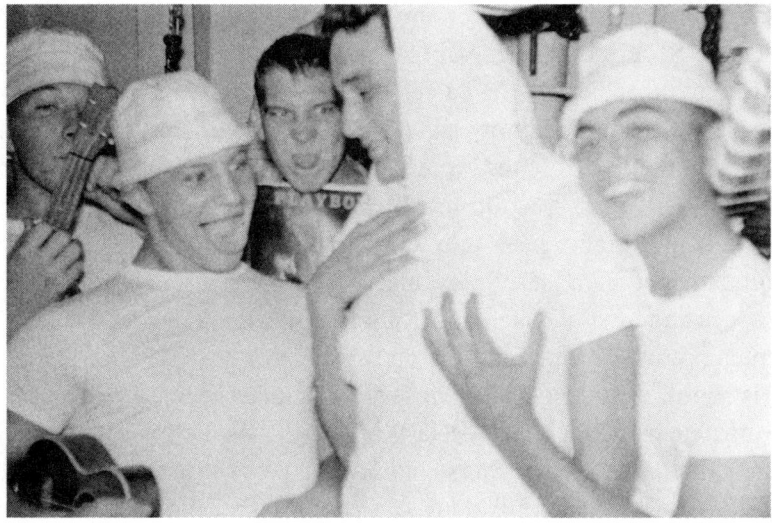

Snapshot 9.8

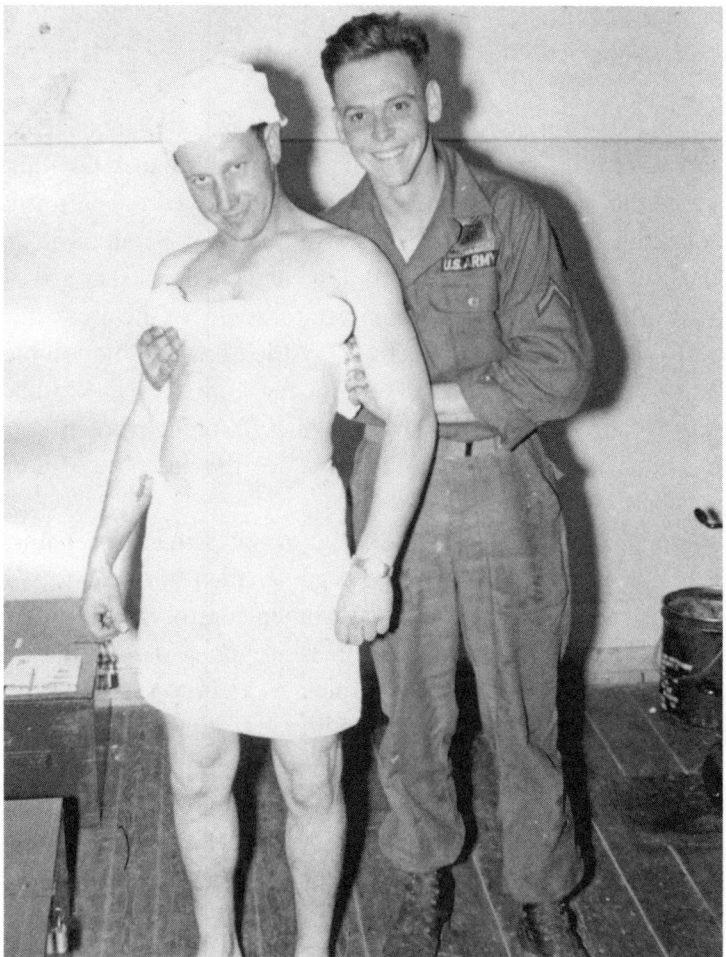

Snapshot 9.9

Snapshots 9.8 and 9.9 also show buddies touching the fake breasts of a cross-dressing soldier or sailor, and in Snapshot 9.8 the expressions on the faces of the men surrounding the cross-dresser show mock enjoyment that is best called "leering."

The *Playboy* magazine cover in Snapshot 9.8 signals one referent for the live performance, and I shall get to the matter of pinups and graffiti next, but the intimate touching in so many snapshots deserves some discussion. In most cases the men cross-dressing in the more informal settings do not put together an elaborate and persuasive female "costume"; at best they improvise a bra or perhaps even borrow one from a female, and they may use other costume props (a grass skirt, a towel over the head) to signal "female." Put simply, in most of these snapshots the illusion is thin, merely suggestive.

The still photograph does not capture whatever body language beyond gesture the cross-dressing soldier might perform to enhance the illusion. I certainly saw this sort of kinetic acting when I observed the performances of the adolescent boys who dressed as girls for the Boy Scout camp theatricals. In those cases, I was watching adolescent boys dressed as girls trying to mimic how teenage girls walk and gesture. A few of the cross-dressing boys tried to act "sexy" and "seductive." While I have no motion pictures of the adult soldiers also cross-dressing for fun, I imagine they often tried to reproduce their own versions of how they thought women use their bodies to attract and seduce men. You can see this in some of the body language caught by the still photos.

Speculating more still, I imagine the cross-dressing soldier might be enjoying his brief experiment with the power men attribute to women. Young men often express the view that women control men through their sexual flirting and teasing. The cross-dressing young men in these snapshots might feel they are turning the tables in the brief time and space of the play performance; they might play with the flirting in order to feel the pleasure and power they imagine (and just imagine) girls and women have over men.

The other men in these snapshots may not be behaving in the way they would with real women. Certainly they are grabbing the cross-dressers' fake breasts in ways that seem more aggressive than how we hope they treat women. The play frame permits the groping because it does not mean what it would mean in interacting with a real women. This amounts to saying that men in this cross-dressing play frame feel free to engage in stylized, exaggerated, even aggressive flirting behavior most of them would not try with real women. As we shall see in Chapter 10, the play frame is a safe space for stylized aggression, which takes the place of real aggression and avoids the harm to the bonding in the male friendship group.

Analysis of the behavior of the cross-dressing military men in the snapshots profits from paying attention to the body language in the images in this chapter. This would be a good place to examine three other genres of images of women we find in many military snapshots—(1) pinups of scantily dressed or even naked women on the walls of barracks, tents, and other sleeping spaces, and graffiti; (2) "nose art" painted on aircraft, ships, and armored vehicles; and (3) hand-drawn graffiti on about every surface a male soldier sees blank.

PINUPS, NOSE ART, AND GRAFFITI

Most of the male soldiers in twentieth-century wars had little or no access to sex with women (Roberts 2013). Those soldiers tended to be young and in the prime of their sexual lives. In World War I, World War II, the Korean War, and the Vietnam War, heterosexual and bisexual soldiers had some access to prostitutes and local women, and we have evidence of some consensual sexual relations between service men and women, but that is against regulations and carries a lot of risk. Gay and bisexual male soldiers, who also might have sexual excitement watching a buddy cross-dress, likewise may have had some opportunities for same-sex experiences (Bérubé 1990). In most cases, though, the only sexual outlet for male soldiers was masturbation.

John Paul Wallis and I (2019) devote an entire chapter of our book, on post-traumatic stress disorder and folk therapy, to masturbation as one of those vernacular activities resembling formal prolonged exposure therapy, a common professional therapy for sufferers with PTSD. Many snapshots of the living spaces of twentieth-century soldiers show sexy images of women adorning the walls. Men miss women, but who would doubt that a major function of these images from magazines and even publicity photos from movie stars (Betty Grable's swimsuit photo is the classic example) is to provide visual stimulation for masturbation in private.

The images of sexy women in magazines and other places also provide the models for "nose art," a phrase based on the paintings of women on the noses of airplanes, often with a women's name alongside the figure. Military snapshots also make it clear that "nose art" appeared on ships and on other vehicles.

The function of nose art is to bring luck and safety to the flyers, sailors, soldiers, and Marines, but many of these paintings of women (sometimes of cartoon characters) feature the poses we see in the pinups. I introduce these genres not to make a point about masturbation in the military but to draw our attention to the body language, to the poses of the women in the photographs and paintings. Those images and the body language captured by a still photo provide templates for the performances by cross-dressing

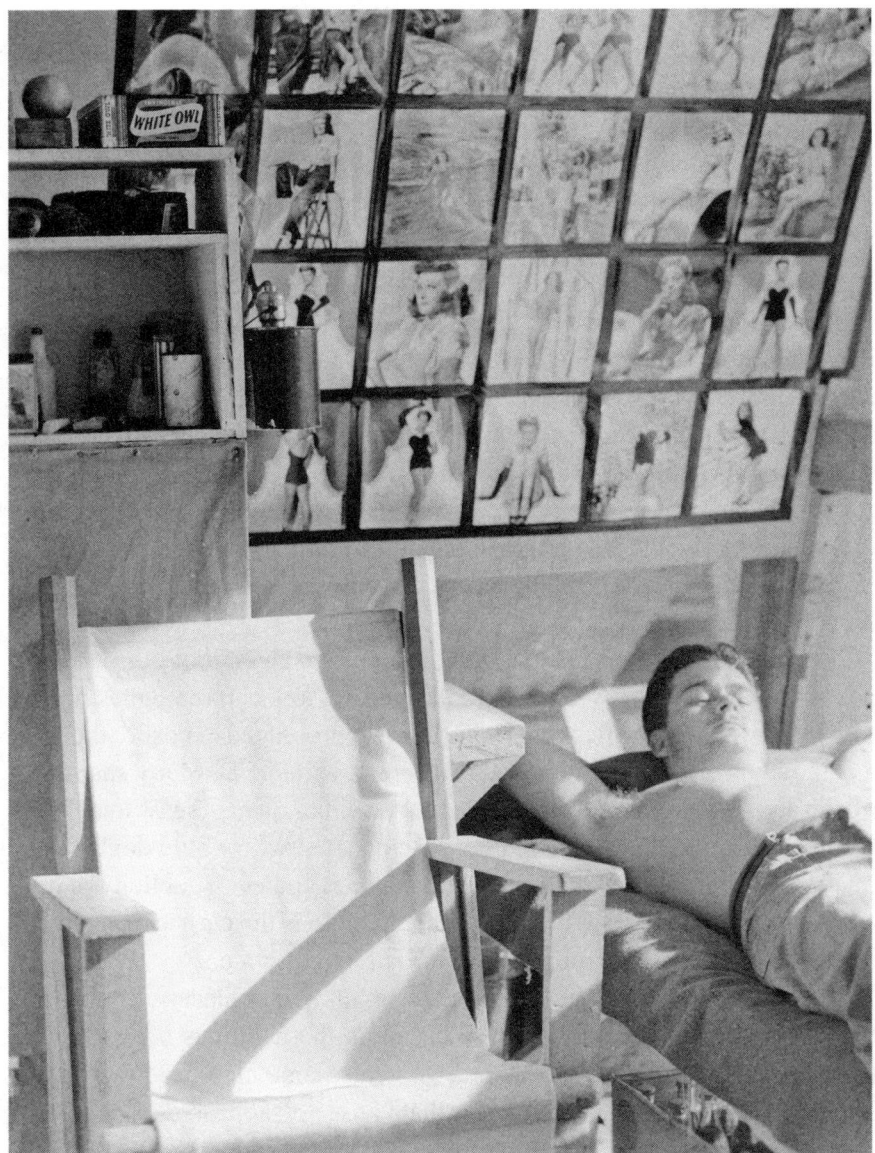

Snapshot 9.10

men, but the closer the performance is to the body language in the familiar images of sexy, seductive females on the walls and machines, the more "real" is the performance and the more sexually arousing is the performance for the male buddies watching and even touching.

Graffiti on the walls of latrines and on any flat surface (such as the side

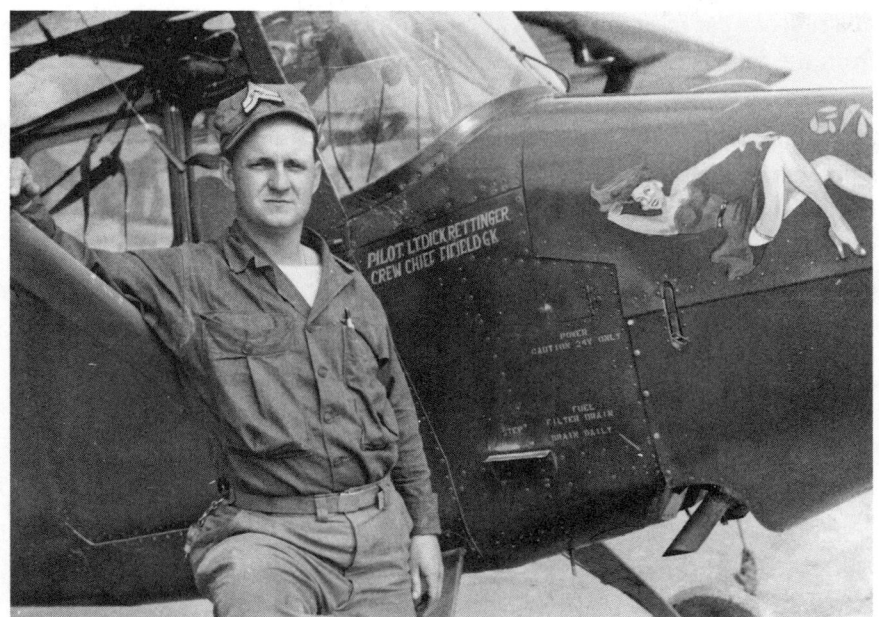

Snapshot 9.11

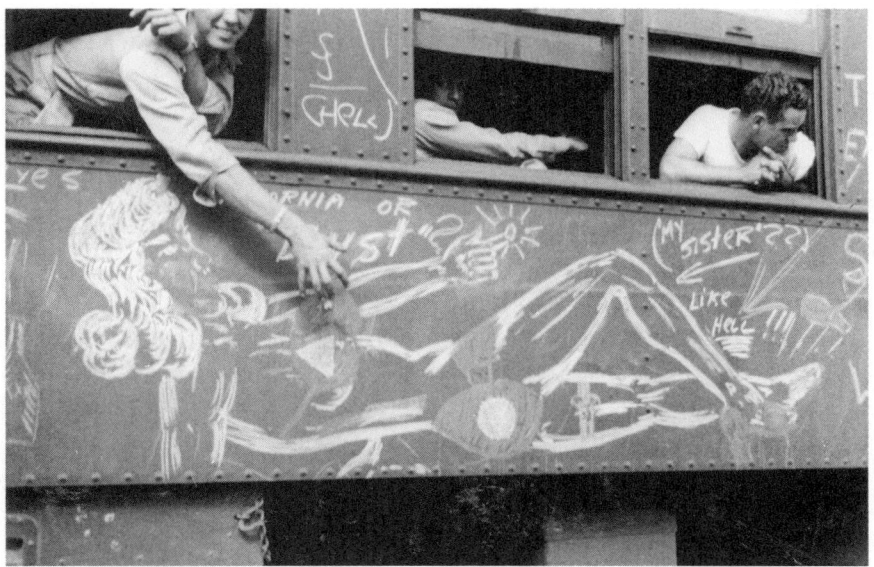

Snapshot 9.12

of a railroad car in Snapshot 9.12) constitute the folk version of the images from the magazines and those painted by talented artists onto planes and ships and vehicles. One Marine said that where others see the blank wall of a "shitter," the Marine sees a blank canvas. Among the graffiti images soldiers draw on walls are genitals, but also women's bodies, again echoing what they see in the pinups and nose art. Snapshot 9.12 resembles the snapshots in which men are touching the bodies, especially the fake breasts, of cross-dressing men.

10

Playfighting

John Paul Wallis and I first collaborated on the journal article "Devil Dogs and Dog Piles" (Wallis and Mechling 2015, reprinted in Wallis and Mechling 2019) as a way of understanding a color photograph by famed war photographer Tim Hetherington. The photo appears on the back dust jacket for the hardback edition of Sebastian Junger's book *War* (2010). Junger was on a writing assignment for *Vanity Fair* magazine, embedded (June 2007–June 2008) in Afghanistan with the Second Platoon, B Company, 1st Battalion, 6th Marine Regiment. Junger and Hetherington were at a small mountain outpost the platoon named "Outpost Restrepo" to honor a loved medic who was killed. Hetherington took video and color photographs during that time at Camp Restrepo. Their award-winning documentary film, *Restrepo* (2010), Hetherington's book of his color photographs and commentary from their time at Restrepo, *Infidel* (2010), and Junger's book combine to document the experiences of that platoon of Marines working and playing and fighting at an extremely dangerous outpost. Later, covering the war in Libya, Hetherington was killed.

Hetherington's photo on the *War* dustjacket can also be viewed in *Infidel* (2010, 127). It is a photo taken outdoors of a free-for-all, rough-and-tumble (R&T) playfight among the Marines. It is one of a few photos of playfighting at Restrepo in Hetherington's book, and he adds some commentary about the photos. Playfighting out in the open in that dangerous

place, where enemy fighters can take high positions in the mountains surrounding the post and shoot down at the Marines, is an unnecessary risk
and might even be classified as "deep play," the focus of Chapter 12, a
form of play in which the stakes are so high that it is irrational to continue
playing. And yet, the Marines at Restrepo did engage in R&T playfighting
out in the open in daylight. And the smiles on their faces tell us they were
having great fun.

Hetherington, of course, was a professional war photographer, but the
soldiers themselves also capture moments of playfighting in their vernacular photographs; indeed, we published one of Wallis's snapshots of the
playfighting in his platoon in Iraq (Wallis and Mechling 2019, 67). Such
snapshots are plentiful in my collection. None, as far as I can tell, was
taken in a hot combat zone, as were Hetherington's photographs at Restrepo, and none has the contextual advantage of the Hetherington and
Wallis photographs, where we have verbal accounts to help make sense of
not only the playfight but possibly even the feelings of the men fighting.
As I have indicated, snapshots often reveal the emotions of the participants
in the folk customs.

The snapshots of soldiers playfighting are plentiful, but also repetitive.
I shall reproduce just a few here as texts for my analysis, though another
batch of playfighting snapshots—with weapons—provides more insight
into the very deep drive for men to playfight in male friendship groups.

PLAYFIGHTING IN THE MALE MILITARY GROUP

Wallis and I (2015, 2019) go into detail about the evolutionary history of
R&T playfighting, and I refer the reader to those discussions. Here I shall
touch on the relevant points and get to the snapshots of play with weapons.

Recall that Gregory Bateson formulated his ideas about the play frame
watching mammals play at the Fleishhacker Zoo in San Francisco, It helped
that he was working at the time with a team of psychiatrists at the Veterans Administration Hospital in Palo Alto, California, on a "double bind"
theory of schizophrenia. As we saw in Chapter 3, what puzzled Bateson
about the mammal playfighting was that it features many of the nonverbal
messages one might see in real fights in the species, but somehow the
animals understand that the snarls and bared teeth and other clues meant
something different in the play session; they did not mean what they would

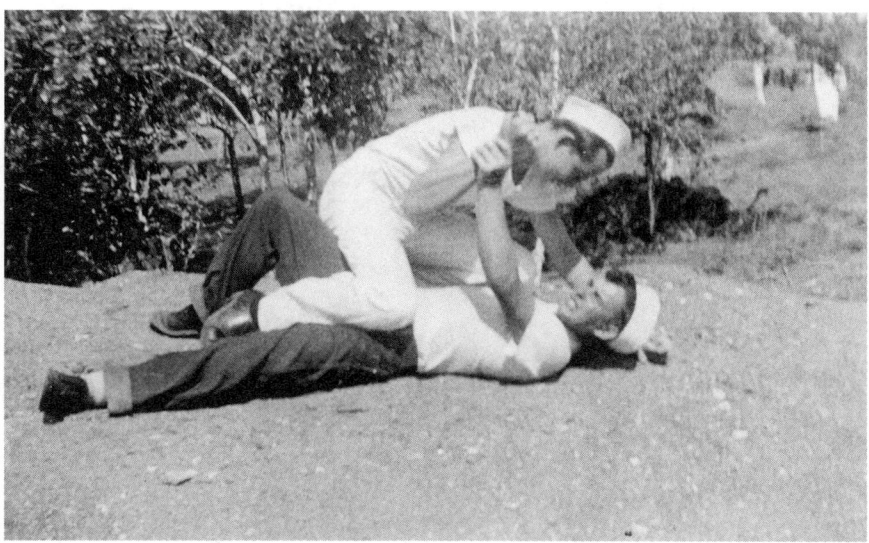

Snapshot 10.1

mean in a real fight. Bateson's great insight was to see that the animals had exchanged a metamessage, a message about messages, and in that case the metamessage was "This is play," which signaled that all of the messages in the play frame do not mean what they would mean outside that frame.

Bateson notes that just entering a play frame communicates to the players important information about their relationship. It takes trust to enter a play frame, though, as I have indicated, Bateson misses the point that not everyone is in the play frame voluntarily. Bateson also misses the fact that people can use the play frame to "mask" other motives. Both of these addenda to Bateson's idea of the play frame help us understand R&T playfighting in the male friendship group.

Watching boys and then men doing R&T playfighting is so common we never really reflect on it much; as Brian Sutton-Smith (1970) said about children's folklore, it seems so trivial that scholars do not bother to understand the psychological and social functions of the folklore. The same is true of R&T playfighting. Boys do it all the time. In fact, a pile of boys playfighting resembles a pile of puppies playfighting.

Snapshots 10.1 and 10.2 are representative of many I could show here—young male soldiers and sailors, usually in pairs, grappling each other, often smiling. Some snapshots capture a larger pile of playfighting men (a "dogpile" in folk jargon).

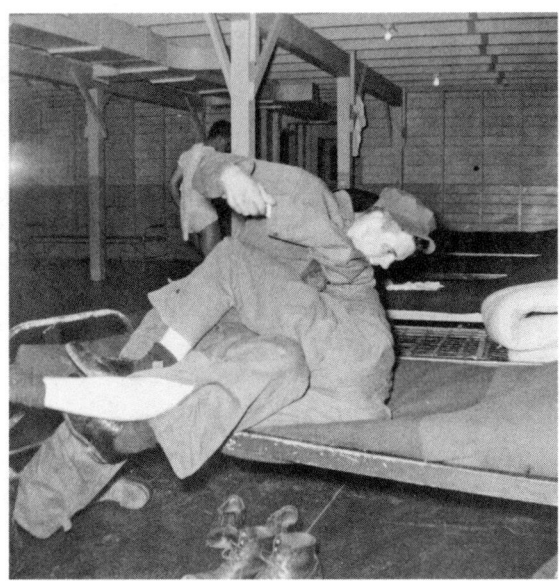

Snapshot 10.2

We have to guess at the event captured in Snapshot 10.3. The eBay seller identified the snapshot as sailors in the 1940s. This appears to be a more formal game of some sort—possibly with a single sailor in the middle or some version of "the "class scraps" Simon Bronner describes as a custom at college and universities (Bronner 2012). Whether this photo shows informal grappling or a more formal R&T playfighting game, the psychological and social functions are similar.

First we must note that playfighting is "stylized" aggression. Men are capable of real aggression and real violence, but the real thing would destroy a friendship group. So boys learn how to interact in the group through stylized aggression in the play frame, aggression that is not real because it is play. As a primatologist and evolutionary psychologist, Robert Sapolsky (1997) sees a strong resemblance between the hierarchies human males establish in their groups and the patterns of male hierarchy in primate groups, especially chimpanzees and bonobos, the primates whose DNA is most similar to ours. And like the primates, humans use playfighting in the group to test boundaries and to get some pleasure from aggression without dire consequences.

Many sociologists, anthropologists, psychologists, and folklorists have noted that much of the play and formal games of boys and men are simply

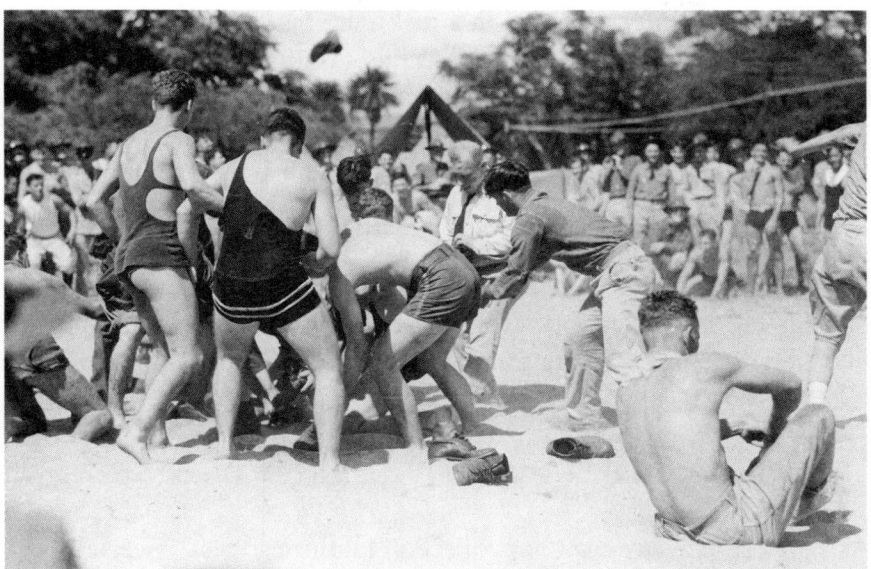

Snapshot 10.3

safer, less-disruptive forms of aggression and even war. Barbara Ehrenreich (1997) notes this in blood sports, while Alan Dundes (1978) argues
that games like football not only substitute for real combat but actually
unconsciously act out forbidden homosexual desire. More on that shortly.

I argued in Chapter 8 that an important function of the human pyramid
is that it creates a "safe" play frame where touching another male, even
touching his butt or genitals, does not carry a sexual meaning. In American
culture men can touch each other in public only on those occasions where
a play frame (building a pyramid, a playfight, cross-dressing, etc.) creates
a safe time and space. Humans need touching, as a great deal of research
shows, and they suffer when denied the touch of other humans. In a hy-
per-masculine social setting like a military male friendship group, the need
for touching is strong, and the play frame makes it safe.

Keep in mind, though, that the play frame of R&T playfighting can be
used by one or more participants to mask other motives. For example,
someone might actually want to hurt another man, but do it under the cover
of "it's just play." Consider, as well, the possible sexual motives of a player
who initiates or joins a R&T playfight.

The likelihood is great that in building, holding, and deconstructing a
human pyramid one or more participants will experience pain, in most

cases not the pain experienced in a real fight, but pain nonetheless. The "birthday beatdown" described by Wallis (Wallis and Mechling 2015, 2019) is a ritual playfight in the play frame, and he testifies that the "victim" of the "birthday beatdown" actually gets pleasure from the beatdown, a pleasure resulting mainly from the knowledge that the play frame itself conveys close bonding and trust. In Chapter 11, I explore the eroticization of pain and how theories about social masochism might unlock the meanings of a soldier's taking pleasure in pain; it is worth noting in this R&T playfighting discussion, however, that soldiers and sailors and Marines often report getting pleasure and pain from playfighting.

PLAYFIGHTING WITH SHARP WEAPONS

As I was sorting my snapshot collection into categories, I puzzled over where to put a pile of snapshots of soldiers playfighting with weapons. At first I had them in with the snapshots for Chapter 12, "Deep Play," but then I realized that playfighting with sharp objects (knives and bayonets, sometimes axes) really was not the same as the irrational risk of play with firearms. Perhaps that is because my brother-in-law was accidentally shot in the face (he survived) while in the army and goofing off with friends. So the playfighting with firearms will show up in Chapter 12. Here I present and analyze a few snapshots of playfighting with sharp objects.

One relevant context for these snapshots of R&T playfighting with knives and bayonets is the inclusion of hand-to-hand combat in basic training. That type of training seems to be a remnant of past combat, in that present-day weapons enable most combat to take place at a distance, rarely at the three closest ranges discussed by Dave Grossman (2009, 120–137): "killing at edged-weapon range," "killing at hand-to-hand combat range," and "killing at sexual range." Wallis's hunch is that, even though the close combat training probably has little practical use in the current wars, the recruits in basic training hunger for close contact with fellow recruits. We analyze the primary form of close combat training—pugil stick fighting— and the satisfaction it brings to the recruits (Wallis and Mechling 2019, 78–79), satisfaction grounded in part by the chance (finally) to get physical with each other, especially in a "stylized" version of combat, featuring competition between recruits and between their platoons. We also point to the phallic nature of the pugil sticks themselves, tapping an unconscious pleasure in the physical fighting. I shall have more to say about that shortly.

Pugil stick fighting aims to prepare the recruit for a combat situation he is unlikely to face in the current wars—bayonet combat. Bayonet training seemed pointless enough to the US Army that it eliminated those skills from basic training in 2010, though the Marines still train their recruits for bayonet use in close combat (Stone 2012, 885).

Snapshots 10.4 and 10.5 are typical in their capturing of moments of play with bayonets. Use of the bayonet in combat was common for hundreds of years, beginning in the early seventeenth century, but its use began to wane in the late nineteenth century. There was some limited bayonet fighting in both world wars, but only one bayonet charge in the Korean War (Stone 2012, 888–889). In his scholarly article about the history and meaning of the bayonet, Stone accounts for the continuing training in bayonet combat long past its actual usefulness by speculating that the purpose of the bayonet training was "to forge strong associations between bayonet and aggressive behavior, thereby bolstering the moral fortitude of soldiers in times of battlefield crisis" (Stone 2012, 885–886).

Snapshot 10.6 shows two soldiers having a playfight using bayonets as if they were knives, and Snapshot 10.7 is a genuine play knife fight. From my own experience as a Boy Scout and then studying teen boys (ages eleven to eighteen) in Boy Scout troops at summer camp, I know

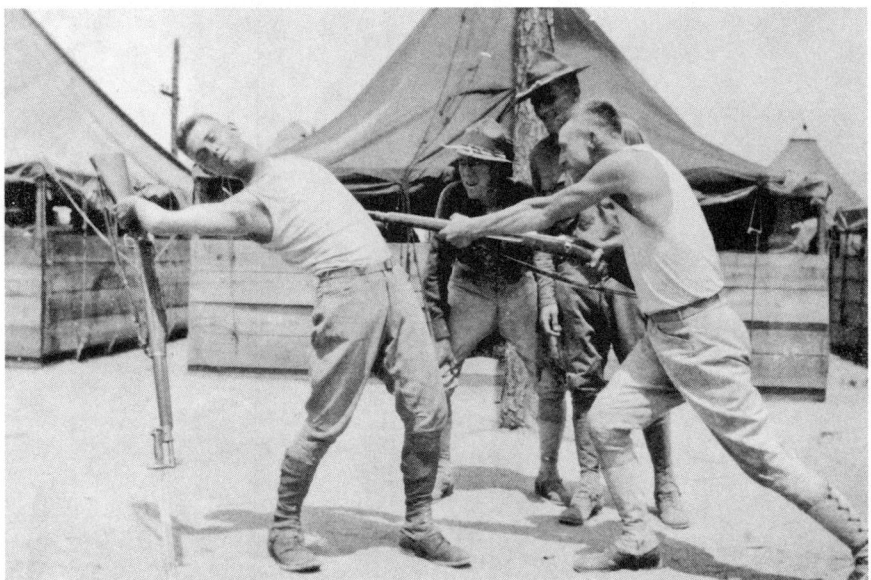

Snapshot 10.4

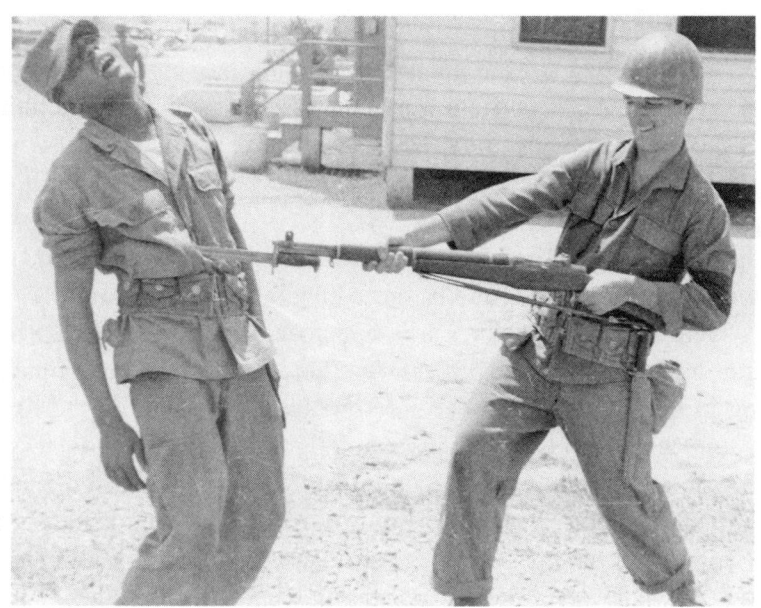

Snapshot 10.5

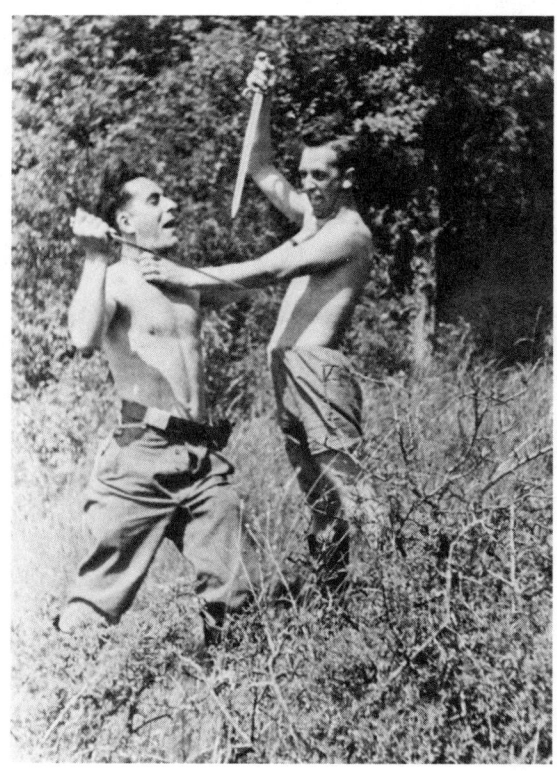

Snapshot 10.6

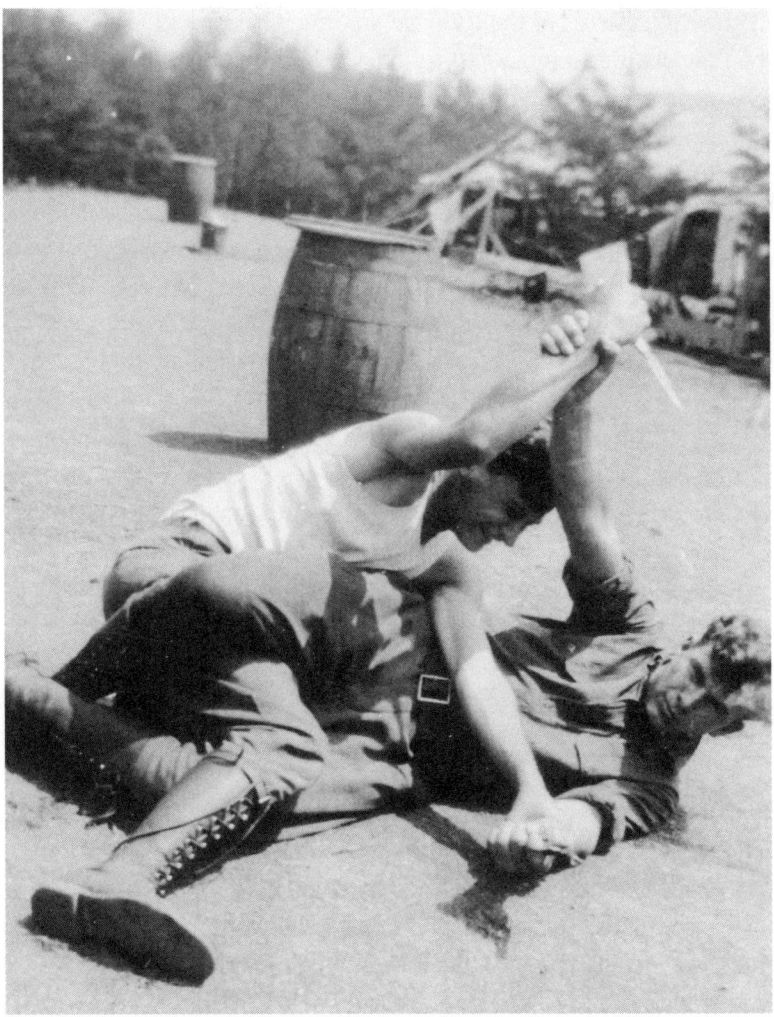

Snapshot 10.7

that young boys have a strong fascination with knives. Play with bayonets and knives, therefore, must be tapping some strong feelings. The danger is mild and unlikely fatal, as it could be with play with firearms, but even the mild danger probably heightens the fun.

We cannot ignore the sexual meanings of male playfighting with sharp objects. In his excellent, thoughtful book, *On Killing* (2009), Lieutenant Colonel Dave Grossman describes the experience of killing at various distances (ranges), finally ending with a chapter on "Killing at Sexual Range:

'The Primal Aggression, the Release, and the Orgasmic Discharge.'" The title of that chapter announces frankly his argument that fighting at extremely close range—hand-to-hand combat with the two combatants virtually wrestling—resembles sex.

In writing about rough-and-tumble playfighting in the combat zone, Wallis and I (2019, 67–87) draw upon Bateson to note that the paradoxical nature of the frame for playfighting means that the experience resembles real fighting but is not fighting, resembles sex but is not sex. With regard to the film *Hans Christian Andersen* (1952), Bateson writes:

> The hero starts out accompanied by a boy. He tries to get a woman, but when he is defeated in this attempt, he returns to the boy. In all of this, there is, of course, no homosexuality, but the choice of these symbolisms is associated in these fantasies with certain characteristic ideas, e.g., about the hopelessness of the heterosexual masculine position when faced with certain sorts of women or with certain sorts of male authority. In sum, the pseudohomosexuality of the fantasy does not stand for any real homosexuality, but does stand for and express attitudes which might accompany a real homosexuality or feed its etiological roots. The symbols do not denote homosexuality, but do denote ideas for which homosexuality is an appropriate symbol. (Bateson 1955/1972, 183–184)

Bateson is describing that paradoxical aspect of the play frame in which play engages "a special combination" of primary (unconscious) and secondary (conscious) processes. "In primary process," he writes, "map and territory are equated; in secondary process, they can be discriminated. In play they are both equated and discriminated" (Bateson 1955/1972, 185). Andrew Delfino and I (2017) make the same point about scholastic wrestling: it both is and is not fighting; it both is and is not sex. That young male wrestlers sometimes get embarrassing erections while wrestling proves the point.

Grossman goes beyond this resemblance between playfighting, real fighting, and sex to explore the strange conjunction of two fundamental instincts—sex and death—in close combat at the sexual range. These instincts, of course, were formulated by Sigmund Freud—the pleasure principle and the death instinct (Freud 1920/1961). I shall return to discussing these instincts in Chapter 11. In discussing "killing as sex" and "sex as killing" (2009, 135–137), Grossman quotes an Israeli military psychologist, who describes the "pleasures of combat" as lying in "the primal aggression, the release, and the orgasmic discharge" (Ben Shalit, quoted in Grossman 2009, 136). Grossman himself likens the experience of shooting a weapon in battle to the sexual experience: "Many men who have carried and fired a gun—especially a full automatic weapon—must confess in their hearts that the power and pleasure of explosively spewing a stream of bullets is akin to the emotions felt when explosively spewing a stream of semen" (2009, 136).

In Chapter 12, I shall return to the view of Grossman and combat veterans that shooting weapons, especially automatic weapons, "feels" like the discharge of semen from a very hard penis. In this discussion of playfighting with sharp objects, though, of interest is Grossman's description of close combat with a bayonet or knife as resembling rape. "Thrusting the sexual appendage (the penis) deep into the body of the victim," he writes, "can be perversely linked to thrusting the killing appendage (a bayonet or knife) deep into the body of the victim" (Grossman 2009, 137).

Of course, the sexual pleasures Grossman describes, caused by thrusting a knife or bayonet into an enemy's body, are wholly unconscious but "felt" nonetheless. The resemblance of R&T playfighting to sexual grappling adds to the unconscious meaning, but it is also true that male folk speech about knives and swords and bayonets equates the knife with the penis. Peter Murphy (2001) wrote an entire book on male folk speech about their bodies and about sexual acts, and we must note that a condom is called a sheath and a penis is often called a sword.

11
Hazing

Masculinity is a fragile construction always at risk. "Proving" one's manhood is an ongoing project for most men. Timothy Beneke (1997) draws upon the same ideas from feminist psychoanalytic theory (e.g., Chodorow 1978) I presented in Chapter 2 (see also Mechling 2005a). Recall that a major idea in that body of theory is that the separation of the male child's identity from the mother means that he must define "male" as a negative, as "not female" (Frosh 1994). So much of the everyday (folk) culture of boys' friendship groups features misogyny and homophobia as strategies for distancing themselves from the female, and that need to define masculinity as "not female" extends well into adulthood.

One of the ways a man proves his masculinity is by facing and passing a "test." This is an idea enshrined in Western mythology, in those grand stories told and passed on to make sense of the world and of the customs of a particular culture. Joseph Campbell (1949) sees a formula in most of those mythologies, a formula he calls the Monomyth. In the United States, a version of the Monomyth shows up in American popular culture, the medium for telling large, mythological stories in our modern, large, complex society where the written word and then the electronic image have replaced oral storytelling. I shall return to discussing the American Monomyth below.

White American men experienced a masculinity crisis in the late 1980s, prompting a mythopoetic men's movement in the 1990s. The publication of poet Robert Bly's book *Iron John: A Book about Men* (1990), soon became a famous manifesto for the movement. Elizabeth Mechling and I (1994) offer a cultural analysis of that social movement, the nature of the crisis in white middle-class masculinity, and the "solution" proposed by Bly and other writers. As a poet, Bly knows the power of Western mythologies to give men a narrative for understanding their lives. Adhering to the Campbell formula, Bly sees the heroic quest as a narrative worth reviving for men in end-of-century America. It is against the long history of heroic quest stories in Western civilization and the pervasive appearance of the American Monomyth variant in many genres of electronic storytelling (film, television, video games) that the actual enactment of the test of manhood in the American male friendship group takes place.

In this chapter I examine military snapshots that show ways men "test" each other. Sometimes the tests are informal, truly folk customs. Others are more formal rituals, the tests we encounter when we study hazing in fraternities, sports teams, and the military.

INFORMAL FOLK TESTS

Men must prove to the other males in their friendship group that they can "take it like a man" (Savran 1998). The "it" can be many things. For example, being able to "take a joke" is a common, fundamental test within the male friendship group. Successful joking requires a play frame, a joking frame, a "license to joke" (Mechling and Mechling 1985). As in most play frames, the frame itself tells the participants much about their relationship. Joking frames, like play frames, require trust, and (also like other play frames) the joking frame is fragile, easily broken; usually friends will work quickly to repair the frame. And, like other play frames, everyone in the joke frame might not be there voluntarily and might not enjoy the same power. Jokes can be used to mask aggressive or forbidden motives (Sutton-Smith and Kelly-Byrne 1984). "I was just joking" is a common defense kids use to cover the torment of a sibling or an excuse supervisors use to explain sexual harassment on the workplace.

Men in friendship groups tease each other and taunt each other and insult each other, all forms of a test to see if the target can stand it. Boys learns these interpersonal genres of testing in the friendship group, and they learn, as well, the negative consequences of responding to teasing and taunts and insults with anger rather than good humor and a reciprocal verbal attack. This is all part of a young man's learning how stylized aggression works in the male friendship group.

Young men also learn to test each other's masculinity with dares. The Boy Scout troop I studied for many years always began its day-long "Insane Day" set of contests on an island in the middle of the lake with each boy taking the "rope slide" from the high rocks at the campsite down to the lake level where the canoes waited for them to paddle out to the island. The ride involved climbing up to where the rope was attached to a "X" of poles, grabbing a rope hold on a pulley, and then letting gravity take him down the slide to the water, where the other end of the rope was attached to a sunken tree stump. Sometimes a boy (the youngest scout campers there are eleven and twelve) pauses at the top of the X and freezes, "chickening out." He is not so much teased for that if he soon grabs the pulley and slides down the rope. If he did chicken out, the humiliation would probably mean he would not stay with the troop long (Mechling 2001, 69).

Men in the military folk group continue this custom of testing comrades with dares. John Paul Wallis and I (2019, 76–77) discuss the game of "gay chicken" played in his platoon and widely known in the military. Two men stand apart, facing each other, then walk slowly toward each other and when close enough are to kiss each other on the lips. The soldier who chickens out and breaks the game has lost. In the play frame, the game of gay chicken poses a complex paradox. To prove he is masculine, the male player must kiss another man. Proving one's presumably heterosexual masculinity in that game requires that you embrace that paradox. I have seen no snapshots of soldiers playing gay chicken, but in previous chapters we have seen snapshots of men kissing buddies when the frame permits, meaning that the kiss does not mean what it would mean outside the play frame.

Refusing or failing a dare amounts to failing a test of masculinity and would likely lead to true humiliation in the group. This brand of humiliation differs from the stylized humiliation of formal hazing events, as we shall see below.

Photographs do not capture verbal jokes, of course, but there is a genre of joking that does lend itself to being memorialized in snapshots. "Practical jokes" and "pranks" show up in military memoirs and snapshots. In Anthony Swofford's memoir of his experience in the Gulf War (1990–1991), *Jarhead* (2003), for example, he relates an episode in which some of his buddies grab him and pretend that they are about to brand him with a hot wire hanger (2003, 50–51).

Snapshot 11.1 captures a barracks prank, and the smile on the "victim's" face tells us that he can "take" the joke, that his response is laughter rather than anger.

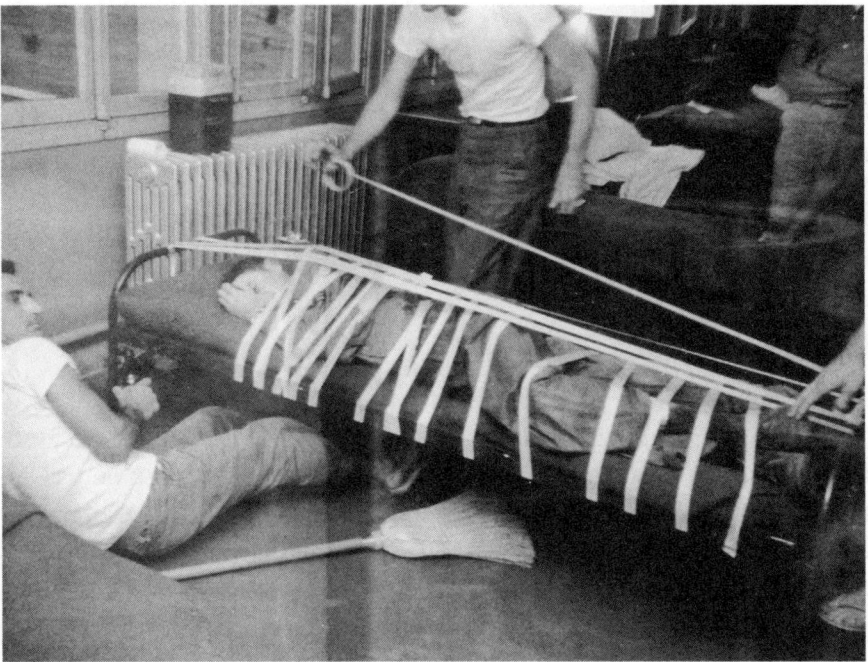

Snapshot 11.1

Written on the back of Snapshot 11.2 is a list of the names of the army buddies giving the birthday boy "twenty-one hits." This folk tradition of delivering a spanking to someone on his birthday, one blow for every year, begins in early childhood in the United States (Bronner 1988, 172, 338). This tradition extends into the military, as Snapshot 11.2 attests, and, as in Snapshot 11.1, the smiles on all faces tell us this is a playful interaction and that the birthday boy can take the spanking in good humor, not anger. Wallis recounts his own "birthday beatdown" during his deployment in Iraq in 2007, and he even reports missing the tradition after he left the Marine

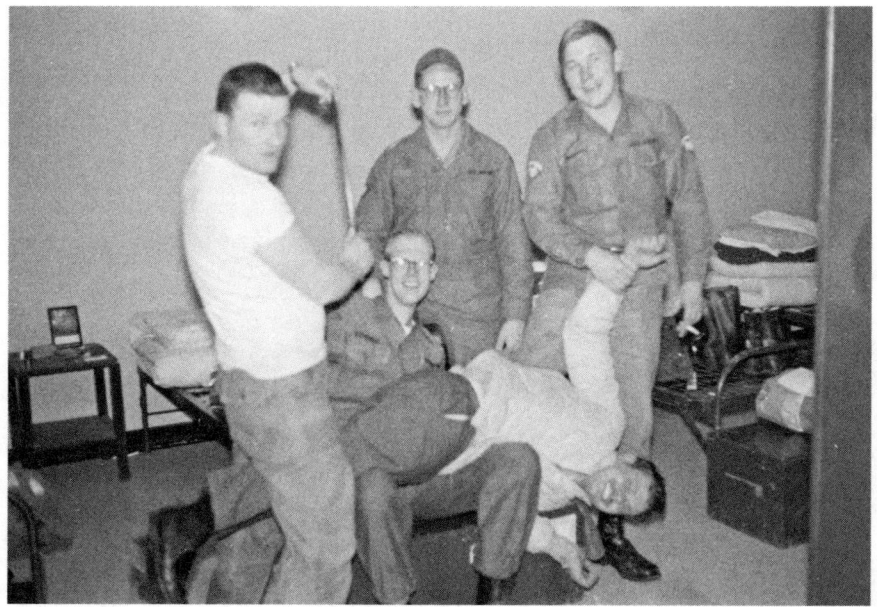

Snapshot 11.2

Corps, went to college, and then went to law school (Wallis and Mechling 2019, 72–73). Paradoxically, he "missed" the birthday beatdowns because he recognized the stylized beating signaled the close bonding he had in his male friendship group in the military, and by the time he was married, had children, and was in law school he was missing the camaraderie of the male friendship group. Fortunately, another law student, also a Marine veteran, punched Wallis playfully in the halls on his birthday, saying, "Happy Birthday, Motherfucker," and they both enjoyed a laugh. The test was administered and passed.

The role of pain in a test of manhood is worthy of a discussion here. A common slogan coming out of the mouths of drill instructors (DIs) in basic training is "pain is weakness leaving the body." Physical training (PT) at boot camp and beyond in the military involves physical tests of the body, and invariably those tests involve pain. Taking it like a man, therefore, includes being able to endure pain for the group. This reflects the distinction between friendship and comradeship I made in Chapter 4. The man in the military endures pain for the group. Wallis describes an actual nostalgia for pain when he and his fellow Marine veterans gather. The stories they tell almost always come around to stories about shared, painful experiences.

The initial pain bonded them, and their stories about those painful experiences rekindle the intense bonding (Wallis and Mechling 2019, 73). We might even talk about the "eroticization" of pain in the male military friendship group. I return to that notion at the end of this chapter.

So far we have been looking at the informal, everyday, folk versions of the ways men test each other's manhood. Evolutionary psychology and culture come together in these everyday tests, forces driving the process of proving one's masculinity. These same forces of nature and nurture show up in more formal tests of manhood in male friendship groups. In the more formal organizations where men bond—notably sports teams, fraternities, and military units—the members often test prospective members (recruits, pledges) to see if they are worthy of joining the brotherhood. And unlike the informal ways men test other men to confirm their continuing worthiness to belong to the male friendship groups, the more formal hazing and then initiation follow a pattern or formula familiar to anthropologists.

CROSSING THE LINE

Cultures tend to create rituals around the gaps between categories. Those gaps, what anthropologists call "liminal" zones of culture, use the metaphor of the "limin" or "limen," Latin for "threshold," the border between two places, such as the border between outside and inside or the threshold between rooms in a house (Turner 1969, 1974).

The transition from boyhood to manhood is one of the events that draw sometimes elaborate rituals. As early as 1908 the French-Dutch anthropologist, Arnold van Gennep (1960), outlined a formula anthropologists and folklorists still find useful in studying male initiations. Typically a male initiation separates the initiate from his usual primary group, puts him through tests in the liminal time and space, and then reincorporates him into the group with his new status as a member. Every member of the American military who goes through basic training (boot camp) will recognize this sequence, having experienced it firsthand. The recruit is separated from his family and friends. The military erases his old identity, taking away his civilian clothes, shaving his head, giving him a new nickname, and infantilizing him by totally controlling when and where he sleeps and eats and even his basic bodily functions, defecating and urinating. One might say that the entire experience of basic training is one of being hazed, of being tested. At the center of basic training are two key elements in testing manhood—pain and humiliation. I discussed pain above regarding informal tests of manhood, or "taking it like a man." Now I explore the humiliation almost always present in hazing.

The move in several states to make hazing illegal often includes in its definition of hazing "humiliation." Such a legal move wholly misunderstands the meanings of humiliation in the male friendship group (Mechling 2009). Men certainly are capable of humiliating other men with tests and dares such as the rope slide and gay chicken. That humiliation is harmful and its unpleasantness is what keeps men "in line," motivating them to take and pass the tests to "prove" that their manhood is strong.

The meaning of "humiliation" changes in the play frame, though, and if we view hazing as acts and messages in the play frame, then the stakes change. In the play frame a pledge or recruit can "take humiliation like a man" at the hands of his fellows because the humiliation is stylized, not real. As Ray Raphael puts it in his book on "rites of passage in male America," in a society like the United States, which has few cultural rituals for the transition from boy to man, initiation rituals can "offer dramatic definitions of manhood that are otherwise lacking" (Raphael 1988, 12). He goes on to say that "the function of hazing, in this context, is to provide a threat of potential failure while simultaneously insisting that the novitiate must actually succeed" (Raphael 1988, 13). In fact, notes Raphael, the extensive ethnographic literature on male initiations across cultures reveals no cases where a novitiate actually failed the test. Young men certainly can decide to quit pledging a fraternity and walk away from the hazing of "Hell Week." But you can't walk away from the military without severe consequences. That means that both the recruits and the elders who are hazing them have a heavy investment in the recruits' passing the tests. This fact is very clear from the remarkable series of three documentary videos about basic training for Marines—the drill instructors, as harsh as they can be, clearly want the recruits to shape up and pass every physical and mental test the DI throws at them (Black Friday 2012, 2014, 2015).

Although there are other folk versions of hazing and then initiation in military groups, the best-known and best-documented military hazing custom is the Crossing the Line (or Neptune) Ceremony, triggered when a ship crosses the equator. This is a general maritime tradition found in the merchant marine as well as the navy, and the vernacular photography and even film records of the ceremony are plentiful. John Ibson (2002, 81–83) has a few examples of the Neptune Ceremony, but the best history and analysis of Crossing the Line comes from Simon Bronner (2006).

Given the impetus to create elaborate cultural responses to encounters with anomalous things and events threating order, crossing the equator seems like the sort of transition in need of taming by ceremony and ritual. Bronner outlines the van Gennep formula in detail, showing how the behavior of both the veterans (called Shellbacks) and the initiates (called Pollywogs) fits the pattern. I'll not reproduce Bronner's excellent description and analysis here, but I can add some of the snapshots of Crossing the Line in my own collection to show some key elements the photographs capture.

Snapshots 11.3 and 11.4 give the viewer some idea of the organized chaos of a Crossing the Line Ceremony. It lasts for hours and requires the construction of props for the dramatic hazing. Snapshot 11.3 appears to be taken from the bow of an aircraft carrier. Apart from the interesting fact that one of the sailors is standing precariously on the bow taking snapshots of the proceedings, we see in this snapshot the long tube the Pollywogs are required to crawl through as part of the hazing. One Pollywog is beginning to crawl into the tube, while two Shellbacks are holding the soft clubs they

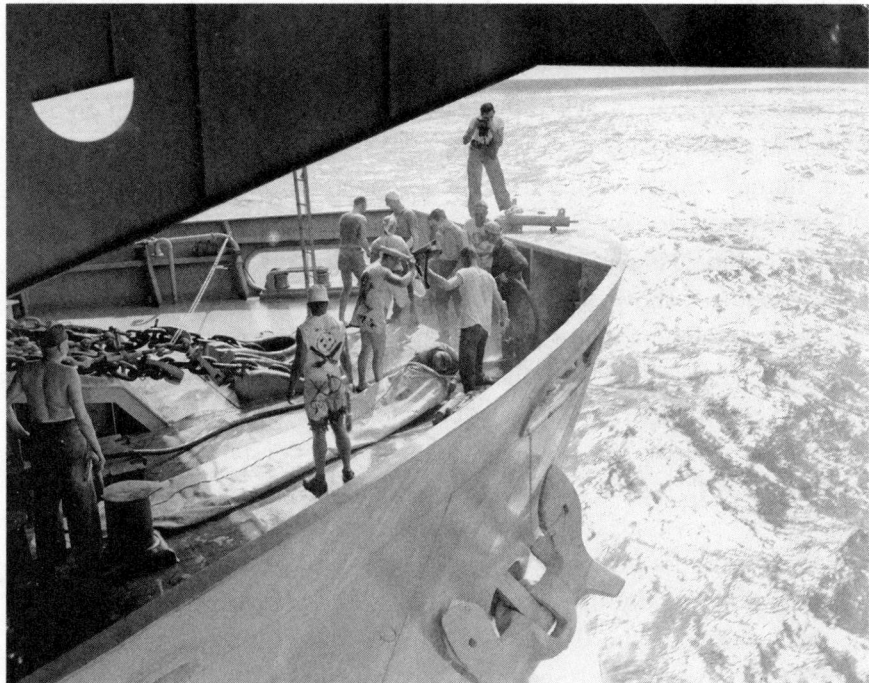

Snapshot 11.3

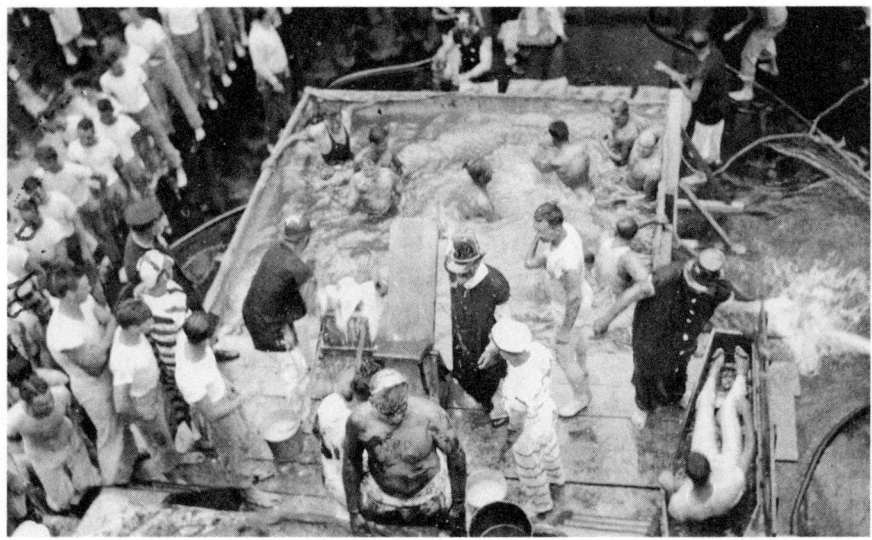

Snapshot 11.4

are "beating" the Pollywogs with throughout the ceremony. We also see in this snapshot the sorts of Neptune-themed folk costumes fashioned by the Shellbacks.

Snapshot 11.4 equally shows us several things going on simultaneously in the ceremony. Shellbacks often construct a portable swimming pool on deck, and this snapshot shows a long line of Pollywogs taking their turns being dumped into the water from the wooden chair at the edge of the pool. On the lower right corner of this snapshot we see a Pollywog lying in a wooden coffin, also part of the hazing.

Snapshot 11.5 shows us another common element of the staged chaos of the Crossing the Line Ceremony. This snapshot (taken on the USS *Indiana*) is of a fake "operation" with the Shellbacks in two very different sorts of costumes working on a Pollywog "patient."

This very old naval tradition, at its simplest, is a physical and mental test, and as with hazing in other male groups, taking the test and passing it carries the novitiate from one status to another, the new status usually signaling mature masculinity. Crossing the Line is a hazing ritual more elaborate and lengthy than most, and the somewhat bizarre scenarios in the folk "script" for this dramatic enactment of the passage from neophyte Pollywog to experienced Shellback feature details that the folklorist and anthropologist wants to, needs to, explain.

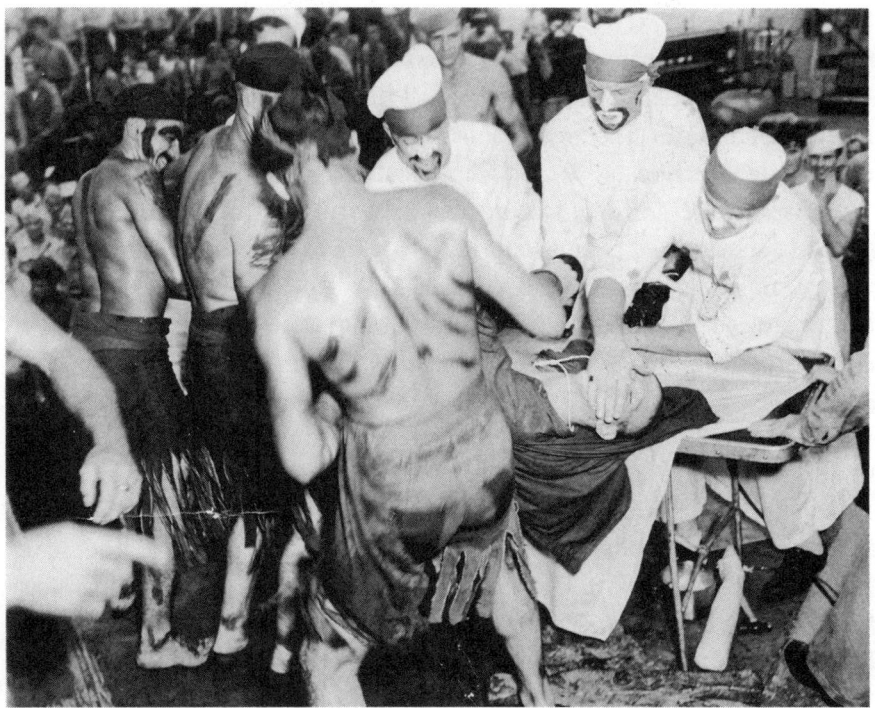

Snapshot 11.5

Bronner certainly is attuned to the symbolic meanings of the Crossing the Line Ceremony. He sees in the structure of the implied "narrative" of the ritual the hero quest so familiar to folklorists (Campbell, again). I would point the reader to Bronner's fine book for elaborate details of his analysis, but here are some highlights.

Prevalent in this extended hazing drama are experiences enacting symbolic death and rebirth, which pretty much characterize male initiation rites altogether. For example, crawling through a tube (Snapshot 11.3) represent passage from the womb to the new world. At every turn the Shellbacks (their very name signals "hard" masculinity) infantilize the Pollywogs (their name signals immaturity), including making them wear their underwear outside their clothing (Bronner 2006, 10). The Shellbacks carry "cudgels made from rope, rubber hose, and paddles" to hit and spank Pollywogs (p. 12). The initiates are forced to crawl through garbage and eat disgusting things (p. 12). Then, after these acts of humiliation and more, the theatrical dimension of the ritual begins: "Neptune arrives with his Royal Court: Davy Jones, his Queen or Aphrodite (or Amphitrite), Royal

Bay or Belly, Royal Navigator, and Royal Barber amid fanfare. Other figures that accompany them in various accounts are Royal Executioner, Lawyer, Counsel, Herald, Policeman, Priest, Chaplain, Devil, Princess, Doctor, Undertaker, Electrocutionist, Pallbearer, Torturer, Cannibal, Skeleton, Hangman, Dentist, Taster, Clerk, and Scribe" (pp. 12–13).

We see these costumed characters in various snapshots. The Royal Court hears charges against the Pollywogs and then metes out punishments, launching another series of tests—fake operations (Snapshot 11.5), and executions, including coffins for the dead, as in Snapshot 11.4, lower right (Bronner 2006, 14). Once they have passed all the tests (and everyone passes), the Pollywogs are permitted to dress in clean clothes, participate in "Neptune's Ball," and receive certificates or diplomas attesting to their new membership in the fraternity of men who have crossed the equator and survived the tests (Bronner 2006, 14–15).

The tradition of the Royal Court accounts for some of the male cross-dressing we saw in Chapter 9. Snapshot 11.6 has its all: King Neptune wearing his crown, holding his trident, and bending over to speak to the Pollywog groveling before the King. Two cross-dressing Shellbacks sit to the King's left, enjoying the humiliation of the Pollywogs. Historians do have some written and oral accounts of the Crossing the Line Ceremony, but the visual record in snapshots provides details not found in other evidence. Moreover, the snapshots provide evidence about the emotional meanings of the ceremony; we can read the body language and facial expressions of both Shellbacks and Pollywogs. Everyone is having a good time; some Pollywogs may be faking it to prove they can "take it like a man," but most of the smiles look genuine.

I want to layer another interpretive scheme on top of Bronner's already very insightful analysis of the symbolism of the Crossing the Line Ceremony. In my book looking at the rituals and play invented by a troop of Boy Scouts at their annual summer encampment (Mechling 2001), I warned readers just ahead of a section of that book that I was going to offer a psychoanalytic interpretation of the adolescent boys' folk customs and that if the reader objected to psychoanalytic interpretations of cultural behavior, he or she could skip past that section and still understand the basic argument in the book about the social construction of masculinity. I also noted, however, that the psychoanalytic approach makes sense of some of the puzzling details of the boys' games and rituals, uncovering meanings that are not obvious to those using interpretive approaches from the social

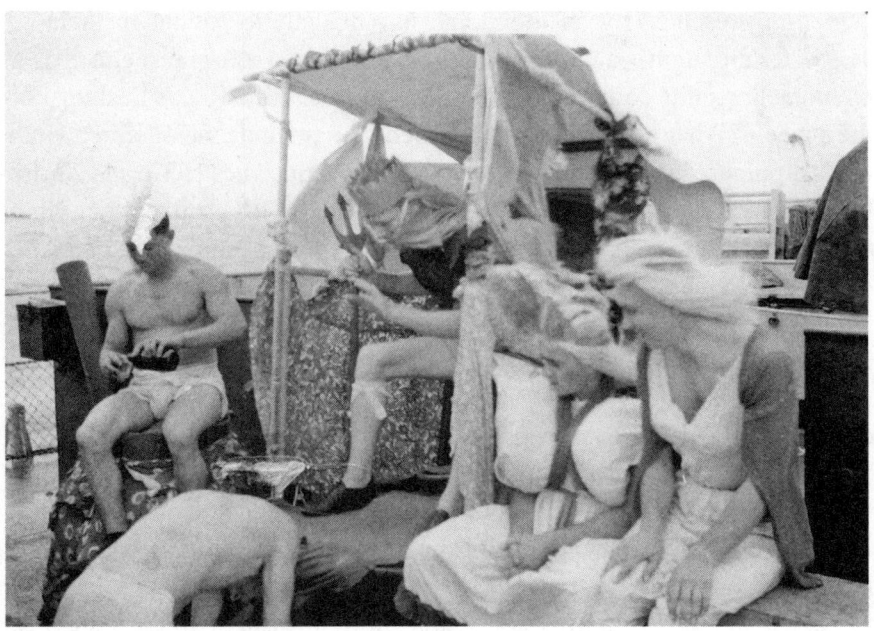

Snapshot 11.6

sciences, especially without the addition of depth psychology. The same warning and promise applies here, as I turn to psychoanalytic theory to understand how it is that young men can experience pleasure in the pain and humiliation of hazing.

HAZING AND SOCIAL MASOCHISM

Theodor Reik's 1941 book, *Masochism and Modern Man* (translated and published in the United States in 1962 as *Masochism in Sex and Society*), guides my thinking about hazing practices in male groups in the United States. Sigmund Freud had introduced the concept of masochism in 1905, initially thinking masochism was a turning of sadism back upon the self, but when that idea seemed inadequate to understanding masochism Freud eventually formulated the death instinct as an instinctual force as important as the pleasure principle (1920/1961) and a key to understanding the masochistic impulse. In subsequent years, other psychoanalysts took the concept of masochism in two different directions. One direction was concerned with masochism as a sexual "perversion" and, therefore, as a symptom presented by an individual psychoanalytic patient in therapy. The other direction—and the one that interests me—sees masochism as a phenomenon quite common in everyday, "normal" life. Reik's fleshing out the shape of what he calls "social masochism" reminds me of Karen Horney's argument in *The Neurotic Personality of Our Time* (1937) and Christopher Lasch's in *The Culture of Narcissism* (1979)—namely, that what was once seen as a clinical neurosis in patients has become characteristic of the culture as a whole, a set of symptoms no longer a pathology but a feature of everyday life. Both Horney (one of the founders of feminist psychoanalytic thinking) and Lasch (a historian and cultural critic famous for writing psychohistory) see in this "pathology of everyday life" important clues to understanding American culture. Writing in 1941, Reik seems to have been making the same argument with reference to social masochism.

Reik, a therapist, wrote his book for a general audience of readers, but also with his fellow psychotherapists in mind. His thoughts attempt to fill in the gaps and puzzles Freud left in his too-brief writings about masochism and about the dynamics of pleasure and "unpleasure," of the dynamics between the sexual drive (Eros) and the death instinct (Thanatos). Like Freud and others, Reik sees the paradox of finding pleasure in pain a fascinating puzzle to solve.

Keep in mind that I am mustering ideas about masochism in order to understand why American young men voluntarily submit to hazing as a test of masculinity and worthiness to join a band of brothers in a fraternity, sports team, or military unit. Why do the men being hazed smile in so many snapshots of hazing? Why do these initiates embrace the pain and humiliation involved in so many hazing customs? How does shared pain become so crucial in the construction of male comradeship, such that when Wallis and his Marine Corps veteran buddies gather to chat and play video games, the memories in their stories are so often about the shared experience of pain?

As Reik explains, Freud distinguishes three forms of masochism: (1) moral masochism, a "certain attitude toward life," an "unconscious desire for punishment"; (2) feminine masochism, "the expression of femininity" in the male patient, the desire to take the female role and submit to the male; and (3) erotogenic masochism, a "mode of sexual excitement" evident early in childhood (Reik 1962, 9). Although there are aspects of all three forms that help explain male hazing, clearly the idea of moral (social) masochism is most relevant. At its core masochism names the drive to find pleasure in pain, the person's "need for punishment," a reaction to "the forbidden wishes of the ego" (p. 10). Reik bluntly writes that "any psychological explanation of masochism would have to answer two questions: What is feared? What is longed for?" (p. 131), two questions I shall return to shortly.

In fleshing out a cultural understanding of moral masochism, which Reik prefers to call "social masochism," Reik uses his own and others' therapeutic experiences with patients to discuss three "constituent elements which can be demonstrated in masochism as a perversion as well as its desexualized form" (p. 44). The elements are "phantasy," "suspense," and "the demonstrative feature" (p. 44).

Given Reik's psychoanalytic work with "the talking cure" and the prominent role of dreams and fantasies in that therapeutic approach, it is not surprising that Reik discusses the role of phantasies in masochism. In both the sexualized and desexualized versions of masochism, the basic phantasy/ fantasy is of being punished. To understand hazing, our interest here is in the desexualized version, though (as we shall see) sexuality is not entirely lacking. The distinction made back in Chapter 4 between friendship and comradeship is relevant because while the sexualized versions of masochism usually involve two people and, therefore, resemble friendship in the focus on individuals, the desexualized version relevant to hazing really is about comradeship, about connections with a group of men, and, therefore, might involve desexualized moral masochism. The fantasy in moral masochism is unconscious, general (pp. 57–58).

The second element, "suspense," describes what Reik calls "the masochistic tension curve," the tension between pleasure and anxiety (p. 59). The pleasure goal is the orgasm, and the masochist tends to prolong the tension. The masochist embraces "punishment, humiliation, discomfort" as procedures prolonging the tension curve (p. 65). In fact, argues Reik, masochism "is not characterized . . . by the pleasure in discomfort, but by pleasure in the *expectation* of discomfort" (p. 67). Anxiety becomes "an element of pleasure" (p. 67).

The third feature of masochism, the "demonstrative" feature, recognizes that for the masochist, the pain and humiliation must be on display. There is a theatrical aspect to masochism, a dramatistic aspect. In the sexualized version of masochism, role-playing helps enact the fantasies. In the desexualized version of everyday moral (or social) masochism, there are many ways in which the masochist can make his (or her) discomfort and humiliation a public performance. And what is hazing but a very public (even if private, behind the closed doors of a fraternity house) demonstration of pain and humiliation in tension with pleasure?

In applying these ideas to male hazing, I need to make a preliminary observation. It is important to realize that American culture, with the exception of some subcultures, is more usefully understood as a fratriarchy rather than a patriarchy, a society where phallic authority lies not in a father but is shared in a band of brothers. In *Totem and Taboo* (1913) and *Civilization and Its Discontents* (1930), Freud saw the desire to kill the father and sexually possess the mother as the source of guilt driving a sense of the need for punishment in the patricidal brothers. Freud's ideas might work well for understanding patriarchal societies, but understanding a fratriarchy forces a modified set of questions.

Put simply, and returning to the questions Reik says a cultural understanding of moral masochism must ask and answer, what do the young men submitting themselves to hazing fear and what do they long for?

Fear and longing. In American culture young men fear that they are not masculine enough. At the same time, they long for intimate bonding with other males. That longing conjures its own fear and anxiety. To meet the demands of normative heterosexual masculinity, regardless of the young man's sexual orientation, male friends and comrades must carefully frame their intimate experiences in groups, often using the play frame, as we have seen in previous chapters. If, following Reik and other psychoanalytic theorists, we look at the details of the ritual of male hazing through the lens of moral masochism, we discover the likely unconscious meanings delivered by the ritual customs.

Phantasy/fantasy, the first factor in masochism discussed by Reik, suggests that perhaps we should think of hazing as a dreamlike experience. Some aspects of hazing are actually dreamlike, such as blindfolding the participants or making them enter dark spaces. Even the ritual nudity or near-nudity of those being hazed not only infantilizes them but also echoes common dreams in which the dreamer is naked in front of others. The word "magical" is not far off the mark in describing the experience of hazing. As in all masochism, the content of the phantasy/fantasy is punishment.

The suspense factor, the factor describing the tension between pleasure and unpleasure, is ever-present in hazing. The neophyte expects the pain and humiliation—the punishment. On the conscious level the neophyte doubtless understands the punishment as a "test"; it is that, certainly. If we press further into the unconscious meanings of the punishment, that is where we encounter the masochistic impulse.

The young male initiate represses three thoughts and their related feelings. First, the initiate represses aggression and anger toward his tormenters. He must repress the "fight or flight" response triggered in his brain and endocrine system in response to physical assault. He experiences guilt in connection with those powerful feelings; of course he cannot lash back at the brothers. He has to "take it like a man." In his own mind (all unconscious, of course), the initiate deserves punishment. So the pain and humiliation experienced in hazing satisfy that need.

The second thought necessarily repressed in the initiate is identification with the female. Details of many hazing practices not only infantilize the initiate but also feminize the initiate. Recall that Reik's second category of masochism (based on Freud) is feminine masochism, "the expression of femininity" in the male patient, the desire to take the female role and submit to the male. The experience of infantilization and feminization in the initiate being hazed evokes anxiety (even fear). The construction of a normative heterosexual masculine identity requires the repression of a male's feminine side; he needs to push the female impulse deep down into his psyche, which often results in the emergence of "symptoms," many settling on a fixation on the anus, a conclusion borrowed from Freud's famous "Wolf Man" analysis in which the cost of his patient's repression of the female in his psyche was intestinal problems and anal fixations (Mechling 2001; Mechling 2008b).

Taking the symbolic female role in hazing actually invokes anxiety in the initiate in two ways. Enacting the female role raises too close to consciousness the feminine nature the young man works so hard to repress. Further, enacting the female role might even spark a truly taboo desire, the wish to take the female role in sex with a brother in the group. Again, the hazing ritual delivers the "deserved" punishment for these unconscious, taboo impulses raised close to the surface of consciousness by the hazing.

The third thought necessarily repressed in hazing, and related to the second, is of incest, the unconscious desire for sexual relations with the brother. In American culture many young men long for the close friendships and comradeship promised by belonging to the male group, the band of brothers. As we saw in Chapter 2, the social construction of normative heterosexual masculinity in American culture often depends upon misogyny and homophobia, both distancing the young man from the feminine, even at the cost of repressing the feminine aspects of his own self (Mech-ling 2008b). At the same time, the closer he gets to male friends and the more he experiences the pleasure of "intimacy" with those male friends, the more he must interpret his feelings as not sexual. "I love you, man" is an expression often heard in closely bonded male groups, and that broth-erly love feels as real as romantic love and might even share some of the endocrinological aspects of romantic love. The young man must negotiate these feelings of intimacy with male friends.

If we think of these unconscious feelings as taboo desire for sexual re-lations with the loved brothers, then we come to appreciate how guilt for those feelings arises in the initiate and why the initiate might embrace pain and humiliation as suitable punishment for those taboo feelings and thoughts. Reik even mentions the fear of castration as a "punishment for forbidden incestuous wishes" (Reik 1962, 128). This is social masochism.

Thinking about hazing as a ritual of social masochism makes sense of many details in hazing. The nudity in so many male hazing customs creates the suspense Reik writes about, the masochistic tension between pleasure and pain. The naked neophyte unconsciously anticipates playing the fe-male role in a sexual congress with the brother, but that consummation of pleasure (the orgasm, Reik would say) never happens. I make a similar point in my analysis of the custom of paddling the buttocks of the initiate in hazing (Mechling 2008b). The paddle represents the phallus of the "adult" brother, and it is a symbolic phallus delivering pain, creating suspense over the pleasure that never happens. The paddle and the older brother's penis never penetrate the neophyte.

The anticipation of pain and humiliation and the actual pain and humil-iation itself provide the longed-for punishment for taboo thoughts about sex with the brothers. The power of the hazing ritual is that it holds out the possibility of the sexual congress but substitutes the symbolism for the real thing, just as stylized violence in the male friendship group substitutes for real violence between the brothers. Actual sex in the American male friendship group would be as destructive as would violence.

And so we get to the third element in masochism discussed by Reik—the demonstrative, dramatistic dimension in which the pain and humilia-tion must be public, must have an audience. The psychological usefulness of many customs is that they dramatize deep psychological anxieties. In the case of male hazing, the anxieties are these. The young man worries that he is not masculine enough. He worries that he will not pass the test of manhood. He worries that he cannot manage intimate bonding with other males in the group while maintaining the normative heterosexual mask. The play space and time of ritual hazing takes these anxieties away from being personal and individual, and collectivizes the anxiety, a process Kenneth Burke (1937/1959, 181) calls "the socialization of losses." The military motto so often shouted at recruits by drill instructors in basic training, "Pain is weakness leaving the body," might also be phrased as "Pain is guilt (anxiety) leaving the body."

Recall that Reik is interested in the ways social masochism has become a normal feature of everyday life in the United States. He echoes Freud's thesis offered in 1930 in *Civilization and Its Discontents* that the development of culture, especially modern culture, has required the repression of instincts. Reik sees in the formula of social masochism the dynamic Freud sees in the creation of civilization: "Fear of the consequences of a forbidden action, the anticipation of punishment, the identification with the suffering victim, and the guilt-feeling—these factors are at the same time important forces of cultural development" (Reik 1962, 386).

In making this point about masochism and modern society, Reik returns to phantasies/fantasies as one of the "constituent elements" in social masochism. The mythologies of cultures, the large stories people tell and hear explaining the meaning of life, provide narrative understanding of masochistic behavior in the service of the group. Reik points to the classic hero quest (Campbell 1949) as an example, and he cites examples of famous novels "into which masochistic phantasies develop and in which pain and discomfort are suffered for national or altruistic aims" (Reik 1962, 386–387). Reik then describes this element in words strikingly apt when thinking about the masochistic fantasies of soldiers: "By serving the family, the nation, mankind, by his own suffering, by sacrificing himself for others in phantasy, by undergoing discomfort and humiliation for them, the masochistic character has replaced the goal at hand by a distant goal which he is hardly ever able to attain. Moreover we must not forget that the satisfaction is mostly anticipated in phantasy and rarely enjoyed materially" (Reik 1962, 388).

The point hinted at by Reik's brief mention of the masochistic plot formula in novels deserves elaboration when we consider the experience of young American men offering themselves for hazing. American mythologies are found in popular culture, in comic books, films, television, and video games, and the formulaic mythology relevant to our thinking about hazing is the American Monomyth (Jewett and Lawrence 1977; Lawrence and Jewett 2002; Mechling and Mechling 1999). In the American Monomyth, a variant of the Classical Monomyth described by Campbell (1949), "A community in a harmonious paradise is threatened by evil: normal institutions fail to contend with this threat: a selfless superhero emerges to renounce temptations and carry out the redemptive task: aided by fate, his decisive victory restores the community to its paradisal condition: the superhero then recedes into obscurity" (Jewett and Lawrence 1977, xx).

Readers will recognize in this description the formula plot familiar in so many popular culture narratives. Young American men entering the military have encountered the American Monomyth in the popular culture narratives they consume. An analysis of the Western film genre by Will Wright (1977) shows how in the 1970s this formula expanded to allow the place of the lone Monomythic hero to be filled by a male group, each member especially skilled in one type of the violence necessary for the redemptive outcome of the formula plot. A fratriarchy, a band of brothers.

Relevant to my argument here about social masochism in hazing is the development in the 1980s of increased suffering by the Monomythic hero in films and comic books consumed largely by young men. Susan Jeffords (1993) analyzes a number of 1980s films with attention to the assaults on the bodies of the heroes. What happens to the body of the hero played by Bruce Willis in the five *Die Hard* films (1988–2013) is just a sampling of the pain and humiliation experienced by present-day heroes in American popular culture, including films, comics, and films made from comics.

I have taken this slight detour into American popular culture and the formulaic narratives consumed primarily by young men to make the point that the eighteen-year-old male entering the hazing experience brings with him years of experience with the idea that it is noble to suffer pain and humiliation for the good of the group. The narrative gives purpose to the suffering; it makes the suffering redemptive. If the masochistic elements of the hazing experience deliver wished-for punishment for the individual's taboo feelings and thoughts of violence and incest, a punishment alleviating the guilt, then both the formulaic hazing ritual and its similarity to American cultural mythologies of the hero quest serve to take the feelings and thoughts out of the individual, personal realm and dramatize the feelings and thoughts symbolically in the ritual. Bronner (2006, 8–15) casts the typical Crossing the Line Ceremony into a plot formula closely following the hero tale, and we could do the same structural analysis of the plot of most hazing events.

For those readers who chose to skip the foregoing analytical discussion of social masochism in hazing, the now-familiar interpretation of hazing from anthropology and folklore studies tells us plenty about how men in groups create both informal and formal rituals for testing the manliness of each other. If the reader doubts the psychoanalytic interpretation, though, a central puzzle of hazing remains unsolved. Why do young men willingly subject themselves to rituals involving pain and humiliation? The reader who rejects the psychoanalytic answer to that question seems to me somewhat obliged to offer an alternative theory and interpretation of the meanings of the pain and humiliation. A test need not consist of these qualities. After all, the test administered by the Sphinx of legend was a riddle, and one can imagine any number of tests men can invent in their groups to test the worthiness of the neophytes wishing to earn their right to membership in the brotherhood. In American culture, young men have chosen pain and humiliation over and over again as the qualities of the test of manhood, and the resistance of these practices to extinction testifies to their deep psychological functions in the male group. As of this writing over forty states in the United States have passed laws against hazing, and yet hazing persists. Institutions from universities to the US military have banned hazing, only to see hazing move underground, persisting in even greater secrecy. The smiles in the snapshots of young men being hazed tell us that these men take pleasure in pain. Psychoanalytic theory and analysis tells us why that is.

12

Deep Play

The social anthropologist, Clifford Geertz, whose ideas about the interpretation of cultures (Geertz 1973b) we encountered in my Introduction, famously used the notion of "deep play" to interpret a Balinese cockfight he attended doing fieldwork in Indonesia (Geertz 1973a). He borrowed the notion of deep play from the English utilitarian philosopher, Jeremy Bentham, and Geertz explains that for Bentham deep play "means play in which the stakes are so high that it is, from his utilitarian standpoint, irrational for men to engage in it at all" (Geertz 1973a, 432). And yet the players play. Geertz uses the notion of deep play to interpret the Balinese cockfight, but Brian Sutton-Smith and Diana Kelly-Byrne (1984) in turn borrow Geertz's use of deep play in their description of the ways people use the play frame to "mask" other goals and motives, including cruelty, violence, power, danger, and even work (pp. 187–194). The two authors elicited stories from university students in their classes about all these forms of play that mask other motives, and in the chapter subsection "Masks for Danger" (pp. 191–193) they offer examples of very risky play.

In my 2012 article that is a precursor to this book, I offered some examples of snapshots showing evidence of deep play. John Paul Wallis and I (2019) elaborate that point in our treatment of deep play as a form of folk therapy to cope with the trauma of living, working, and fighting in the combat zone. Deep play is a practice akin to what we might call "dark play," which includes what folklorists call "gallows humor"—humor in the face of horrible events and death, humor invoked as a kind of charm to protect the jokers from harm, but also humor invoked to share the thought that there is nothing you can do about your fate so you may as well laugh at the devil.

Deep play and dark play provide play frames for dealing with the feelings of dread and horror and guilt in the combat zone. Much of gallows humor is oral and not captured in snapshots. Soldiers joke about death, including jokes about "last words" (Finkel 2009, 121). They adopt folk speech—proverbs—to comment on the irrationality of war and specifically the irrationality of who lives and who dies in combat. In the Vietnam War, the two phrases that appear again and again in the war memoirs are "There it is" and "It don't mean nothin'." Kurt Vonnegut has his protagonist in *Slaughterhouse-Five* (1969) utter the phrase "So it goes" continuously throughout this novel. The novel reflects his own experience living through the firebombing of Dresden as a prisoner of war in World War II. I have not been able to establish whether this phrase is unique to Vonnegut; that seems so. Clearly Vonnegut uses it the same way a grunt in Vietnam used "There it is" or "It don't mean nothin'": resignation in the face of an irrational world, a calm acceptance of and surrender to fate.

Although a lot of dark play is oral, some does lend itself to visual representation. This is because the warrior has some control over his body—his skin and clothing, for example—so he can make his body the site of ideas and gesture of resistance against military discipline (Wallis and Mechling 2020). For example, professional war photographers in Vietnam captured several examples of soldiers and Marines wearing helmets and flak jackets with words and symbols we might call "resistant" to authority. The famous helmet worn by the character Joker in Stanley Kubrick's 1987 film, *Full Metal Jacket,* sports both the words "Born to Kill" and a peace symbol. When quizzed about this apparent contradiction by an officer, Joker replies, "It's a Jungian thing, sir" (Burton 2017).

The antiwar sentiments on Joker's helmet reflect actual practices of warriors in the combat zone in Vietnam. I have no snapshots of these gestures, but a few press photos from the era record examples. I do have in my collection a large print of a photo that may or may not be a snapshot, so I am not including it here in case it is a copyrighted press photo (it has none of the usual stamps on the back). It is a close-up photo of the back of a soldier's jacket, on which he (or a buddy) has written: CAUTION: BEING A MARINE IN KHE SANH MAY BE HAZARDOUS TO YOUR HEALTH. 3D BN. 26TH "NEWSWEEK."

Some tattoos placed on their bodies by soldiers also provide visual examples of dark play (and gallows humor). Wallis and I discuss the practice in our article on the soldier's use of his or her body as a site of "microresistance" (small gestures of resistance) in the American military (Wallis and Mechling 2020). Again, I have no snapshots of such tattoos, though doubtless such snapshots exist. Wallis and I rely, in part, on a 2009 documentary film, *Tattooed under Fire* (directed by Nancy Schiesari), filmed in a tattoo parlor in Killeen, Texas, near Fort Hood, and the filmmaker interviewed both the married team of tattoo artists who own the establishment and the male and female soldiers who get tattoos on the way to deployment in Iraq and Afghanistan and on their way back. One example can suffice here. A medic headed for Iraq designed and had tattooed on his upper arm the image of a fetus in a blender. He took some heat from some noncommissioned officers who had children and objected to the tattoo; his reply was that his tattoo was an apt metaphor for the experience he was about to have in Iraq.

I do have snapshots of what we might call a minor genre of gallows humor.

Snapshot 12.1 literally enacts in the play frame a hanging of a sailor by two of his friends. We know nothing of the context for this snapshot, but it is difficult not to see them as enacting their helpless feelings as they all face "the gallows." Snapshots 12.2 and 12.3 are just a few of the snapshots I own and have seen of soldiers and sailors gesturing with the middle finger, the "digitus impudicus," originally an obscene gesture in ancient Rome. The middle finger represents the penis and the two knuckles on either side represent the testicles, and this gesture still carries the meaning in American usage of "fuck you" or "fuck this" (Nasaw 2012). The meaning of the gesture has evolved to be an expression of protest and displeasure, a gesture protected as free speech by the First Amendment (Robbins 2008). A common saying in the Marines, "Eat the apple and fuck the Corps," plays on the homonyms core/corps. Matt Young even titled his war memoir/novel *Eat the Apple* (2018). I would argue that the folk gesture is a kinesic version of "There it is."

Even though I have no snapshots of gallows humor written on the helmets and jackets of warriors or snapshots of tattoos of the sort seen in

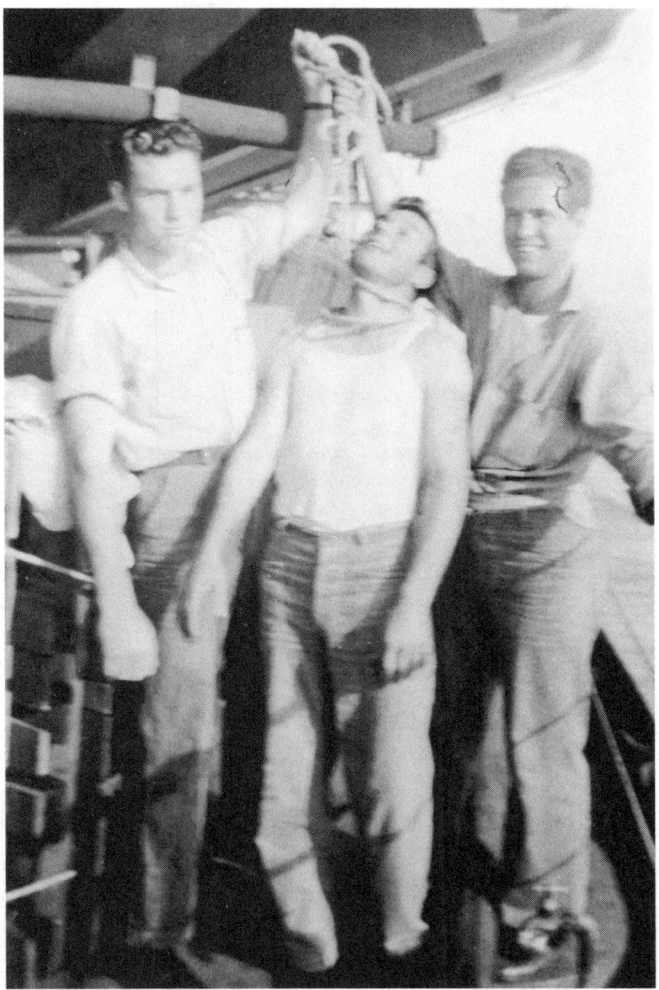

Snapshot 12.1

Tattooed under Fire, I can present here snapshots picturing two sorts of deep play—some of play with firearms and some of play with dead bodies, particularly human skulls.

PLAY WITH FIREARMS

My first thought in sorting snapshots was to lump together those showing playfighting with sharp objects and those showing playfighting with

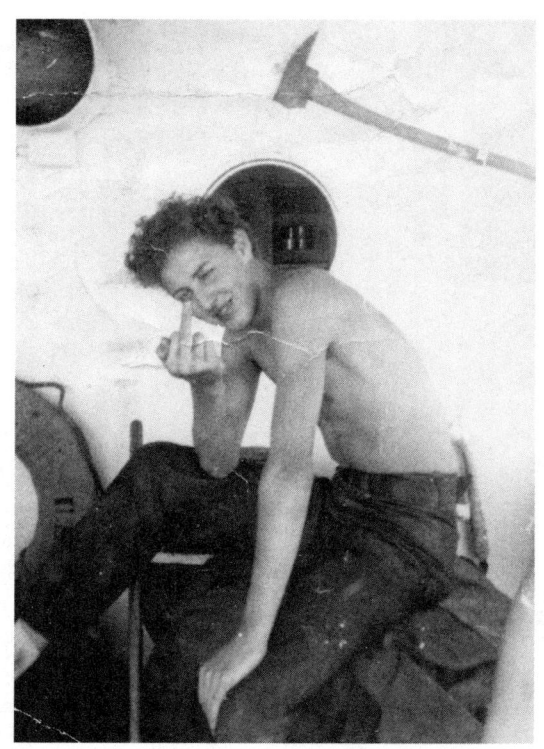

Snapshot 12.2

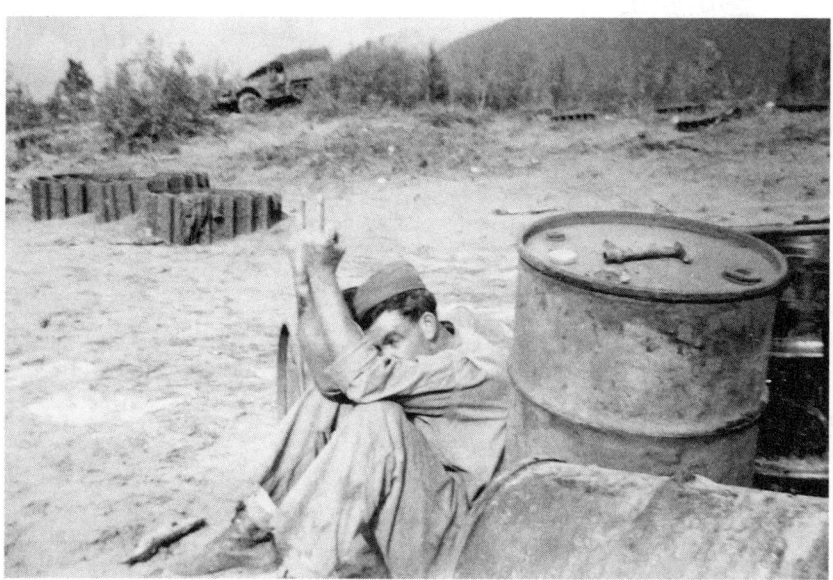

Snapshot 12.3

firearms, for Chapter 10. Always at the back of my mind, however, was the experience of my brother-in-law, who actually was shot in the face accidentally while on Army duty in Germany in the 1970s. He and his buddies were playing around with a loaded pistol and one accidentally shot him in the mouth, shattering teeth and palate; the bullet lodged in his neck. He survived; he easily could have been killed. So the play with firearms I see in so many snapshots deserves to be in this chapter on deep play, as the results of the play can be fatal.

Snapshot 12.4 says so much and so little that I devoted some space in the original "Soldier Snaps" article to my "reading" of the photo. We have no context for this photo, though I suspect it was taken in Vietnam. We do not know which of the soldiers pictured here saved the snapshot; perhaps it was saved by the soldier who took the picture. Whoever he was, he wrote KILL THE BEAST in the top white margin.

The race of each soldier is a factor in what makes this a fascinating snapshot of the lives of these soldiers, as are the gestures by the two soldiers. The standing African American soldier is holding the pistol waist high and pointing it directly into the face of the kneeling white soldier, who appears to be begging for his life. It is no mystery why and how this snapshot conjures my own thoughts about my brother-in-law's brush with death engaging in deep play with a pistol.

For me, this snapshot is a perfect example of the power of a vernacular photograph to make us, the viewers, construct in our minds a "story," a continuous narrative of the everyday lives of these two men of which the snapshot records a split-second moment. Some snapshots are candid, true "snapshots" taken spontaneously in the moment, while some are posed, staged. Snapshot 12.4 appears to be staged, almost as a dramatic *tableau vivant,* a living drama. The handwritten caption, KILL THE BEAST, forces us to speculate on the motives and meaning of this staged event. We have to assume that this sort of deep play both signals and requires the trust found in friendship, which itself may be remarkable, given the voluntary racial segregation solders in Vietnam often practiced. In the snapshot the white soldier is "the beast," and we wonder what that means. Certainly the snapshot reverses American stereotypes that African American men behave more "beastly" than do white men. Here a white man is "the beast" and one possible meaning is that the white man has acted beastly toward the African American man. The snapshot turns the table, much as the slave

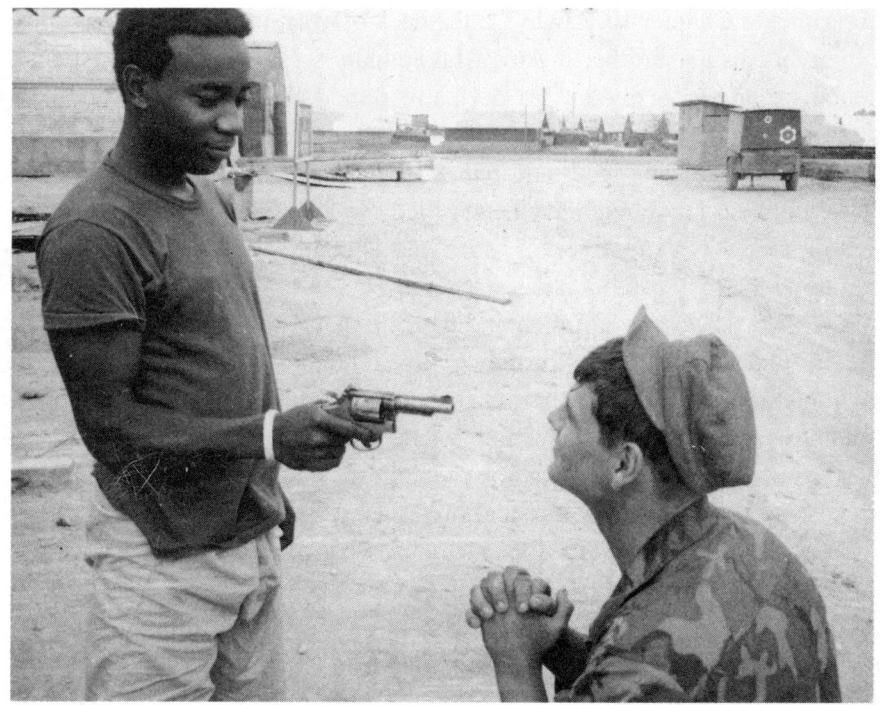

Snapshot 12.4

rebellions so feared by white slaveowners in the Western hemisphere turned the table. The oppressed becomes the oppressor.

Still speculating on the unconscious and unintended meanings of this snapshot, though, I see two other messages. The racial reversal in the snapshot might also point us to the racial drama being fought altogether in the Vietnam War. As Dave Grossman (2009) and many others observe, it is easier to kill enemy soldiers if you think of them as less than human, as animals. American soldiers daily experienced, in both their training and in their everyday folk cultures, language dehumanizing the Vietnamese people. Many African Americans in uniform and back home during the Vietnam War noticed the paradox; they were drafted and sent to fight Asians who were not their oppressors. "No Vietnamese ever called me a nigger," said many protestors, and that statement is the title of a 1968 documentary film by David Loeb Weiss about the particular stance taken by African Americans protesting the war (Hoberman 2018). The heavyweight boxing champion Muhammed Ali famously expressed the same idea as he refused to be drafted in 1967, claiming that as a convert to Islam he was a conscientious objector to the war. "I ain't got no quarrel with them Vietcong, anyway," he said. And he might have added, although this is disputed, "No Viet Cong ever called me nigger" (Fatsis 2016). In any case, the phrase "No Vietnamese Ever Called Me Nigger" certainly appeared quite often on antiwar protest signs carried by African Americans at protests. Given this context for a snapshot I think was taken in Vietnam, the racial reversal also indicts both white and Black soldiers who treated the Vietnamese like animals.

I see one more, possibly unconscious meaning in this snapshot. "The beast" needing killing lives within those soldiers. For some soldiers, the understanding that they had a beast inside them had surfaced to the conscious level. In his "rap groups" with Vietnam veterans, Robert Lifton (1973) heard this often. The beast-like capacity for aggression and violence, especially in the berserk state of warriors committing hot atrocities in war (more on this below), lurks in every person. Is the white soldier in this snapshot begging for his life? Or is he begging to be killed as punishment for the killing he has done in the war? Does he deserve death as expiation for his guilt? And more, perhaps the beast in both soldiers in the snapshot is the post-traumatic stress syndrome both are experiencing, which would be one more reason to read the white soldier's pose as a plea to be executed, ending the pain of his PTSD. One thing we know from the present wars in Iraq and Afghanistan is that veterans commit suicide at tragic rates when they return home, suffering from the symptoms of PTSD.

RACE

Snapshot 12.4 is only the third image in this book, so far, including an African American soldier (Snapshot 5.8 is the first, Snapshot 10.5 is the second, and Snapshot 12.5 is the fourth), so perhaps this is a good time to talk about race in the snapshots. These photographs prove that play with weapons in the snapshots can mix the race of the aggressor and the victim, and show us that the laughter signals the play frame of this pose; the actors are having fun.

I have very few snapshots in my collection featuring African American (Black) soldiers alone or in pairs or in groups. I have no way of knowing the source of the "sample bias." When I was collecting snapshots I was interested in what was being shown in the image as evidence of the everyday,

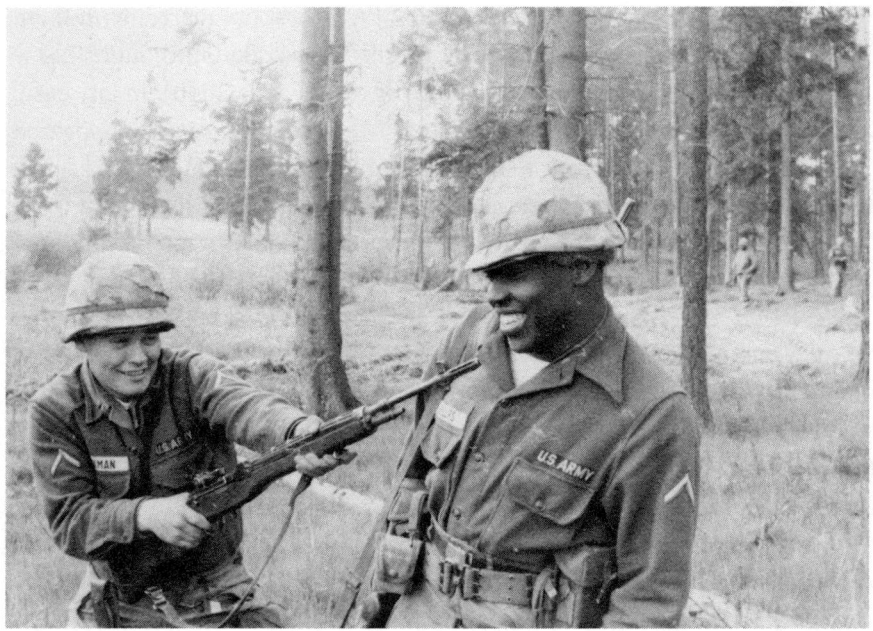

Snapshot 12.5

folk, vernacular cultures of soldiers, and I have no reason to believe that I avoided collecting images featuring Black service members. If I had extended my collection past those taken on film to include those taken with digital cameras and smartphones in the Gulf War and the wars in Iraq and Afghanistan, doubtless I would have a better set of images to make some guesses about what the images tell us about race relations in those male friendship groups.

I have a few more snapshots of Black soldiers playing with weapons or just showing off their weapons for the snapshot. I also have a few of Black soldiers doing mundane things, like writing letters home and doing KP ("kitchen police," cooking and cleaning).

Dian Hanson's book (2014), which is mostly snapshots, has only three images including Black members of the military (pp. 31, 55, 98) among the hundreds of photographs in the book, and two of those do not seem to be snapshots of American soldiers at all. When one turns to collections of official war photography, there are not many more images of Black soldiers, at least before the arrival of digital photography. In Evan Bachner's (2004, 2007) two collections of official war photographs by photographers in Edward Steichen's Naval Aviation Photographic Unit, there are only a few photographs with Black soldiers (2004, 82, 103, 127), including one of naked Black soldiers showering together (p. 127).

A fact relevant to the scarcity of soldier snaps featuring Black men is the racial segregation of the American military for almost half of the twentieth century. Black soldiers were segregated in their own units, often given support roles rather than combat roles, until 1948, when President Harry Truman issued Executive Order 9981 integrating the US military. Some of the official photographs, therefore, are of Black soldiers among other Black soldiers in their segregated units. By the Vietnam War the images, both official and in the snapshots, are of Black and white soldiers working, playing, and fighting together, but the historian looking at the photographs from that era is mindful of the state of race relations back home in the 1960s and 1970s, just as the Black and white soldiers in Vietnam were mindful of those tensions, riots, and assassinations.

As evidence of the everyday lives of both Black and white soldiers in the military, the snapshots do not seem to suggest many differences. The play with weapons—the most common theme in the snapshots I have of Black and white soldiers playing together—puts an object, a killing machine, between the two men. Put differently, I have seen no snapshots in my collection or in others of white and Black soldiers engaging in simple R&T playfighting, nor are there any in Hetherington's collection of photographs he took while at Restrepo, *Infidel* (2010). The weapon must create a "safe" way in the play frame for Black and white soldiers to engage in stylized aggression. I see the pattern; I just am not clear as to the meaning of the pattern.

THE DEATH INSTINCT

Of course, my interpretation of both Snapshots 12.4 and 12.5 is highly speculative and posits unconscious meanings in the dark play captured by the snapshots. Many historians and other scholars "reading" vintage snapshots would not dare to speculate as I have here in interpreting the layered meanings of Snapshots 12.4 and 12.5. Snapshot 12.6 is from an earlier period and bears a strong resemblance to Snapshot 12.4. The simplest explanation for these and other snapshots of play with firearms, I suppose, is that boys in American culture grow up playing with guns and the popular culture they consume is filled with guns (Mechling 2008c). Perhaps gun

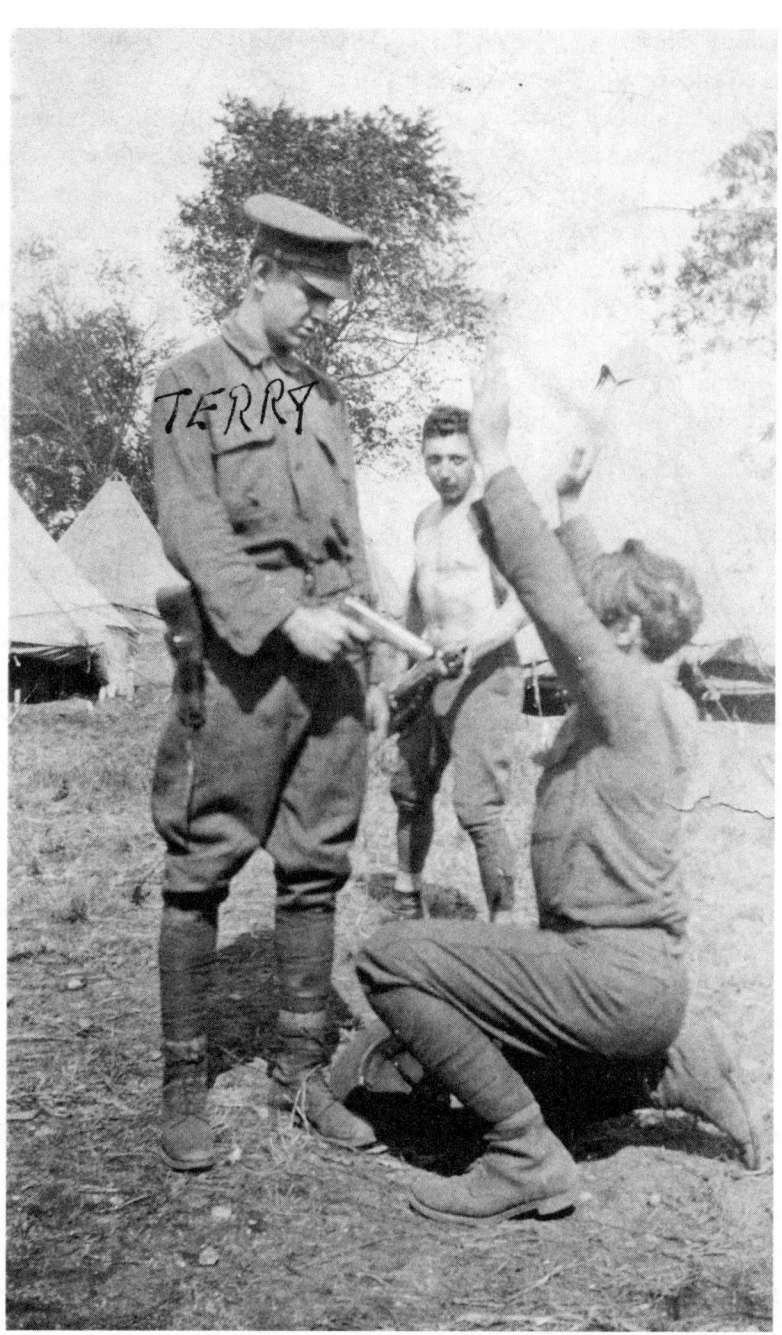

Snapshot 12.6

play among older males in the military is simply an extension of the boy's fascination with guns as instruments of power, but that seems to me to be one of those "thin descriptions" Geertz and Niobe Way write about. A "thick description" of the play with guns in the soldier snapshots, it seems to me, really must take into account the fact that these are not toy guns, that soldiers are trained to kill with guns, and that the complex play with guns, pretending to shoot a friend, must bring to the surface strong emotions. As Brian Sutton-Smith (2017) teaches us, play helps us manage emotions and their expression in feelings. Soldiers' play with guns is not child's play.

The thought that deep play with firearms might even suggest an unconscious desire for death warrants some discussion. Recall that in Chapter 11 we saw that Freud modified his original concept of masochism to see the death instinct at work in the unconscious. Wallis and I (2019, 126–130) devote considerable attention to "self-harm" as a form of deep play by warriors in the combat zone. I shall not reproduce that analysis here, in large part because I have no snapshots of the sorts of self-harm Wallis and I discuss in that book. But I do offer Snapshot 12.7 for more speculation along these lines.

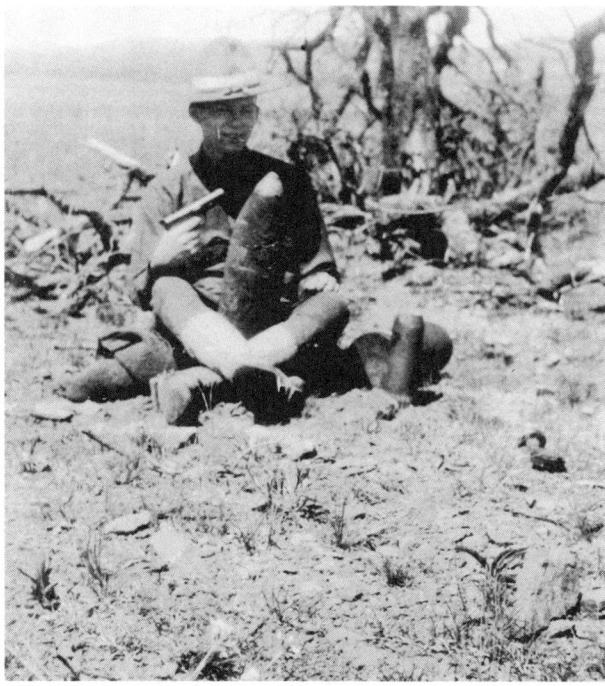

Snapshot 12.7

This snapshot, mostly likely from the World War I era based on the uniform, features a different sort of play with a firearm. The soldier is not pointing the handgun at his head or body, but toward the triggering tip of the bomb (or artillery shell) he holds between his legs. Straddling a bomb or artillery shell actually is a common pose in military snapshots, as in Snapshot 12.8 (dated on the back "Aug. 4, 1945," with the handwritten caption, "Two things that win wars"). Even dime-store psychoanalytic analysis easily sees the phallic meaning of a soldier's posing with a hard, powerful weapon (a "tool" of war) between his legs.

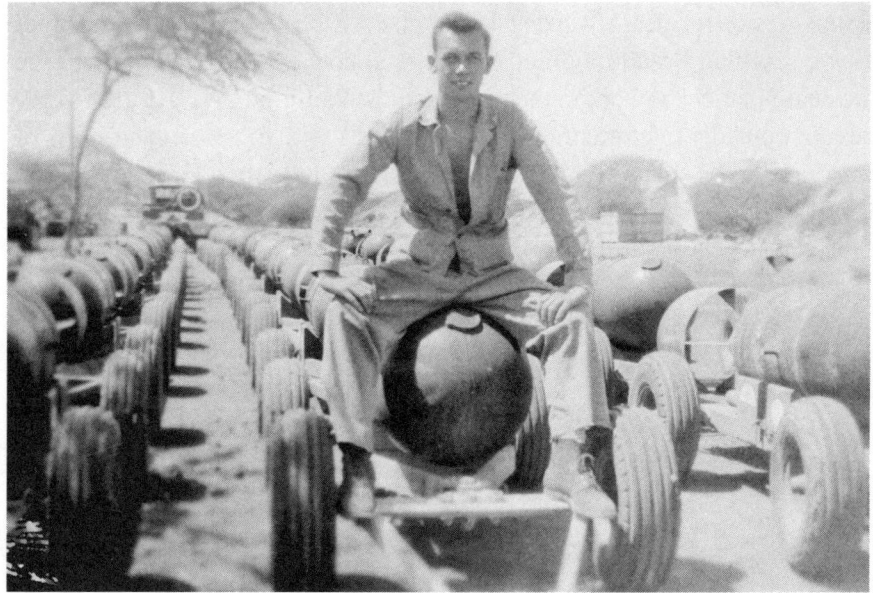

Snapshot 12.8

Returning to Snapshot 12.7, though, we can find more there. If we speculate that the bomb or artillery shell in the snapshot, given its location, stands for the soldier's penis (and I am not at all sure these are unconscious meanings for the soldiers posing this way), then the soldier is pointing the sidearm at his symbolic penis. Perhaps he is showing off two "weapons," both with phallic meanings. Or perhaps the snapshot captures him in a momentary thought of committing suicide by shooting the tip of the artillery shell.

I admit that my analysis of Snapshots 12.4 and 12.7 (and others, but especially those) has been speculative, but as I discussed back in the

Introduction, following Geertz's lead, the process of interpreting cultural texts resembles the method of clinical inference in that the analyst forms a tentative hypothesis meant to make "best sense" of the data. Is this case, the data are the details in the image. I believe the analysis I offer here makes some sense of the images. An alternative hypothesis needs to meet the same criterion—does it make better sense of the details of the images than the hypothesis I offer?

For me a satisfactory hypothesis for the meanings in Snapshots 12.4 and 12.7 cannot be "Well, this is play and they are having fun." That explains nothing; that simply declares the starting point that people get pleasure from the activity captured by the snapshot. The soldiers in these two and any other posed scenes have made choices. They choose to pose in a particular way, and they choose to have a friend take the photograph. Choices imply underlying motives.

DEEP PLAY WITH DEAD BODIES

My article on vernacular photography taken by hunters (Mechling 2004) begins with an analysis of a snapshot taken on a hunting trip, probably in the 1920s or 1930s, judging from the car, and of interest for this discussion of soldier snapshots is the way the hunters have posed the small dead bear. That pose reminds me of a scene in Stanley Kubrick's 1987 film, *Full Metal Jacket,* in which the platoon is taking a break after a battle (in the Vietnam War) and one of the Marines has seated the dead Vietnamese fighter beside him and animates the corpse by moving its arms. The scene is shocking, as are many others in the film, which is based on Gustav Hasford's 1979 semi-autobiographical Vietnam War novel, *The Short-Timers.* Many viewers of the film probably assume that the play with the enemy body is a fiction, but play with bodies and body parts by American warriors has not been uncommon. Wallis and I devote a section of our chapter on deep play as folk therapy to play with body parts (Wallis and Mechling 2019, 130–133). Most of what we know of such dark play, which is also deep play in that it is against military regulations and subject to severe punishment if discovered, we gather from war memoirs and novels. Photographic evidence of soldiers' play with dead bodies is scarce, for good reasons, but relatively recently there have been two very public and scandalous episodes. One was the release of digital snapshots taken by American soldiers treating Iraqi prisoners cruelly at Abu Ghraib prison (Hersh 2004; Morris 2011). And in 2012, a video taken by American Marines urinating on dead Taliban fighters in Helmand Province hit the Internet, causing consternation and courts-martial (Bowley and Rosenberg 2012). As I write these words, the trial, acquittal, and pardon of Navy SEAL Edward Gallagher and their aftermath still are news. Most sensational is that Gallagher posed for a snapshot holding up a dead ISIS fighter in Mosul, Iraq (Bates and Law 2019).

Wallis (2012) uses the phrase "digital trophies" to describe the video the Marines took and kept of urinating on the bodies of dead Taliban fighters. Wallis and I were surprised to find that we both arrived at the insight from different directions, and we pick up on that convergence in our book (2019, 131–132). Those snapshots at Abu Ghraib and the video at Helmand Province bear a strong resemblance to the hunting snapshots I collected and analyzed, and the desire to have a "digital trophy" of the kill must be strong in both cases. The digital trophy snapshots of a kill serve as more than just a souvenir (Stewart 1984) of a pleasant experience, like a holiday or family gathering. I have a few thoughts on what that something more might be.

Both hunting snapshots and the snapshots of warriors' deep play with the bodies of dead enemy combatants stand as evidence of a test passed. In both cases the test is one of manhood.

What these two examples suggest is that the ease of digital photography, when every soldier carries a smartphone capable of taking snapshots and videos, makes possible photographic capture of forbidden deep play, like play with the bodies and body parts of enemy fighters. In the age of film photography, it would have been rare for a snapshot of deep play, like play with body parts, to survive all of the editing I discussed earlier. There is, however, a class of snapshots on film that does fit.

SKULLS AS MEMENTO MORI

I present here a gallery of four snapshots (12.9–12.12) featuring human skulls. Such snapshots are more plentiful than snapshots of other sorts of forbidden play with dead bodies. Elliott Oring (2012, 50) calls the human skulls displayed in wartime snapshots "totems," a term easily linked with Wallis's use of "digital trophies." Oring uses a snapshot of a human skull on a stake taken by his friend, a Vietnam veteran (tour 1969–1970), and

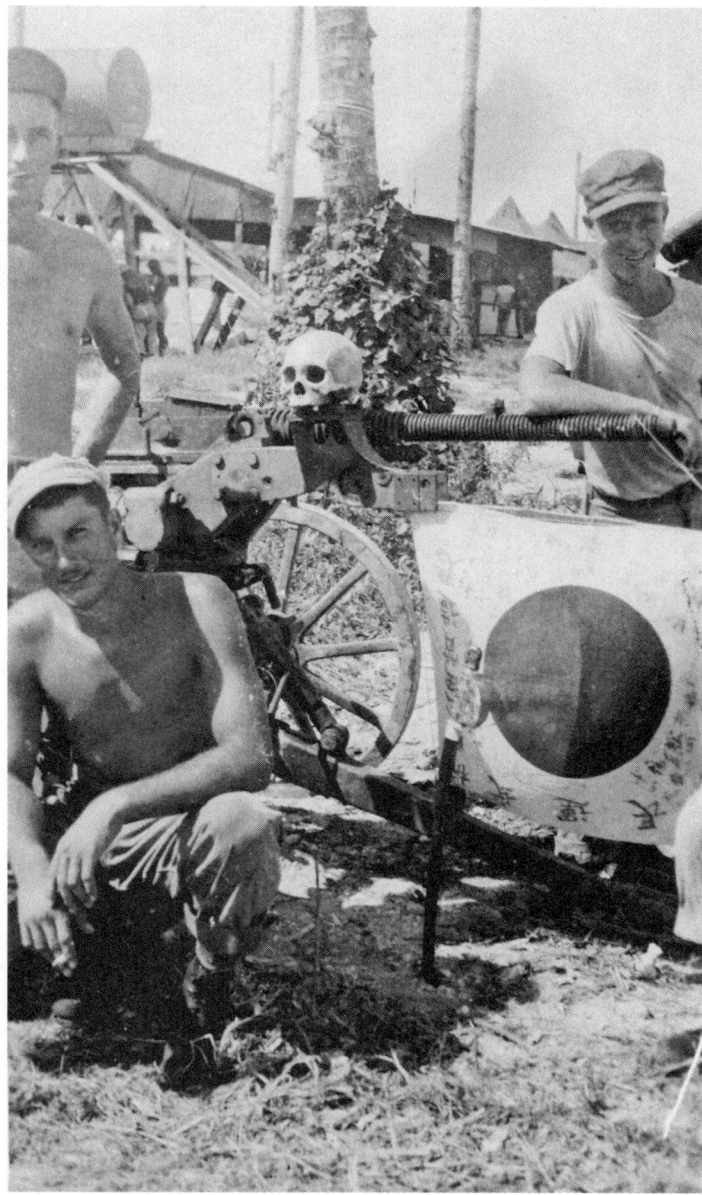

Snapshot 12.9

Oring quotes his friend as saying that his platoon carried the skull around
with them, named him "Bruce," and would sometimes dress up the skull
and pike in a hat, sunglasses, and even pants (Oring 2012). Even Steichen's
Naval Aviation Photographic Unit produced a photograph of a human skull

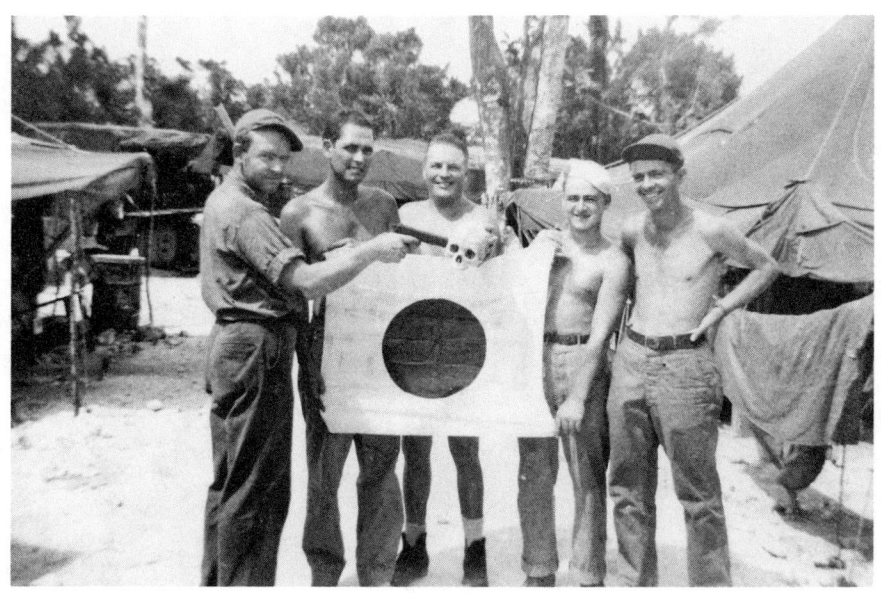

Snapshot 12.10

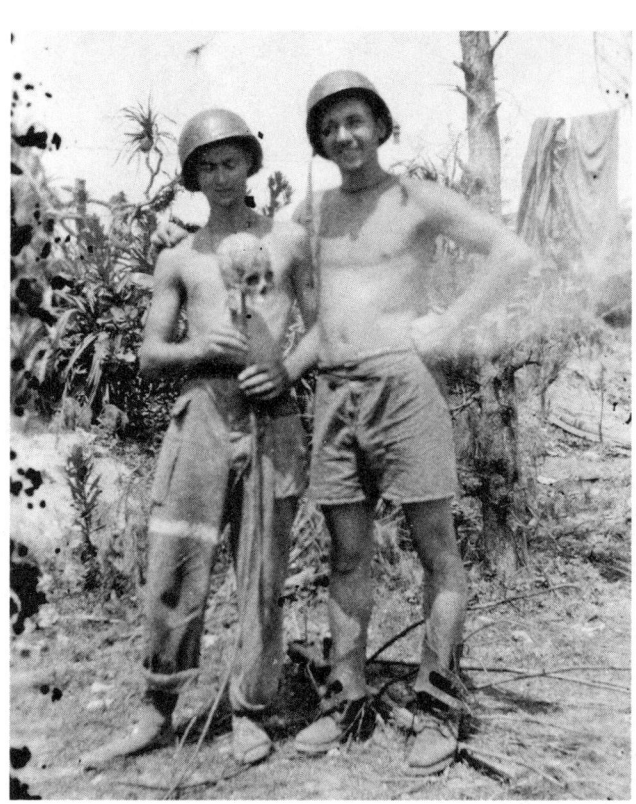

Snapshot 12.11

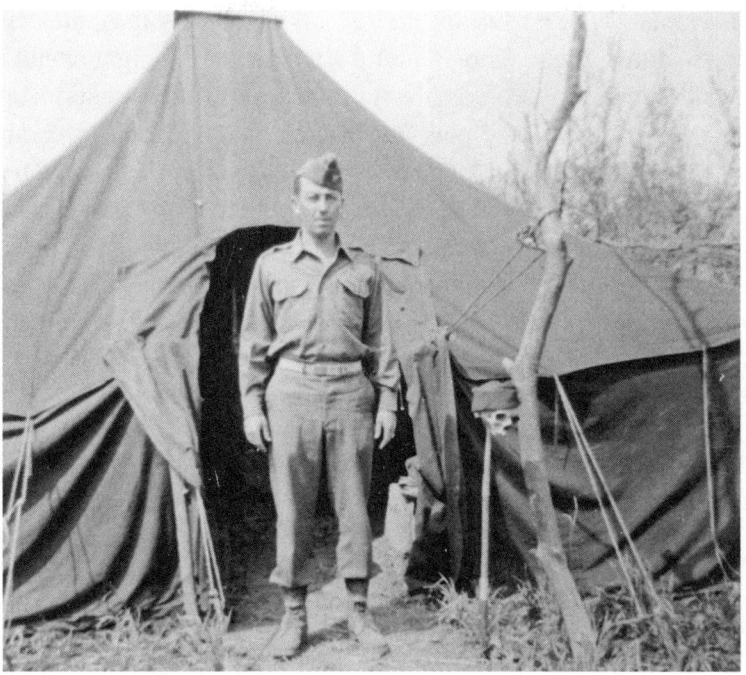

Snapshot 12.12

marking a sardonic sign reading TARAWA RECRUITING OFFICE (Phillips 1981, 188).

Snapshots 12.9 and 12.10 show the play with a human skull along with other items—notably the Japanese flag—captured as trophies of battle. The skulls perched on tall stakes in Snapshots 12.11 and 12.12 repeat that motif found in Oring's friend's snapshot, so the display of the enemy skull as a more permanent reminder than a snapshot posed with other trophies seems to have been a common practice. A "permanent reminder" of what?

Art historians document well the visual and cultural history of the use of skulls by painters and sculptors as "memento mori," a Latin phrase meaning "Remember that you will die" (Stewart 2019). The use of the skull as that sort of reminder of the death that awaits us all shows up, of course, in Hamlet's famous musings while he is holding Yorick's skull, and that scene not only foregrounds the "memento mori" meaning but also foretells the deaths coming for so many characters at the end of the play.

It seems paradoxical that the constant presence of a human skull would be at all comforting to people engaged in mortal battle, but that is the most useful function of dark humor and deep play. Recall that I said that in the case of anomalies, as in unexpected events or objects that threaten the order of the culture, a common cultural strategy is not to ignore and bury the anomaly but to put the anomaly at the center of ritual attention, taking away its power in ritual and play with the anomaly (Babcock-Abrahams 1975). The human skulls on long sticks, guarding the entrance to a tent or carried around as a companion, as was "Bruce," rob the power of daily reminders of death in the combat zone. These folk practices are risky, violating military regulations and subject to severe penalties if caught, and still the warriors take the risk. The risk might be irrational, but so are the deaths in combat.

PART IV
Coda

Coda

This is a "Coda" and not a traditional "Conclusion." I began to write a conventional conclusion, a concise summary of the arguments in the book, returning to the central idea that the men in the snapshots use the male folk practices documented in the snapshots to manage their friendships, and then my brain went in a different direction. This Coda is the result.

That reminds me of a story.

Not so long ago a longtime friend and I were talking about both the *PTSD and Folk Therapy* (2019) book John Paul Wallis and I were finishing and the "Soldier Snapshots" book project underway. I told him that when I went off to college at Stetson University (Florida) in the fall of 1963, I had every intention of taking the Army Reserve Officer Training Corps (ROTC) program Stetson offered, but it turns out that I got so involved with debate and theater and my studies that I left no time for ROTC, even though I was dazzled by the fancy uniforms and weapons drills performed by the Pershing Rifles Drill Team.

"Do you regret not doing ROTC?" he asked me.

I replied, "I think I would have liked it too much."

That reply is pregnant with meaning. One of the meanings is my uncertainty about what would have been my fate had I completed ROTC and been commissioned as a second lieutenant upon graduation in May 1967.

The year 1967–1968 was not a good one to head for Vietnam in a uniform. Years later I helped spearhead a Stetson Alumni Vietnam and Vietnam Era Veterans Remembrance Project, and my role was to find and communicate with as many Stetson alumni veterans as we could find. In that correspondence (many from my class of 1967, of course, as the war was heating up considerably by then), I discovered the many different paths those veterans took after graduation. Not all took ROTC and began as commissioned officers; others were drafted. What became clear was that our veterans served in many different ways. Some became infantrymen and humped in the jungle. A friend who was a geography major spent his year in Vietnam reading maps in an air-conditioned trailer. Another was sent to medical school by the army. Another worked in a Veterans Administration hospital in South Carolina (where he met a friend from my high school class of 1963, both drafted). A few worked in Army intelligence. There was no one "Vietnam war experience."

So I never knew what fate awaited me if I had been commissioned a second lieutenant in the US Army in May 1967. But I do think I would have liked it "too much."

Snapshot C.1 is not of me and my Boy Scout buddies, but it might as well be. That snapshot conveys why I would have liked ROTC so much and, eventually, military service. I was in the Boy Scouts from age eight to sixteen, earned the rank of Eagle Scout, and worked as a Boy Scout camp counselor for three years. I loved the male camaraderie in the scouts, and I loved the elements of scout camp that resembled the military (two Virginia Military Institute college students were on the camp staff and brought that school's military culture to the staff—I know that one, James Rogan, died in Vietnam and his name is on the Wall). I am sure I would have loved ROTC and the military.

If one reason why I replied to my friend, "I would have liked it too much," is the lingering thought that I might have died in military service, the other reason is that I think I would have experienced military service as one big Boy Scout adventure, which it both is and is not.

One of the themes moving through this book has been the importance of friendship and of comradeship for young men. The never-ending "masculinity project" undertaken by boys and young men, a project meant simultaneously to mask and to bolster the actual fragility of masculinity and a project driven by constant tests of manhood, is made bearable by male friendship. When I read Niobe Way's book, *Deep Secrets* (2011), reporting

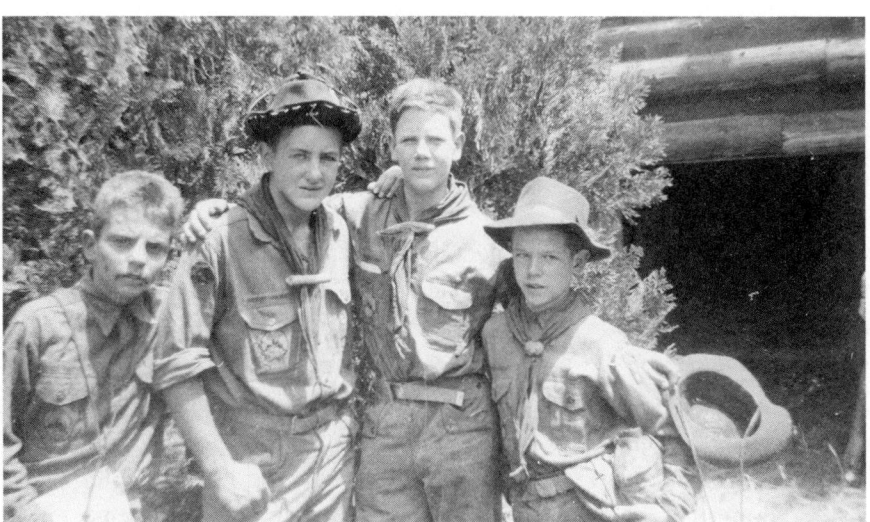

Snapshot C.1

years of research on adolescent male friendship by her and by her colleagues and others, I was startled by her main thesis that boys experience strong, emotional friendships in early and late adolescence, but that their experience in late adolescence is of betrayal and loss and grief for the lost intensity of friendship with other males.

That observation described my own experience.

At age sixteen debate and other high school activities drew me away from active participation in my Boy Scout troop. Our great success in debate in my junior year of high school (1961–1962) meant that I would not be able to return to the South Florida Boy Scout Council summer camp staff in the summer of 1962, as I was scheduled to do, because we were headed for the national tournament in Montana that summer. At age sixteen I felt very sad realizing that I had spent my last summer with those buddies I had in the Boy Scouts.

Suddenly, reading Way's book, I realized that the young men entering military service, usually in late adolescence, were seeking to repair the same loss and grief I had experienced at age sixteen. Recruits to the volunteer army have many reasons for enlisting (you can read Wallis's own story about being called out for his "bullshit" explanation to his Marine Corps senior drill instructor about why he joined the Marines, in Wallis and Mechling 2019, 20). One reason for joining the military, the true one in many cases but one rarely spoken or written, is "I miss having close male friends." In fact, when asked why they reenlist, even a few years after leaving the service, many men will finally admit that close bonding in a male group is what they miss most and hope to regain.

In his book, *The Mourning After* (2018), which picks up in the 1950s the story begun with his examination of the vernacular photography of men "together and apart" up until 1950, John Ibson writes that "in regard to men's relationships, the immediate postwar period, roughly a decade and a half, may meaningfully be characterized as a prolonged period of mourning after the war, with an attendant sense of loss and longing" (2018, xvii). *The Mourning After* aims to continue what he began in *Picturing Men* (2002), that is, using vernacular photography to help write the history of American male emotions (Ibson 2018, 4).

All of this sheds new light on what we are seeing in the soldier snapshots. Young men in the military are trying to recover the intense emotional friendships they experience in early and middle adolescence. The "tools" they have at hand to reconstruct those intimate friendships are the folk practices I see in the snapshots, mostly folklore performed in the play frame. Brian Sutton-Smith (2017) elevates the importance of play for the expression and regulation of the emotions (feelings). I go one step further (Mechling 2019), extending Sutton-Smith's insight to claim that all folklore makes our feelings available to others and to ourselves. It is the management of the feelings men have for one another that we see in the snapshots.

Although I have taught and written for nearly two decades now about the experience of being in the military, my only access to that experience is by reading war memoirs and fiction and by looking at documentary films and war photography. I am not a veteran, having taken advantage of a student deferment and then a high number on the draft lottery in December 1969. I have always been looking at the everyday male experience in the military from the outside. I do not regret missing that experience ("I would have liked it too much"), but as I taught and still write about warriors and veterans, I am ever-mindful of the fact that I have not had that experience.

The Boy Scouts is not military service. I do not equate the two experiences. At the end of this project looking at the soldier snapshots, though, I now feel a new understanding of and affinity for the young men in these photographs. I understand their sense of loss of deep friendships and their search for recovering those feelings in the all-male military group. It's all there in the photographs, if you know how to look.

References

Abrahams, Roger D. 1982. "The Language of Festivals." In *Celebration: A World of Art and Ritual,* ed. Victor W. Turner, 161–177. Washington, DC: Smithsonian Institution Press.

———. 2005. *Everyday Life: A Poetics of Vernacular Practices.* Philadelphia: University of Pennsylvania Press.

———, and Richard Bauman. 1978. "Ranges of Festival Behavior." In *The Reversible World: Symbolic Inversion in Art and Society,* ed. Barbara A. Babcock, 193–208. Ithaca, NY: Cornell University Press.

Arluke, Arnold, and Lauren Rolfe. 2013. *The Photographed Cat: Picturing Human-Feline Ties, 1890–1940.* Syracuse, NY: Syracuse University Press.

Babcock, Barbara, ed. 1978. *The Reversible World: Symbolic Inversions in Art and Society.* Ithaca, NY: Cornell University Press.

Babcock-Abrahams, Barbara. 1975. "Why Frogs Are Good to Think and Dirt Is Good to Reflect On." *Soundings* 58:167–181.

Bachner, Evan. 2004. *At Ease: Navy Men of World War II.* New York: Harry N. Abrams, Publishers.

———. 2007. *Men of World War I: Fighting Men at Ease.* New York: Harry N. Abrams, Publishers.

Bates, Josiah, and Tara Law. 2019. "After Contentious Trial, Navy SEAL Edward Gallagher Found Not Guilty of the Murder of an ISIS Fighter." *Time Magazine,* July 2. Accessed January 17, 2020. https://time.com/5610116/navy-seal-edward-gallagher-isis-murder-trial/

Bateson, Gregory. 1955. Reprinted in 1972. "A Theory of Play and Fantasy." In *Steps to an Ecology of Mind,* 177–193. New York: Ballantine.

————. 1979. *Mind and Nature: A Necessary Unity.* New York: E. P. Dutton.

Beneke, Timothy. 1997. *Proving Manhood: Reflections on Sex and Sexism.* Berkeley: University of California Press.

Berger, Peter L., Brigitte Berger, and Hansfried Kellner. 1974. *The Homeless Mind: Modernization and Consciousness.* New York: Vintage.

Berger, Peter L., and Thomas Luckmann. 1967. *The Social Construction of Reality: A Treatise on the Sociology of Knowledge.* New York: Anchor Books.

Bernstein, Adam. 2007. "Al Chang, 85: Soldier Captured Combat Photos." *Los Angeles Times*, October 8. Accessed January 17, 2020. https://www.latimes.com/archives/la-xpm-2007-oct-08-me-chang8-story.html.

Bérubé, Allan. 1990. *Coming Out under Fire: The History of Gay Men and Women in World War Two.* New York: Free Press.

Bettelheim, Bruno. 1954. *Symbolic Wounds: Puberty Rites and the Envious Male.* New York: Free Press.

Black, Jonathan. 2009. "Charles Atlas: Muscle Man." *Smithsonian Magazine*, August. https://www.smithsonianmag.com/history/charles-atlas-muscle-man-34626921/. Accessed January 17. 2020.

Black Friday: Dark Dawn. 2012. Los Angeles: Moto Entertainment.

Black Friday: Dark Dawn II. 2014. Los Angeles: Moto Entertainment.

Black Friday: Dark Dawn III. 2015. Los Angeles: Moto Entertainment.

Bly, Robert. 1990. *Iron John: A Book about Men.* Reading, MA: Addison-Wesley.

Bonser, Frederick G. 1902. "Chums: A Study in Youthful Friendships." *Pedagogical Seminary* 9 (2): 221–236.

Bordo, Susan. 1993. "Reading Male Bodies." *Michigan Quarterly Review* 32 (4): 606–737.

————. 1999. *The Male Body: A New Look at Men in Public and in Private.* New York: Farrar, Straus and Giroux.

————. 2002. "Does Size Matter?" In *Revealing Male Bodies*, ed. Nancy Tuana, William Cowling, Maurice Hamington, Greg Johnson, and Terrance MacMullan, 19–37. Bloomington: Indiana University Press.

Bouissac, Paul. 1976. *Circus and Culture: A Semiotic Approach.* Bloomington: Indiana University Press.

Bowley, Graham, and Matthew Rosenberg. 2012. "Video Inflames a Delicate Moment for U.S. in Afghanistan." *New York Times*, January 12. Accessed January 17, 2020. https://www.nytimes.com/2012/01/13/world/asia/video-said-to-show-marines-urinating-on-taliban-corpses.html.

Brannon, Robert, and Deborah David. 1976. "Introduction." In *The Forty-Nine Per Cent Majority.* Reading, MA: Addison-Wesley.

Bronner, Simon J. 1988. *American Children's Folklore.* Little Rock, AR: August House.

————, ed. 2005. *Manly Traditions: The Folk Roots of American Masculinities.* Bloomington: Indiana University Press.

————. 2006. *Crossing the Line: Violence, Play, and Drama in Naval Equator Traditions.* Amsterdam: Amsterdam University Press.

————. 2012. *Campus Traditions: Folklore from the Old Time College to the Modern Mega-University*. Jackson: University Press of Mississippi.

————. 2017. *Folklore: The Basics*. London: Routledge.

Brummet, Barry. 1991. *Rhetorical Dimensions of Popular Culture*. Tuscaloosa: University of Alabama Press.

————. 2004. *Rhetorical Homologies: Form, Culture, Experience*. Tuscaloosa: University of Alabama Press.

Burke, Kenneth. 1937. Reprinted in 1959. *Attitudes toward History*. Boston: Beacon Press.

————. 1945. Reprinted in 1969. *A Grammar of Motives*. Berkeley: University of California Press.

Burton, Roland. 2017. "Full Metal Jacket—Pvt Joker's Born to Kill/Peace Sign and the Jungian Duality of Man." Roland's Civil War blog, June 24. Accessed January 17, 2020. https://rolandscivilwar.wordpress.com/2017/06/24/full-met al-jacket-pvt-jokers-born-to-killpeace-and-the-jungian-duality-of-man/.

Butler, Judith. 2006. *Gender Trouble: Feminism and the Subversion of Identity*. New York: Routledge.

————. 2011. *Bodies That Matter: On the Discursive Limits of Sex*. New York: Routledge.

Caillois, Roger. 1961. *Man, Play, and Games*. Trans. Meyer Barash. New York: Free Press.

Campbell, Joseph. 1949. *The Hero with a Thousand Faces*. New York: Pantheon.

Chappell, Bill. 2019. "Navy SEAL Demoted for Taking Photo with Corpse of ISIS Fighter." National Public Radio, July 3. Accessed January 17, 2020. https://www.npr.org/2019/07/03/738463353/jury-reduces-navy-seals-rank-for-taking -photo-with-corpse-of-isis-fighter.

Chodorow, Nancy. 1978. *The Reproduction of Mothering: Psychoanalysis and the Sociology of Gender*. Berkeley: University of California Press.

————. 1994. *Femininities, Masculinities, Sexualities: Freud and Beyond*. Lexington: University Press of Kentucky.

Cole, Sarah. 2003. *Modernism, Male Friendship, and the First World War*. Cambridge: Cambridge University Press.

Collins, Max Allen. 2000. *For the Boys: The Racy Pin-Ups of World War II*. Portland, OR: Collectors Press.

Connell, R. W. 1995. *Masculinities*. Berkeley: University of California Press.

Coons, Sean. 2011. "Documentary 'Under Fire' Shows That War Is Hell for Journalists." *Atlantic*, November 10. Accessed January 17, 2020. https://www.theat-lantic.com/entertainment/archive/2011/11/documentary-under-fire-shows -that-war-is-hell-for-journalists/248232/.

Coupland, Douglas. 1991. *Generation X: Tales for an Accelerated Culture*. London: St. Martin's Griffin.

Crawford, John. 2005. *The Last True Story I'll Ever Tell: An Accidental Soldier's Account of the War in Iraq*. New York: Riverhead Books.

Csikszentmihalyi, Mihaly. 1975. *Beyond Boredom and Anxiety: Experiencing Flow in Work and Play.* New York: Jossey-Bass.

Deitcher, David. 2001. *Dear Friends: American Photographs of Men Together, 1840–1918.* New York: Harry N. Abrams, Publishers.

Delfino, Andrew, and Jay Mechling. 2017. "Wrestling with Masculinity." *Children's Folklore Review* 38:57–77.

Douglas, Mary.1966. *Purity and Danger: An Analysis of Concepts of Pollution and Taboo.* London: Routledge and Kegan Paul.

———. 1970. *Natural Symbols: Exploration in Cosmology.* London: Routledge and Kegan Paul.

Dundes, Alan. 1978. "Into the Endzone for a Touchdown: A Psychoanalytic Consideration of American Football." *Western Folklore* 37 (2): 75–88.

———. 1997. "Traditional Male Combat: From Game to War." In *From Game to War and Other Psychoanalytic Essays on Folklore,* 25–45. Lexington: University Press of Kentucky.

———, Jerry W. Leach, and Bora Özkök. 1970. "The Strategy of Turkish Boys' Verbal Dueling Rhymes." *Journal of American Folklore* 83:325–349.

Ehrenreich, Barbara. 1997. *Blood Rites: Origins and History of the Passions of War.* New York: Metropolitan Books.

Faram, Mark D. 2009. *Faces of War: The Untold Story of Edward Steichen's WWII Photographs.* New York: Berkley Caliber.

Fatsis, Stefan. 2016. "'No Viet Cong Ever Called Me Nigger': The Story behind the Most Famous Quote Muhammed Ali Probably Never Said." *Slate,* June 8. Accessed January 17, 2020. https://slate.com/culture/2016/06/did-muhammad-ali-ever-say-no-viet-cong-ever-called-me-nigger.html.

Feintuch, Burt, ed. 2003. *Eight Words for the Study of Expressive Culture.* Champaign: University of Illinois Press.

Finkel, David. 2009. *The Good Soldiers.* New York: Picador, Farrar, Straus and Giroux.

Fox, Robert. 1996. *Camera in Conflict.* Köln, Germany: Könemann.

Freud, Sigmund. 1913. Reprinted in 1950. *Totem and Taboo.* Trans. James Strachey. New York: W. W. Norton.

———. 1918. Reprinted in 1955. *From the History of an Infantile Neurosis (Wolfman).* Trans. James Strachey. New York: W. W. Norton.

———. 1920. Reprinted in 1961. *Beyond the Pleasure Principle.* Trans. James Strachey. New York: W. W. Norton.

———. 1930. Reprinted in 1989. *Civilization and Its Discontents.* Trans. James Strachey. New York: W. W. Norton.

Friedman, Devin, et al. 2006. *This Is Our War: A Soldier's Portfolio.* New York: Artisan.

Frizot, Michel. 1998. *The New History of Photography.* Cologne: Könemann.

Frosh, Stephen. 1994. *Sexual Difference: Masculinity and Psychoanalysis.* London: Routledge.

Gabor, Mark. 1972. *The Pin-Up: A Modest History.* New York: Universe Books.

Garber, Marjorie. 1992. *Vested Interests: Cross-Dressing and Cultural Anxiety.* New York: Routledge.

Geertz, Clifford. 1973a. "Deep Play: Notes on the Balinese Cockfight." In *The Interpretation of Cultures,* 412–453. New York: Basic Books.

———. 1973b. "Thick Description: Toward an Interpretive Theory of Culture." In *The Interpretation of Cultures,* 3–30. New York: Basic Books.

———. 1983. "Common Sense as a Cultural System." In *Local Knowledge: Further Essays in Interpretive Anthropology,* 73–93. New York: Basic Books.

Gibson, James William. 1994. *Warrior Dreams: Violence and Manhood in Post-Vietnam America.* New York: Hill and Wang.

Goffman, Erving. 1956. *The Presentation of Self in Everyday Life.* New York: Doubleday.

———. 1961. *Asylums: Essays on the Condition of the Social Situation of Mental Patients and Other Inmates.* New York: Vintage Books.

———. 1963. *Behavior in Public Places.* New York: Free Press.

———. 1967. *Interaction Ritual: Essays on Face-to-Face Interaction.* New York: Aldine.

———. 1974. *Frame Analysis: An Essay on the Organization of Experience.* New York: Harper Torchbooks.

———. 1976. *Gender Advertisements.* New York: Harper & Row.

Gottschalk, Louis, ed. 1963. *Generalization in the Writing of History.* Chicago: University of Chicago Press.

Gould, Stephen Jay. 1987. "What, If Anything, Is a Zebra?" In *Hen's Teeth and Horse's Toes: Further Reflections in Natural History.* New York: W. W. Norton.

Gray, J. Glenn. 1959. Reprinted in 2015. *The Warriors: Reflections on Men in Battle.* Lincoln: University of Nebraska Press/Bison Books.

Greenberg, Jay R., and Stephen A. Mitchell. 1983. *Object Relations in Psychoanalytic Theory.* Cambridge, MA: Harvard University Press.

Greenough, Sarah, et al. 2007. *The Art of the American Snapshot, 1888–1978.* Princeton, NJ: Princeton University Press.

Grier, Katherine C. 2006. *Pets in America: A History.* Chapel Hill: University of North Carolina Press.

Grossman, Dave. 2008. *On Combat: The Psychology and Physiology of Deadly Conflict in War and Peace.* N.p.: Warrior Science Publications.

———. 2009. *On Killing: The Psychological Cost of Learning to Kill in War and Society.* New York: Back Bay Books.

Hall, Edward T. 1959. Reprinted in 1973. *The Silent Language.* New York: Anchor Books.

Hall, G. Stanley. 1904. *Adolescence.* 2 vols. New York: D. Appleton and Company.

Handelman, Don. 1977. "Play and Ritual: Complementary Frames of Meta-Communication." In *It's a Funny Thing, Humour,* ed. A. J. Chapman and H. Foot, 185–192. Oxford: Pergamon.

Hanson, Dian. 2014. *My Buddy: World War II Laid Bare.* Köln, Germany: Taschen.

Hasford, Gustav. 1979. *The Short-Timers.* New York: Harper & Row.

Hersh, Sidney M. 2004. "Torture at Abu-Ghraib." *New Yorker,* May 10, 42–47.

Hetherington, Tim. 2010. *Infidel.* London: Chris Boot.

Hirschfeld, Magnus. 1941 [1934]. *The Sexual History of the World War.* New York: Cadillac Publishing.

Hoberman, J. 2018. "G.I.s 'without a Country,' Protesting the Vietnam War." *New York Times*, January 31. Accessed January 17, 2020. https://www.nytimes .com/2018/01/31/arts/no-vietnamese-ever-called-me-nigger-documentary.html.

Horney, Karen. 1932. "The Dread of Women." *International Journal of Psycho-Analysis* 13: 348–360.

———. 1937. *The Neurotic Personality of Our Time.* New York: Norton.

Howe, Neal, and William Strauss. 1993. *13th Gen: Abort, Retry, Ignore, Fail?* New York: Vintage.

———. 2000. *Millennials Rising: The Next Generation.* New York: Vintage.

Howe, Peter. 2002. *Shooting under Fire: The World of the War Photographer.* New York: Workman Publishing.

Hughes, Linda A. 1993. "'You Have to Do It with Style': Girls' Games and Gaming." In *Feminist Theory and the Study of Folklore,* ed. Susan Tower Hollis, Linda Pershing, and M. Jane Young, 130–148. Urbana: University of Illinois Press.

Huizinga, Johan. 1949. *Homo Ludens: A Study of the Play-Element in Culture.* London: Routledge and Kegan Paul.

Ibson, John. 2002. *Picturing Men: A Century of Male Relationships in Everyday American Photography.* Chicago: University of Chicago Press.

———. 2007. "Picturing Boys: Found Photographs and the Transformation of Boyhood in 1950s America." *THYMOS: Journal of Boyhood Studies* 1 (1):68–83.

———. 2018. *The Mourning After: Loss and Longing among Midcentury American Men.* Chicago: University of Chicago Press.

James, William. 1902. *The Varieties of Religious Experience: A Study in Human Nature.* New York: Longmans, Greer.

———. 1907. Reprinted in 1975. *Pragmatism: A New Name for Some Old Ways of Thinking.* Cambridge, MA: Harvard University Press.

Jarvis, Christina. 2004. *The Male Body at War: American Masculinities during World War II.* DeKalb: Northern Illinois University Press.

Jeffords, Susan. 1993. *Hard Bodies: Hollywood Masculinity in the Reagan Era.* New Brunswick, NJ: Rutgers University Press.

Jewett, Robert, and John Shelton Lawrence. 1977. *The American Monomyth.* Garden City, NY: Anchor Press/Doubleday.

Jones, Howard. 2017. *My Lai: Vietnam, 1968, and the Descent into Darkness.* New York: Oxford University Press.

Jones, James. 1962. *The Thin Red Line.* New York: Charles Scribner's Sons.

Junger, Sebastian. 2010. *War.* New York: Twelve.

Kimmel, Michael. 2008. *Guyland: The Perilous World Where Boys Become Men.* New York: Harper.

King, Graham. 1984. *Say "Cheese": Looking at Snapshots in a New Way.* New York: Dodd, Mead.

Kinsey, Alfred C., Wardell B. Pomeroy, and Clyde E. Martin. 1948. *Sexual Behavior in the Human Male.* Philadelphia: W. B. Saunders.

Kirshenbaum, Sheril. 2011. *The Science of Kissing: What Our Lips Are Telling Us.* New York: Grand Central Publishing.

Knightley, Phillip, and John Keegan. 2003. *The Eye of War: Words and Photographs from the Front Line.* Washington, DC: Smithsonian Books.

Kouwenhoven, John A. 1982. *Half a Truth Is Better Than None.* Chicago: University of Chicago Press.

Kuhn, Thomas. 1970. *The Structure of Scientific Revolutions.* 2nd ed. Chicago: University of Chicago Press.

Lacdan, Joe. 2019. "First Enlisted Female to Graduate from Ranger School Reflects on Experience." Army News Service, August 26. Accessed January 17, 2020. https://www.army.mil/article/226137/first_enlisted_female_to_graduate_from_ranger_school_reflects_on_experience.

Lakoff, George. 1987. *Women, Fire, and Dangerous Things: What Categories Reveal about the Mind.* Chicago: University of Chicago Press.

Lakoff, George, and Mark Johnson. 1980. *Metaphors We Live By.* Chicago: University of Chicago Press.

Laquer, Thomas W. 2003. *Solitary Sex: The Cultural History of Masturbation.* New York: Zone Books.

Lasch, Christopher. 1979. *The Culture of Narcissism.* New York: Norton.

Lawrence, John Shelton, and Robert Jewett. 2002. *The Myth of the American Superhero.* Grand Rapids, MI: William B. Eerdmans Publishing.

Lifton, Robert Jay. 1973. *Home from the War: Vietnam Veterans, Neither Victims nor Executioners.* New York: Basic Books.

MacMullan, Terrance. 2002. "Introduction: What Is Male Embodiment?" In *Revealing Male Bodies,* ed. Nancy Tuana et al., 1–16. Bloomington: Indiana University Press.

Manning, Frederic. 1930. *Her Privates We.* London: Peter Davies.

Mansfield, Nick. 1997. *Masochism: The Art of Power.* Westport, CT: Praeger.

March, William. 1933. *Company K.* New York: Smith and Haas.

Marotta, Michael E. 2002. "Short Snorters: Keeping the Memories Alive." *The Numismatist.* Accessed January 17, 2020. http://shortsnorter.org/files/November_2002_NUMISMATIST_Snorter_Article.pdf.

McKay, Brett, and Kate McKay. 2018. "Bosom Buddies: A Photo History of Male Affection." *Art of Manliness,* November 7. Accessed January 17, 2020. https://www.artofmanliness.com/articles/bosom-buddies-a-photo-history-of-male-affection/.

Mead, Margaret. 1975. *Culture and Commitment: A Study of the Generation Gap.* London: Bodley Head.

Mechling, Elizabeth, and Jay Mechling. 1985. "'Shock Talk': From Consensual to Contractual Joking in the Workplace." *Human Organization* 44 (4): 339–343.

———, and Jay Mechling. 1994. "The Jung and the Restless: The Mythopoetic Men's Movement." *Southern Communication Journal* 59 (2): 91–111.

———, and Jay Mechling. 1999. "American Cultural Criticism in the Pragmatic Attitude." In *At the Intersection: Cultural Studies and Rhetorical Studies,* ed. Thomas Rosteck, 137–167. New York: Guilford Press.

Mechling, Jay. 1985. "Introduction: William James and the Philosophical Foundations for the Study of Everyday Life." *Western Folklore* 44: 303–310.

———. 1986. "The Jamesian Berger." In *Making Sense of Modern Times: Peter L. Berger and the Vision of Interpretive Sociology,* ed. James Davison Hunter and Stephen Ainlay, 197–220. London: Routledge and Kegan Paul.

———. 1989. "'Banana Cannon' and Other Folk Traditions between Human and Nonhuman Animals." *Western Folklore* 48 (4): 312–323.

———. 1997. "Some [New] Elementary Axioms for an American Cultur[al] Studies." *American Studies* 38: 9–30.

———. 2000. Republished in 2015. "Children's Folklore, Children's Brains." *New Directions in Folklore* 4 (2). https://scholarworks.iu.edu/journals/index .php/ndif/article/view/19874/25944.

———. 2001. *On My Honor: Boy Scouts and the Making of American Youth.* Chicago: University of Chicago Press.

———. 2004. "Picturing Hunting." *Western Folklore* 63 (1–2): 51–78.

———. 2005a. "The Folklore of Mother-Raised Boys and Men." In *Manly Traditions: The Folk Roots of American Masculinities,* ed. Simon J. Bronner, 211–227. Bloomington: University of Indiana Press.

———. 2005b. "Found Photographs and Children's Folklore." *Children's Folklore Review* 27: 7–31.

———. 2008a. "The Cultural History of the Penis." In *The Cultural Encyclopedia of the Body,* Vol. 2, ed. Victoria Pitts-Taylor, 384–390. Westport, CT: Greenwood Publishing.

———. 2008b. "Paddling and the Repression of the Feminine in Male Hazing." *THYMOS: Journal of Boy Studies* 2 (1): 60–75.

———. 2008c. "Gun Play." *American Journal of Play* 1 (2): 192–209.

———. 2009. "Is Hazing Play?" In *Transactions at Play,* ed. Cindy Dell Clark, 45–61. Lanham, MD: University Press of America.

———. 2012. "Soldier Snaps." In *Warrior Ways: Explorations in Modern Military Folklore,* ed. Eric A. Eliason and Tad Tuleja, 222–247. Logan: Utah State University Press.

———. 2014. "Pissing and Masculinity." *Culture, Society & Masculinities* 6 (1): 19–34.

———. 2016a. "The Erotics of Adolescent Male Altruism." *Boyhood Studies* 9 (2): 92–115.

———. 2016b. "Sandwork." *American Journal of Play* 9 (1): 19–40.

———. 2019. "Folklore and the Emotional Brain." In *Contexts of Folklore: Festschrift for Dan Ben-Amos,* ed. Simon J. Bronner and Wolfgang Mieder, 217–228. New York: Peter Lang.

Metzger, Walter. 1963. "Generalizations about National Character." In *On Generalizations in the Writing of History,* ed. Louis Gottschalk. Chicago: University of Chicago Press.

Mitchell, Juliet. 1974. *Psychoanalysis and Feminism.* New York: Vintage/Random House.

Moeller, Susan D. 1989. *Shooting War: Photography and the American Experience of Combat.* New York: Basic Books.

Montagu, Ashley. 1986. *Touching: The Human Significance of Skin.* New York: Perennial Library.

Morris, Erroll. 2011. *Seeing Is Believing: Observations on the Mysteries of Photography.* New York: Penguin Press.

Mosse, George L. 1998. *The Image of Man: The Creation of Modern Masculinity.* New York: Oxford University Press.

Murphy, Peter F. 2001. *Studs, Tools, and the Family Jewels: Metaphors Men Live By.* Madison: University of Wisconsin Press.

Nardi, Peter M. 1999. *Gay Men's Friendships: Invincible Communities.* Chicago: University of Chicago Press.

Nasaw, Daniel. 2012. "When Did the Middle Finger Became Offensive?" *BBC News Magazine,* February 6. https://www.bbc.com/news/magazine-16916263.

Newton, Judith. 2004. *From Panthers to Promise Keepers: Rethinking the Men's Movement.* New York: Rowman and Littlefield.

O'Brien, Tim. 1990. *The Things They Carried.* New York: Mariner Books.

Olivier, Marc. 2007. "George Eastman's Modern Stone-Age Family." *Technology and Culture* 48 (1): 1–19.

Oring, Elliott. 1986. "On the Concepts of Folklore." In *Folk Groups and Folklore Genres,* ed. Elliott Oring, 1–22. Logan: Utah State University Press.

———. 2012. "Totemism and the A.E.F. Revisited." In *Just Folklore,* 46–54. Los Angeles, CA: Cantilever Press.

———. 2016. *Joking Asides: The Theory, Analysis, and Aesthetics of Humor.* Logan: Utah State University Press.

Orwell, George. 1941. *The Lion and the Unicorn: Socialism and the English Genius.* London: Searchlight Books, Secker & Warburg.

Paret, Peter, Beth Irwin Lewis, and Pail Paret. 1992. *Persuasive Images: Posters of War and Revolution from the Hoover Institution Archives.* Princeton, NJ: Princeton University Press.

Parker, Kim, Anthony Cilluffo, and Renee Stepler. 2017. "6 Facts about the U.S. Military and Its Changing Demographics." Pew Research Center Factank, April 13. Accessed January 17, 2020. https://nclegion.org/wp-content/uploads/2019/10/6-facts-about-the-U.S.-militarys-changing-demographics.pdf.

Phillips, Christopher. 1981. *Steichen at War.* New York: Harry N. Abrams, Publishers.

Pipher, Mary. 1994. *Reviving Ophelia: Saving the Selves of Adolescent Girls.* New York: Random House.

Pollack, Michael. 1998. *Real Boys: Rescuing Our Sons from the Myths of Boyhood.* New York: Owl Books.

Putnam, Robert. 2000. *Bowling Alone: The Collapse and Revival of American Community.* New York: Simon and Schuster.

Raphael, Ray. 1988. *The Men from the Boys: Rites of Passage in Male America.* Lincoln: University of Nebraska Press.

Reik, Theodor. 1962. *Masochism in Sex and Society.* Trans. Margaret H. Beigel and Gertrud M. Kurth. New York: Grove Press. Orig. published as *Masochism in Modern Man,* 1941.

Reimers, L., and E. K. Diekhof. 2015. "Testosterone Is Associated with Cooperation during Intergroup Competition by Enhancing Parochial Altruism," June 12. *Front Neurosci.* Accessed January 17, 2020. https://www.ncbi.nlm.nih .gov/pubmed/26124701.

Robbins, Ira. 2008. "Digitus Impudicus: The Middle Finger and the Law." *University of California, Davis, Law Review* 41:1403–1485.

Roberts, John, Malcolm J. Arth, and Robert R. Bush. 1959. "Games in Culture." *American Anthropologist* (New Series) 61 (4): 597–605.

Roberts, Mary Louise. 2013. *What Soldiers Do: Sex and the American GI in World War II France.* Chicago: University of Chicago Press.

Rockett, Ben, and Sam Carr. 2014. "Animals and Attachment Theory." *Society and Animals* 22: 415–433.

Roeder, George H., Jr. 1993. *The Censored War: American Visual Experience during World War Two.* New Haven, CT: Yale University Press.

Rubin, Patricia Lee. 2018. *Seen from Behind: Perspectives on the Male Body and Renaissance Art.* New Haven, CT: Yale University Press.

Sapolsky, Robert M. 1997. *The Trouble with Testosterone and Other Essays on the Biology of the Human Predicament.* New York: Simon & Schuster.

———. 2004. *Why Zebras Don't Get Ulcers.* 3rd ed. New York: St. Martin's Griffin.

———. 2017. *Behave: The Biology of Humans at Our Best and Worst.* New York: Penguin Press.

Savin-Williams, Ritch C. 2017. *Mostly Straight: Sexual Fluidity among Men.* Cambridge, MA: Harvard University Press.

Savran, David. 1998. *Taking It Like a Man: White Masculinity, Masochism, and Contemporary American Culture.* Princeton, NJ: Princeton University Press.

Scarry, Elaine. 1985. *The Body in Pain: The Making and the Unmaking of the World.* New York: Oxford University Press.

Scherman, David E., ed. 1977. Life *Goes to War.* New York: Pocket Books.

Senelick, Laurence. 2000. *The Changing Room: Sex, Drag and Theatre.* New York: Routledge.

Shay, Jonathan. 1994. *Achilles in Vietnam: Combat Trauma and the Undoing of Character.* New York: Scribner.

Short Snorter Project. Accessed January 17, 2020. http://www.shortsnorter.org.

Slotkin, Richard. 1973. *Regeneration through Violence: The Mythology of the American Frontier, 1600–1860.* Middletown, CT: Wesleyan University Press.

———. 1985. *The Fatal Environment: The Myth of the Frontier in the Age of Industrialization, 1800–1890.* New York: Macmillan.

———. 1992. *Gunfighter Nation: The Myth of the Frontier in Twentieth-Century America.* New York: Atheneum.

Sontag, Susan. 1977. *On Photography.* New York: Farrar, Straus and Giroux.

———. 1978. *Illness as Metaphor.* New York: Farrar, Straus and Giroux.

———. 1989. *AIDS and Its Metaphors.* New York: Farrar, Straus and Giroux.

———. 2003. *Regarding the Pain of Others.* New York: Farrar, Straus and Giroux.

———. 2004. "Regarding the Torture of Others." *New York Times Magazine,* May 23, 25–29.

Stearns, Carol Zisowitz, and Peter N. Stearns. 1986. *Anger: The Struggle for Emotional Control in American History.* Chicago: University of Chicago Press.

Steenhuysen, Julie. 2009. "Kissing: It Really Is All about Chemistry." Reuters, February 14. Accessed January 17, 2020. https://www.reuters.com/article/us-kissing/kissing-it-really-is-all-about-chemistry-idUSTRE51D1MM20090214.

Stewart, Jessica. 2019. "Memento Mori: Life and Death in Western Art from Skulls to Still Life." *My Modern Met,* June 23. Accessed January 17, 2020. https://mymodernmet.com/memento-mori-art/.

Stewart, Susan. 1979. *Nonsense: Aspects of Intertextuality in Folklore and Literature.* Baltimore, MD: Johns Hopkins University Press.

———. 1984. *On Longing: Narratives of the Miniature, the Gigantic, the Souvenir, the Collection.* Baltimore, MD: Johns Hopkins University Press.

Stone, John. 2012. "The Point of the Bayonet." *Technology and Culture* 53 (4): 885–908.

Strauss, William, and Neil Howe. 1991. *Generations: The History of America's Future, 1584–2069.* New York: William Morrow.

Sutton-Smith, Brian. 1970. "Psychology of Childlore: The Triviality Barrier." *Western Folklore* 29:1–8.

———. 2001. *The Ambiguity of Play.* Cambridge, MA: Harvard University Press.

———. 2017. *Play for Life: Play Theory and Play as Emotional Survival.* Rochester, NY: Strong Museum of Play.

Sutton-Smith, Brian, and Diana Kelly-Byrne. 1984. "The Masks of Play." In *The Masks of Play,* ed. Brian Sutton-Smith and Diana Kelly-Byrne, 184–197. New York: Leisure Press.

Swofford, Anthony. 2003. *Jarhead: A Marine's Chronicle of the Gulf War and Other Battles.* New York: Scribner.

Szoldra, Paul. 2018. "'I Got Him with My Hunting Knife': SEAL Allegedly Texted Photo Cradling ISIS Fighter's Head." *Task and Purpose,* November 15. Accessed January 17, 2020. https://taskandpurpose.com/seal-chief-gallagher-isis-execution.

Tannen, Deborah. 2007. *You Just Don't Understand: Women and Men in Conversation.* New York: William Morrow.

Taylor, Charles M. 1902. *Why My Photographs Are Bad.* Philadelphia: George W. Jacobs.

Theweleit, Klaus. 1989. *Male Fantasies.* Vol. 2, *Male Bodies.* Minneapolis: University of Minnesota Press.

Thompson, Sylvia. 2018. "Science of Kissing: Why a Kiss Is Not Just a Kiss." *Irish Times,* February 13. Accessed January 17, 2020. https://www.irishtimes

.com/life-and-style/health-family/science-of-kissing-why-a-kiss-is-not-just
-a-kiss-1.3380704.

Tuana, Nancy, et al., eds. 2002. *Revealing Male Bodies.* Bloomington: Indiana
University Press.

Tucker, Anne Wilkes, et al. 2012. *War/Photography: Images of Armed Conflict
and Its Aftermath.* Houston: Museum of Fine Arts.

Turner, Victor. 1969. *The Ritual Process: Structure and Anti-Structure.* Ithaca,
NY: Cornell University Press.

———. 1974. *Dramas, Fields, and Metaphors: Symbolic Action in Human Society.* Ithaca, NY: Cornell University Press.

Twenge, Jean. 2017. *iGen.* New York: Atria Books.

Uriarte, Maximilian. 2016. *The White Donkey: Terminal Lance.* New York: Little,
Brown.

———. 2018. *Terminal Lance: Ultimate Omnibus.* New York: Little, Brown.

Van Gennep, Arnold. 1960. *The Rites of Passage.* Chicago: University of Chicago
Press.

Vonnegut, Kurt. 1969. *Slaughterhouse-Five, or the Children's Crusade.* New
York: Delacorte.

Wallace, Anthony F. C. 1970. *Culture and Personality.* 2nd ed. New York: Random House.

Wallis, John Paul. 2012. *Reborn to Kill: American Warriors and Digital Trophies.*
Unpublished senior honors thesis in American Studies, University of California, Davis.

Wallis, John Paul, and Jay Mechling. 2015. "Devil Dogs and Dog Piles." *Western
Folklore* 74:275–308.

———. 2019. *PTSD and Folk Therapy: Everyday Practices of American Masculinity in the Combat Zone.* Lanham, MD: Lexington Books.

———. 2020. "Warriors' Bodies as Sites of Microresistance in the American Military." In *Different Drummer: Military Discipline and Its Discontents,* ed. Tad
Tuleja. Logan: Utah State University Press.

Ward, Jane. 2015. *Not Gay: Sex between Straight White Men.* New York: New
York University Press.

Watson, John. 1968. *The Double Helix: A Personal Account of the Discovery of
the Structure of DNA.* New York: Atheneum.

Way, Niobe. 2011. *Deep Secrets: Boys' Friendships and the Crisis of Connection.*
Cambridge, MA: Harvard University Press.

Wells, Liz, ed. 1996. *Photography: A Critical Introduction.* New York: Routledge.

Wiener, Jon. 2018. "Op-Ed: A Forgotten Hero Stopped the My Lai Massacre 50
Years Ago Today." *Los Angeles Times,* March 16. Accessed January 17, 2020.
https://www.latimes.com/opinion/op-ed/la-oe-wiener-my-lai-hugh-thompson
-20180316-story.html.

Williams, Raymond. 1976. *Keywords: A Vocabulary of Culture and Society.* New
York: Oxford University Press.

Winnicott, D. W. 1965. *Maturational Processes and the Facilitating Environment: Studies in the Theory of Emotional Development*. London: Hogarth Press.

Wood, C. E. 2006. *Mud: A Military History*. Lincoln: University of Nebraska Press.

Wright, Will. 1977. *Sixguns and Society: A Structural Study of the Western*. Berkeley: University of California Press.

Young, Matt. 2018. *Eat the Apple*. New York: Bloomsbury.

Zeeland, Steven. 1993. *Barrack Buddies and Soldier Lovers*. Binghamton, NY: Haworth Press.

———. 1995. *Sailors and Sexual Identity: Crossing the Line between "Straight" and "Gay" in the U.S. Navy*. Binghamton, NY: Haworth Press.

———. 1996. *The Masculine Marine: Homoeroticism in the U.S. Marine Corps*. Binghamton, NY: Haworth Press.

———. 1999. *Military Trade*. Binghamton, NY: Harrington Park Press.

Zelt, Natalie. 2012. "Seeing Eye to Eye." In *War/Photography: Images of Armed Conflict and Its Aftermath*, by Anne Wilkes Tucker et al., 18–26. New Haven, CT: Yale University Press.

Index